Talking Feminist Politics

Talking Feminist Politics

*Conversations on Law,
Science, and the Postmodern*

Eloise A. Buker

ROWMAN & LITTLEFIELD PUBLISHERS, INC.
Lanham • New York • London

ROWMAN & LITTLEFIELD PUBLISHERS, INC.

Published in the United States of America
by Rowman & Littlefield Publishers, Inc.
4720 Boston Way, Lanham, Maryland 20706
http://www.rowmanlittlefield.com

12 Hid's Copse Road
Cumnor Hill, Oxford OX2 9JJ, England

British Cataloging in Publication Information Available

Library of Congress Cataloging-in-Publication Data

Buker, Eloise A.
    Talking feminist politics : conversations on law, science, and the
postmodern / Eloise A. Buker.
        p.   cm.
    Includes bibliographical references.
    ISBN 0-8476-9616-2 (cloth : alk. paper).—ISBN 0-8476-9617-0
(pbk. : alk. paper)
    1. Feminism—Political aspects.   2. Feminist jurisprudence.
3. Feminism and science.   I. Title.
HQ1150.B84   1999
305.42—dc21   99-26313
                                                        CIP

Printed in the United States of America

∞™ The paper used in this publication meets the minimum requirements of American
National Standard for Information Sciences—Permanence of Paper for Printed Library
Materials, ANSI/NISO Z39.48–1992.

Dedicated to my mother
Eloise L. Buker

Contents

Acknowledgments   ix

1   Listening to Three Feminist Conversations:
     Law, Science, and the Postmodern   1

Part I: Feminist Jurisprudence: Justice and Politics   17

2   Feminist Legal Discourse: Embodied Laws and Contested Authorities   23

3   Reconstructing Legal Discourse: Feminist Possibilities   47

4   Judgments and Politics: Citizens and Justice in Everyday Life   63

Part II: Feminist Scientific Conversations: Truth and Politics   75

5   Feminist Scientific Discourse: Knowing Metaphors and Images   85

6   Rhetorical Moves: Science As Storytelling   101

7   A Reflective Feminist Science: Scientist-Citizens and Public Policies   117

Part III: Postmodern Feminism: Ethics and Citizenship   137

8   Critical Feminism: Putting-Off and Putting-On the Postmodern   143

9   Gender-Sex Plays: A Metaphorical Reformation of Public Policies   165

10   Talking Our Way Along: Ethics and Politics   189

11   Feminist Stories and a New Politics: Justice, Truth, and Ethics   207

Index   227

About the Author   230

Acknowledgments

It is not so much that the author is dead as it is that authors continue to evolve as they are shaped by their conversation partners, and so books are remnants of such conversations that remind us of them so that we can continue to carry on.

Four universities have provided me with homes for the conversations that have produced this book. First, Gonzaga University gave me my first tenured position where Jesuits, lay colleagues, and students helped me talk about the connection between ethics, gender, and politics. At Gonzaga, Fr. Frank Costello, S.J., gave me the courage to do feminist work even before getting tenure. Second, colleagues at the University of Utah taught me the strength and limits of postmodernism, and friends in political science insisted that I speak about my theories of justice. Third, colleagues at Denison University, especially in women's studies, have encouraged and supported me as they have honored me by permitting me to serve them as director of the women's studies program. Sylvia Brown and Tommy Burkett, from the Denison English Department, have furnished editorial comments that helped me find a more clear and precise voice. Joan Novak's way of being has made it clear to me that critical reflection and kindness are not opposites; Donna Childers has showed me that friendship goes beyond the university walls; and many others have provided the day to day inspiration that makes writing possible. Denison students who have worked in the women's studies office have supplied me with valuable comments on the draft, especially Rachel Haught, whose dedication to scholarship reaches beyond her undergraduate status. Students from all three universities in my feminist theory classes have encouraged me to talk about the connections between thinking and acting. Fourth, support from Ohio State University's Department of Political Science provided me with a home to begin this work and the Ohio State Postmodern Seminar, PMS, gave me the intellectual companionship that got me started. I especially want to thank Laurel Richardson who led this faculty seminar. Feminist scholars from the American Political Science Association and the Western Political Science Association have accorded me the opportunity to participate in and listen to many fine conversations about women and politics. An NEH seminar, "Interpretation and the Human Sciences," granted me a wonderful summer in Santa Cruz, as well as an opportunity to work out connections between postmodernism and feminism in a book with articles by seminar participants. My article "Rhetoric in Postmodern Feminism: Put-Offs, Put-Ons and Political Plays," published in *The Interpretive Turn: Philosophy, Science, Culture*, edited by James Bohman, David Hiley, Richard Schusterman (Ithaca: Cornell University Press, 1991), 218–44, serves as a first version of chapter 8 of this book.

Two conversation partners have played a special role in shaping this book. Robert S. Cahill has loved and annoyed me for twenty-three years by showing me that critical intellectual work requires avoiding any hint that one has all the answers. His dedication to scholarship, politics, and justice continues to inspire me. Jane Rinehart has shown me feminist possibilities that have gone beyond my imagination by living feminism through her everyday life as scholar, teacher, and friend. She has been patient in teaching me about feminism from the first time I had lunch with her in 1981 to the present, and her faith in me has sustained my work.

It is Mother's Day as I finish this manuscript, and so I wish to dedicate this work to my own mother, Eloise L. Buker, who everyday shows me how strength can be gentle and how power can be just.

Chapter 1

Listening to Three Feminist Conversations: Law, Science, and the Postmodern

The successes of the first and second waves of American feminism spectacularly mark the events of the twentieth century. Women have become part of the paid labor force, holding positions in government, art, entertainment, sports, and other fields; public life now includes a multiplicity of female representations. "Public woman" has arrived.[1] While women are increasingly found to compose a good majority of the poor, a phenomenon described as the "feminization of poverty," even this observation manifests that American women have achieved some visibility. Both male and female citizens may now even dream about the feminization of politics. For some this might mean that politics can become more caring, while others believe that changes in the political structure will give women equal representation; many on both the right and the left hope for both. The twentieth century began with women as nonvoters and ends not only with female suffrage, but with women holding two seats on the Supreme Court, major presidential cabinet posts, positions throughout the federal bureaucracy, governorships, key posts in state legislaturers, and 10 percent of congressional seats. However, sexism still prevents women from giving society the full measure of their talents, and women still are held back because they are women. Racism, poverty, ageism, and heterosexism still work their ill on the republic. But even though the work is not done, it is well begun.

Two waves of feminism have made a difference: the first, beginning in 1848, culminated with women gaining voting rights in 1920, and the second, beginning in the 1960s has moved on in the 1990s to build into the third wave. While sexism continues, changes in women's status from 1900 to the end of the twentieth century are considerable: women now constitute over 40 percent of the paid workforce while still providing primary care in the home; women serve in many executive positions including as CEOs of companies; women help shape national

1

political parties; women have been admitted to major universities and graduate schools. Nevertheless, day care, pregnancy benefits, and parental leave support women's dual responsibilities as mothers and workers, and men are increasingly taking responsibility for child care. Women have access to reproductive medical benefits; abortion is available; women are a force in electoral politics, demonstrated by attention to the gender gap, soccer moms, sexual harassment, and other issues previously labeled as "women's issues." Women's issues are now recognized as national political issues. Although the new right with its antifeminist agenda has gained power since 1980, women's issues have remained strong. Feminist issues are on the public agenda; sexual harassment is a serious concern for both public and private sector employers and has even played a part in debates about presidential impeachment. In 1990 "sexual harassment" seemed a vague, nearly meaningless concept, considered by many as an unsuccessful feminist tool; it was more likely to elicit jokes than serious charges. But all of these changes represent only steps toward creating full citizenship for U.S. women. The phrase "Politics is a man's business" is no longer unproblematic. In 1970, 40 percent of women supported changes in women's status, and by 1994, 78 percent of women supported such changes.[2] Perhaps at the end of the twenty-first century, the statement "Politics is a man's business" will wither away to remain only as a historical oddity—preserved in history classes where professors try to convince students that it once was really like that and students puzzle over the bigotries of their foreparents.

The twentieth century has brought a new feminist imagination to American public life that has made public space for women and regenerated politics. At the opening of this century women from so-called privileged families hoped to do the "right" thing and stay at home to be full-time mothers; in 1999 successful women from such families as well as working class families do the "right" thing by having careers and being mothers. While this double burden may not produce more freedom, this shift represents a new image of women that reframes politics, just as politics has reformed images of women with the government recruitment of female workers during World War II, the transition from an industrial to a social service economy, and the end of cold-war militarism. Furthermore, new feminist imaginations have played roles in key political movements—including peace politics, environmentalism, multiculturalism, the Black movement, the Chicano movement, the gay-lesbian movement, disability movements, alternative health organizational efforts, and others. Feminist imaginations have reshaped images of a host of problems associated with public housekeeping: clean air, housing, potable water, employment, education for children, opportunities for self-development, medical care, nutritional standards for food, regulation of drugs, and other matters that nurture and maintain citizens. Women are now voting members of the republic and so have acquired the right and obligation to participate in politics.

Current feminist theories offer American citizens a variety of political conversations. Affecting citizens in both personal and political ways, these conversations raise questions about how citizens form identities, families, and communities. Transforming American public discourse, feminism has brought an intensity to public discussions about gender issues that makes politics a personal everyday matter. Some of that has been very beneficial, and some of it has created more problems than it has solved. Nevertheless, feminism is no longer of interest just to women; men care about feminism and write about their roles in it. Political leaders from the right, middle, and left—from Republican, Democratic, and third parties—pay attention to feminist intellectuals who develop political theories by drawing from conservative, liberal, and radical values. Middle of the road government bureaucrats and marginalized political activists think about gender issues to figure out how to reform public policies to include the half of the population called "women."

In the academy, feminist scholarship has reached into almost every discipline, and feminist theories have questioned basic concepts—for example, work, sex, gender, sexuality, power, parenting, socialization, language, rituals, God, cosmologies, nature, nuclei, pronouns, poetry, performance, and art. As feminist theories intersect with a multiplicity of other theories, feminist discourses continue to revise theories and generate new understandings, new words, new images, and new metaphors. In this sense, feminism offers a new paradigm and alters other paradigms. Sometimes the paradigm shifts offer methods of inquiry, revised vocabularies, new canons, fresh conceptions of the self, and renewed concerns for political deliberation. Certainly, feminist scholars working in concert with feminist activists have enabled American citizens to develop policies and practices that move toward a gender-inclusive democratic society—a society that can enable both women and men to contribute their talents to public life.

WHAT CONNECTS FEMINISTS CONVERSATIONS ABOUT LAW, SCIENCE, AND THE POSTMODERN?

For this analysis, I have selected three conversations that have engaged feminist intellectuals: (1) feminist jurisprudence, (2) feminist science, and (3) postmodern feminism. While most of these intellectuals work primarily within the academy, many understand their work as political in that they hope their efforts will help build a better society. Rejecting the view that the academy is a separate institution untouched by current social values, feminist scholars understand the academy as an important source for critiques of those social values. Scholars working in feminist jurisprudence are especially well positioned to contribute to American politics because the law provides a key discourse for talking about justice. Feminist jurisprudence connects public life and the law by focusing on issues of gender. Thus, it can help citizens develop new ways of understanding justice that enable the courts to serve female and male citizens more fairly. I find this conversation useful in that it helps demonstrate how the courts provide forums for talking about justice in broader social contexts. Because scientific discourse has provided modernity with basic resources for understanding the difference between truth and falsehood, conversations among those in feminist science are important for political work. Feminist scientific scholars examine truth claims, the construction of rules of evidence, and interpretive strategies in order to see how the truth can be useful in building better gender-inclusive epistemologies that have import for social practices. Postmodern feminist discourse is important to politics because postmodernism analyzes the relationships between cultural practices and the ethical codes that construct public life. Cultural habits inscribe ethics into the *constitution* of everyday politics and so guide citizens in ways that may be even more powerful than the U.S. Constitution. For example, cultural habits "tell" students to take seats and professors to stand at the podium, moves that have ethical and political relevance in a classroom. While this example may seem trivial, many such examples work in concert to reshape power relationships and form the basic components of social interactions. When such habits are taken for granted, their power is magnified. Because postmodern feminist philosophy studies how language and culture shape understandings of the self, political life, and moral codes, it can produce new ways of analyzing and speaking about citizenship, ethics, and politics that can in turn offer new strategies for social change. Thus, feminist conversations about the law, science, and the postmodern can invigorate feminist politics by focusing on justice, truth, and ethics.

In the spirit of working toward concrete social changes, I have limited my analysis to writers who either work in the United States or publish their work in the United States. Thus, this project is focused on public practices that shape conversations at the national level in the United States. I am not searching for a political theory or set of practices that will work in all settings. The strength of this focus is that many public policies are discussed at the level of a national dialogue, even though they most often begin in local settings and may well be administered at a local level. The weakness is that local politics may not be given the attention it deserves and international issues that shape domestic policies may be overlooked. I have also limited my examination to works published since 1980 to concentrate on the formulation of current concerns that can set the political agenda for the opening years of the twenty-first century.

WHAT LINKS JUSTICE, TRUTH, AND ETHICS TO POLITICS?

Politics depends on justice, truth, and ethics. Modern America offers citizens order through its laws and justice through its legal system. But maintaining order and achieving justice depend on accurate, true accounts of how things work.

While truth is a necessary condition for a good society, it is not a sufficient condition. Ethical actions depend on more than the true understandings of, and/or commitments to, universal principles. Ethics depends on citizens choosing the better act over the worse act. Unwilling to reject the possibility of metaphysics, I am also unwilling to concentrate my energy on the quest for universal principles. Examining the practices that guide the lives of American citizens is important because everyday practices themselves govern republican states and democratic communities. These everyday practices serve as codes and norms that guide citizen actions. I am less interested in developing grand codes or grand narratives than I am in solving immediate political problems. I find postmodern analyses helpful in this work because they make implicit cultural practices and codes explicit, which opens them up to scrutiny and evaluation. I believe citizens who clearly understand their cultural codes can then more easily choose justice over injustice. In other words, I think reflection can help citizens make ethical public choices. But my interest in ethics is itself more limited. I am concerned about the ethical relationships that shape women's public lives, and to examine this concern I turn to feminist scholarship, which aims at understanding the political position of women. Before the twentieth century, Americans found it difficult even to speak about women as public political figures. At the close of this century, the public now includes women, and so the habits and cultural practices that guide politics need to be reformulated to respond to this new gender-inclusive commitment. Feminist jurisprudence, feminist science, and postmodern feminism can help in the reformulation of politics by helping citizens to rethink justice, truth, and ethics in the new American context, which now assumes that both women and men are normal citizens with public duties.

Of course, my interest in these three feminist conversations has both theoretical and action components. I anticipate that feminist intellectuals can play leadership roles in shaping the politics of the twenty-first century. And I look toward the next wave of feminism to find ways to speak about ethics that avoid narrow fundamentalisms and hollow abstractions. Narrow fundamentalism creates an atmosphere that involves demonizing others in order to aggrandize one's own group, and groups that employ these strategies often discredit politics itself so as to reserve politics for themselves and their kind. Hollow abstractions are used to affirm such issues as diversity, freedom, democracy, equality, and fairness without giving them sufficient content to even make conversations about them meaningful. Throughout my analysis of these three feminist conversations, I examine how the theoretical positions of a variety of feminist authors suggest new policies and practices for American citizens. The question "What can citizens do?" serves as a beginning point for my analysis.

I turn to theories to respond to this question because theories enable citizens to move beyond incremental, immediate responses to problems in order to rework the problem from its basics up. Many feminists work on theories in order to articulate new ways of understanding the world. Because old theories were developed to understand men and male models of public life, they need reframing in order to include women. Because of the ways in which patriarchy has shaped current political theories, incremental responses to the simple question "What can be done?" often merely evoke patriarchal theories without taking account of the political viewpoints that have framed them. Feminist theories offer promise for moving citizens closer to justice for both women and men because they acknowledge their explicit connections to politics, and so encourage their readers to reflect on the politics of their theories. Old theories built on earlier political experiences are not always sufficiently innovative to open up new possibilities. While some think about theory as an ideal that arises out of individual visions, I do not use the word "theory" in this way. I use the word "theory" to refer to explanations that guide actions. Some theories are implicit and are often unnoticed, like the American theory that competition motivates humans. Others are more explicit and contested, like the theory that capitalism depends on exploitation to serve the economic needs of the rich. Still others are more innovative, like the theory that pornography is a violation of the civil liberties of women as a group. All three of these types of theories arise out of political experiences and are designed to shape political life. Theories are not separate from politics. This understanding of theory is often called praxis because its holders argue that practices shape the formulation of theories, and theories shape the sort of actions that believers select. Thus, theories are more accurately the result of political experiences than the wild imaginations of either good or bad visionaries. Theories are connected to the question of "What can be done?" Because political theories can enable citizens to develop new understandings of politics that can lead to transformative cultural practices, theory building is necessary for political work. I give my attention to theory seeking to find new ways of thinking about feminist politics so that I might articulate new ways of acting that will introduce a new gender-inclusive politics. These reflections reform the question from "What can citizens do?" to "How can citizens create justice for women and men?"

HOW DOES FEMINIST POLITICS REFRAME CITIZENSHIP?

In a democratic society, the term "citizen" implies responsibility for civic public life, which includes accountability for the actions of the government. "We" the citizens are the government. While some may attempt to diminish the participation of others in government, the responsibility for public acts rests with all the citizens. This work of carrying out such public obligations bonds citizens together into moments that they experience as "community." In this sense, a citizen's duty involves taking account of the interests of the entire republic, which means considering the common good of the state as well as the good of each individual within the republic. Although in modern America interest group politics has de-emphasized this aspect of citizenship, citizenship is an invitation to transcend narrow interests to find what is good for the whole polity. This means considering the common good—choosing actions, practices, and policies that will produce the best solution for all those in the polity—or at least choosing the actions that will do the least harm. This need not be an invitation to ignore differences and pretend "we" are all alike, and it does not require a singular focus on the things "we" have in common. It does not require all to agree about political matters. Politics thrives on disagreement and the willingness to struggle toward agreements while realizing their transitory nature. While maintaining a diverse collection of identities, individuals need not relinquish those differences to answer the call to citizenship. However, the role of citizen does require reflections on the common good. Such a common good need not be limited to current citizens, for citizens might consider how actions promote a common good that respects the reputations of those who have gone before and the needs of those who are yet to come.

My desire for women to achieve full citizenship motivates my writing. Citizenship is a complicated concept with intellectual import, symbolic weight, and legal-political implications.[3] Throughout this book, I address my remarks to citizens who I imagine as my audience. This term first entered my text because I wished to avoid the ambiguous term "we" that authors often use to entice their reader into believing that the writer and reader exist in a single community. I know that my readers are unlikely to be persuaded by the rhetoric of this pronoun. This left me with no one to whom to address my text, no figure or pronoun to represent my audience or my reader. The use of "I," while handy, does not fill this gap for two reasons. First, this is not a diary in which I am speaking about my life, but an essay in which I am speaking about public matters, about "our" life together as political persons. Second, a focus on an individual, which is suggested by the pronoun "I," can misdirect matters to attend to individuals who live isolated, autonomous lives designed to fulfill the wants and dreams that flow from some separate internal source. Not only do I reject that view of the individual, I reject that view of myself as a person. In a liberal society, individualism is important because individuals are the bearer of rights and the distinctions among individuals serve to check governmental and social forces, but liberalism also teaches that individuals are responsible to and for one another. In fact, individualism is itself meaningless outside the context of social connections. In this classical liberal sense, politics is an essential and unavoidable part of becoming a full adult human being. While totalitarian governments and monarchies often construct the role of citizen as obedient *servant*, democratic and constitutional republics construct the role of citizen as *co-rulers* with civic responsibilities. In a republic, the "buck" stops not with the president, but with the citizens; each citizen has an obligation to participate in public life, in politics. But the construction of public life is not limited to government, for politics includes the variety of means by which citizens act to achieve a good public life together. Politics includes the habits, institutions, cultural patterns, and everyday acts that compose public life, frame nation-states, and construct local as well as worldwide communities. While the concept of citizenship predates the nation-state system and extends beyond state boundaries, one important arena for performing the work of citizenship in the United States is at the national level. Governance is often represented as voting for representatives or expressing views on public policies. I include in my understanding of citizenship such actions as writing multinational corporate executives and organizing boycotts, which can shape economic practices in arenas that stretch beyond a particular nation-state. In this sense I employ the concept of world citizenship as it has been developed by Martha Nussbaum, and I suggest that the obligations of citizenship go beyond the boundaries of the nation-state.[4] If citizenship means taking responsibility for public life, then all persons are citizens who can and do take responsibility for examining public actions, for correcting injustices, and for promoting fair practices. Obviously, this does not mean that citizens have to rule on every act, but it does mean that citizens have a duty to evaluate how actions contribute toward building a good public life. Of course, not all actions have public import and the private/public distinction is vital for understanding how some actions are public, and the wise citizen continually works to understand the proper distinction between public and private matters.

A democratic republic is built through the wise acts of its citizens. Because my hope is to encourage citizens to use their wisdom in politics, I address my story to citizens. I hope that a variety of "we's" might act collectively as citizens in order to build a better life with each other and I hope that that life will include women as full citizens, which will make the next millennium different from the last two.[5]

HOW CAN FEMINIST THOUGHT CHANGE POLITICS?

First- and second-wave feminism brought changes to American public life. But American public life also brought political changes to feminism. While the abolitionist movement provided an initial momentum to the first wave and the civil rights movement provided momentum to second-wave feminism, it has taken some time for feminists to give racism and ethnicity the measure of attention necessary. Furthermore, the early stages of second-wave American feminism were dominated by a heterosexual bias that created conflict within organizations and threatened to undo political gains. While marxist and socialist feminist theory paid attention to class, only more recently have feminist scholars given attention to the intersections of race/class/gender/sexuality. While the political experiences of feminist scholars and activists have brought that intersection into view, those experiences have been and probably will continue to be painful as well as productive. Other intersections loom on the horizon with promise for expanding feminist politics.

To understand this political movement requires drawing from a variety of viewpoints, so I have turned to poststructuralism and hermeneutics to emphasize the role of culture in shaping politics. I use this analytical framework to examine how three conversations in feminist theory—in the law, science, and the post-modern—can be used to develop a feminist politics that eliminates women's secondary status in American politics. My interpretation endeavors to make explicit the ways in which feminist thought involves quests for the good and just life for both women and men. Because the present status of feminist thought is ambiguous—both accepted as philosophy and criticized as a controversial field touched by politics—feminist theorists and others who challenge present value systems have the opportunity to become more reflective about the political dimensions of their work than those whose work primarily supports prevailing belief systems. This reflectivity is an important virtue because it makes it possible for a scholar to articulate his or her own values while engaging in objective social critiques.

In this sense, feminist theories can be thought of as interpretive turns that give both modern and postmodern philosophical frameworks new and decidedly different spins going beyond scientific objectivism and beyond merely adding gender to analyses.[6] By beginning with the simple assumption that women are important, theorists have created major alterations in philosophies such as liberalism, marxism, psychoanalysis, existentialism, and socialism. By assuming that women are as important to society as men, political activists have encountered unanticipated resistance as patriarchy has shown itself to be quite resilient. But feminist politics itself has been creative. Inspired by activists, feminists have changed theories so, that they have almost compelled them to become adjectives that modify the noun "feminism"—that is, liberal feminism, marxist feminism, psychoanalytical feminism, existential feminism, socialist feminism, and postmodern feminism. In similar ways, academic conversations about the law, science, and culture have been challenged and changed by feminist scholarship.

These transformations emerge out of two feminist commitments. First, feminists believe that women are as important to society as men. While seemingly an innocent belief that might well enjoy close to universal agreement, the belief that women are as important as men becomes radical in the context of social situations that have been in play for the last two thousand years. Masculine images, experiences, and metaphors have shaped social understandings—including methodologies, questions, operationalization of variables, vocabularies, and grammars—even though both men and women are misrepresented by such masculinized representations.

Second, feminists stress analyses that move toward constructing a better world. This political commitment to improving the lives of citizens gives feminism an impatient imminent edge. In today's political world, persons, because they are women, are raped, victimized by incest, deprived of equal pay, plunged into poverty, denied equal access to education, prohibited from promotions, forcibly sterilized, excluded from health care benefits, limited in access to national elected positions, and in other ways treated as second-class citizens. All of this is done not on the basis of merit but because they are female. Change is necessary, not only to protect and empower women, but also to achieve the values of a democratic republic that has responsibilities to all of its citizens. It is helpful to remember that the majority of U.S. citizens, which are 52 percent female, were denied the vote until 1920. Not only do women still suffer from the lack of public life, but men and children also suffer because of women's second-class citizenship. Abusing even a minority of the population deprives communities of their richest resources—the talents of their people. It is clear that misogyny targets the majority of United States citizens for abuse just as do racism and other forms of hate. Furthermore, racism, heterosexism, ageism, and other social ills intersect with gender to create hardships for women and for men. Such denigrations damage the public life of all U.S. citizens.

Because feminist political agendas seek a democracy that avoids these denigrations, feminist political theories are directed toward this end. As feminism changes understandings of law, science, and culture, feminist conversations in the areas of jurisprudence, scientific epistemology, and postmodern cultural analyses offer new ways of understanding and enacting public life. These insights can reenergize American politics and provide citizens with new commitments to an ethical public life that will enrich and delight them.

HOW DOES MY STORY PLAY A PART IN THIS ANALYSIS?

Who am I? In many feminist works, it has become customary to provide a lineage of one's historical and social identities. These identities are most often understood as socially constructed. Such a construction is itself a social, not solitary, process. Identity makes sense in the context of a social order and depends on a social order for its meaning. Identities are the result of living in and dialoguing with others. Because I think that one's social position and identity do matter, I fear the way identity politics can reduce persons to reified, even biological categories rather than the products of social interactions. Second-wave feminists were especially concerned with the way biological discourse was used to reify women's roles. Because social interactions and political experiences have shaped my life history, I want to suggest some of the locations that have constructed my relationships with others.

I have lived as a female. I could almost say I am a female even though I have performed in masculine ways, especially when I have been in predominately male situations. But I hesitate to formulate this as a category that can fully represent me. I have two Irish-American grandmothers who told me many stories about my Irish heritage, but I first experienced liberation as an adult by living in Taiwan and working within a Chinese cultural context, which constructed my identity as American. My second major liberation experience as an adult citizen was living in a small rural working-class multiethnic community in Hawaii where whites constituted less than 20 percent of the population and where Native Hawaiian culture was prominent. Here I became a haole, a stranger with a different breath. Some see my skin as white, so I gain some of the privileges that go with that body sign. Because I grew up in a middle-class community, poverty has not been a part of my life's struggle, although I have lived in a poor working-class community. I was married at 21 and did not find myself an independent person until age 33 when independence was thrust on me by divorce. I often experience the privilege of heterosexuality because I am married, but I have directed women's studies programs for the last eight years and so I experience both the privilege of working in a predominately female community setting and the stigma that goes with it. In a democratic society in which women represent slightly more than 50 percent of the population, it might just be that women's issues could as a matter of course become matters for public concern. Nevertheless, my female identity means that I am often taken as less important, and that I need to prove myself over and over, even though I am a tenured full professor. But I am fortunate because I have friends, colleagues in many universities, and family members who correct my mistakes, as well as overlook them when there are too many to correct all at one time. The three universities where I have been tenured all support women's studies and political science and each one has provided intellectual nourishment for me. I have power and yet am also oppressed. I have been helped and harmed as I am sure that I have helped and harmed others. I am sorry for the harm I have done others and regret the anger I still experience toward those who have harmed me.

While I believe that the personal is political, this phrase works when citizens remember that the two are not the same. Radical feminists taught us that politics is not depersonalized activity. To be political is to be involved; what happens in personal lives comes from and can reframe what happens in public life. My quest for justice, truth, and ethics is a personal quest, but more importantly, it is also a political quest that anticipates a world in which public discussions and public matters respect women as citizens without disrespecting men as citizens. Years of treating women as second-class citizens have harmed public life and damaged individuals. So this quest for justice, truth, and ethics begins in a context that is already unequal. This quest, however, is not about my personal situation or my self-interest as a woman. Although my quest involves scrutinizing practices that are unjust to women, my concern is not only about women. Such unfair practices harm everyone. My focus is on how citizens can construct a good life together.

HOW CAN I DRAW TOGETHER THE LAW, SCIENCE, AND THE POSTMODERN TO INFORM FEMINIST POLITICS?

In part I, I examine feminist jurisprudence to explore how this discourse can help citizens talk about the connection between gender and justice. By analyzing how legal rhetoric constructs social practices, I show how feminist jurisprudence illuminates the male bias in legal practices in order to offer new authority patterns that promise justice to both women and men. Using women's situations to locate unjust practices, feminist legal theorists explain how the law can be used to restructure social patterns and create habits that encourage more just practices for women, for men similarly situated, and for others. In the second chapter on the law, I examine the strategies that feminists offer for altering legal methods so they will take account of women's situations. Once citizens can take account of women's situations as well as men's, they are well positioned to make use of the law to glean images of fair, just actions to use in their everyday lives. Thus, in the third chapter on the law, I argue that judgments are a part of everyday life because all actions depend on them. Rather than arguing that citizens should not judge others, I argue that citizens need to talk about judgment differently. Thus, the problem that confronts citizens is not how they might avoid judgments but how they might make them fairly. I argue for contingent judgments acknowledging that citizens continually change and so cannot be classified once and for all as certain types of persons. While judgments need to be made about situations, actions, and circumstances, this need not involve judging the worth of persons. My mother, Eloise L. Buker, says this more directly by teaching that citizens are to judge actions, not persons.[7] In understanding judgment in this way, I am arguing that citizens need to be open to changes in themselves as well as others, while being closed to acts that promote injustice and ill will. By developing understandings of judgments as contingent decisions about actions, citizens can be more effective in making fair decisions, resisting universal claims that attempt to classify persons for their lifetime. Furthermore, I argue that fair decisions rely more on self-conscious judgment than on neutrality. This critique of neutrality has import for courts, for legal discourse, and for public conversations. Equally important is the fact that citizens in a democracy have an obligation to create justice in their everyday lives. Thus, courts and citizens share the responsibility for making justice happen in the American polity. Extending beyond litigation and arbitration, courts serve as political institutions that provide forums for talking about justice and its realization in current social situations. In this understanding of the law, attorneys are not limited to self-centered, or even client-centered advocacy but serve as court officers who facilitate just outcomes. In practice, many attorneys already assume this understanding of their work. This understanding of the law assumes that just solutions benefit all parties, and it makes the courts a regular resource for discussing justice rather than a last resort for conflict resolution. In this way, courts serve as political institutions that enforce good, just decisions for individuals and for the public.

Part II examines feminist scientific conversations to understand how science can offer citizens epistemological insights that connect truth and politics. As pedagogies have become politicized, the politics of knowledge has permeated education in ways that both limit and liberate students. But even before the cultural wars and before debates about curriculum canons, American citizens have known that good politics depends on a good education system. It is so important that state and local governments use public funds to support the education of students from kindergarten to grade 12. A central feature of education is enabling students to distinguish between truth and falsehood, and science has provided one avenue for performing this task. In modern contexts, this search for the truth has often been spoken about as a struggle—articulated in gendered imagery—between objectivity and subjectivity.[8] The objective truth is hard, factually objective, and masculine whereas subjectivity is soft, opinionated, and feminine. Thus, I begin the exploration of the connections between truth and politics by examining how feminists reconstruct scientific methods by reframing scientific metaphors to avoid the representation of truth as a masculine entity. These new metaphors enable feminist scientific discourse to move citizens from simplistic positivist understandings of objectivity to complex understandings of the ways in which social positions and standpoints shape scientific work. Although not alone in this movement beyond positivism, feminists contribute an important dimension to it because they underscore how knowledge has been represented in masculine terms. Standpoint analyses recognize the intimate connections between social practices and knowledge, but even more important, they lead to reflective, hermeneutical analyses that enable scientists to gain self-knowledge in the process of gaining knowledge about the world.[9] Chapter 5 argues not only that truth and accuracy depend on thoughtful methodologies and on careful scientists, but also that truth depends on careful readers. I argue that those who listen to science need to develop new ways of reading and interpreting science that desanctifies it while still honoring the ways in which science promotes clear, critical analyses. The second chapter in my examination of feminist science, chapter 6, offers a new metaphor, science as "storytelling," to support the new epistemologies developed by feminist scientists and others who have urged scientists, intellectuals, and citizens to read science differently. This new understanding of science not only acknowledges how science is already implicated in public matters from the beginning points of each inquiry, but it makes a virtue of this vice. Scientists' connections to their social settings, I argue, makes scientific work meaningful and relevant. In other words, science works not because it can isolate itself from social life but because it is connected to social life. Therefore, such connections should not be understood as pollutants to be controlled in scientific experiments. Chapter 7 uses feminist scientific conversations to reframe the connection between public life and scientific work. Feminist reflections on science do not avoid politics, nor do they reduce science to politics. Instead, they work out ethical links between social power and knowledge. While a variety of philosophers of science have argued for such reflectivity, feminist scientists reveal how gendered images make such reflectivity difficult. Avoiding gendered images of truth and falsehood, these feminist scientists show how to move beyond objectivity and subjectivity to engage in reflective epistemologies. In chapter 7, I develop a model of scientific reflection that can serve as the basis for conversations among a variety of citizens who can draw on a variety of epistemologies, including "women's ways of knowing,"[10] to discuss public policy issues so that knowledge can inform politics.

Chapter 8 begins with an overview of postmodern feminism to examine the ways in which it both challenges feminist thought and is challenged by it in the work of cultural analysis. Following this overview of how feminists are put-off by postmodernism and how they might "put it on," I show how feminists can use postmodernism to develop a new politics that is both playful and progressive. In chapter 9, I show how postmodern feminist rhetoric can build contextualized social analyses that enable feminists to use symbols to reframe American politics. Such symbols are readily at hand for large numbers of women; they are easy to lift, and they are inexpensive. I give particular attention to four sets of metaphors: (1) hybrid selves, (2) the body, (3) geography, and (4) language. This chapter offers a twelve-gender system to demonstrate the deconstructive and reconstructive possibilities for a playful postmodern feminist turn. I close with a discussion of the political gains and losses that can be created by employing ambiguities, which are facilitated by postmodernism. In chapter 10, I offer a feminist model of ethics, which embraces a form of liberalism emphasizing citizen responsibilities, pluralism, the power of everyday discourse, and the possibility of an ever-changing polity that takes itself both more playfully and more seriously. This model offers a discursive process for arriving at ethical decisions that does not eschew rules and principles, but privileges dialogue and deliberation. I close with reflections on my own struggle to use postmodern feminism to develop a moral discourse that can realize the goals of feminist politics and gender justice. I hope my struggles can help feminists use postmodern feminism to advance the cause of full citizenship in the United States for both women and men.

My closing chapter shows how the metaphor of story can be used to bring these three feminist conversations together while respecting their differences. The storytelling metaphor offers a blend of theory and practice that can connect women's experiences with feminist analyses. Stories employ theories but they do so in the context of particular situations. This storytelling praxis shows how explicit articulations of the moral codes revealed through narratives offer ways to speak about politics that support a new feminist conversation and a new form of politics. This feminist politics goes beyond argumentation and debate to build political conversations about moral questions that encourage discussions among citizens. These discussions acknowledge the difficulty of making good decisions while they authorize citizens to take responsibility for creating a good public life. A good public life does not depend so much on uniformity as it does on the ability to deliberate in ways that produce reflections on the multiplicity of values and needs that shape public concerns. Because some values and needs are contradictory, such deliberations require reasoned arguments, careful listening, and compassion.

For me, feminist politics offers a way to transform public life continually by inviting citizens to transform themselves continually as well. Public conversations can draw citizens closer to our/their full potential as individuals, as partners in intimate family groups, as members of a state, and as parts of communities that reach beyond the state. These three feminist conversations about justice, truth, and ethics can facilitate the transformative work already done by the women's movement and by the other citizens who have joined them in reforming laws, public policies, and institutional habits. Thus, they contribute to a better public life in America by encouraging thoughtful deliberations on how the U.S. democratic republic can serve both women and men. My hope is that this book might support discussions about how justice, truth, and ethics can be created in the daily lives of citizens to support new gender-inclusive social responsibilities that can bring forth a new politics. I hope that "we" citizens now includes women, and that we will look to both men and women for political leadership.

NOTES

1. A review of the earlier ways that barred women from politics can be found in the now classic text, Jean Bethke Elshtain, *Public Man, Private Woman: Women in Social and Political Thought* (Princeton, N.J.: Princeton University Press, 1981).

2. Nancy E. McGlen and Karen O'Connor, *Women, Politics, and American Society* (Englewood Cliffs, N.J.: Prentice Hall, 1995), 292, table from Roper Center for Public Opinion.

3. Ruth Lister, *Citizenship: Feminist Perspectives* (New York: New York University Press, 1997); and Paul Barry Clarke, ed. *Citizenship* (London: Pluto Press, 1994).

4. Martha Nussbaum, with respondents, edited by Joshua Cohen, *For Love of Country: Debating the Limits of Patriotism* (Boston: Beacon Press, 1996).

5. For the importance of hope in politics, see Cornell West, *Race Matters* (Boston: Beacon Press, 1993).

6. By interpretive turn, I am referring to feminist methodologies, to feminist readings of a variety of canons, and to feminist strategies for understanding social phenomena. For summaries of the epistemology involved in these turns, see Eloise A. Buker, "Can Feminism Politicize Hermeneutics and Reconstruct Deconstruction?" *Social Epistemology* 5 (1991): 361-69; "Feminist Social Theory and Hermeneutics: An Empowering Dialectic?" *Social Epistemology* 4 (1990): 23–39.

7. Eloise L. Buker, conversation in Columbus, Ohio, April 1996.

8. For summary of arguments, see Richard J. Bernstein, *Beyond Objectivism and Relativism: Science, Hermeneutics, and Praxis* (Philadelphia: University of Pennsylvania Press, 1983).

9. Buker, "Feminist Social Theory and Hermeneutics" and "Can Feminism Politicize Hermeneutics and Reconstruct Deconstruction?"

10. I borrow this phrase from Mary Field Belenky, Blythe McVicker Clinchy, Nancy Rule Goldberger, Jill Mattuck Tarule, *Women's Ways of Knowing: The Development of Self, Voice, and Mind* (New York: Basic Books, 1986).

Part I

❖ ❖ ❖

Feminist
Jurisprudence:
Justice and Politics

Many American citizens think about their own connections with politics and the state in terms of voting and the law. While both are important aspects of American politics, I choose to focus on the law because it can serve as a common point of reference for citizens to talk about public codes of conduct, guidelines for behavior. The law connects codes of conduct and the quest for fair codes (that is, justice) with a governmental institution, the court system (that is, politics). Jurisprudence is an area of the law that concentrates on the connections between the law and social life and so most directly connects justice and politics. Because women were not originally given public power in the founding of the United States, feminists now have a special opportunity to reexamine authority patterns to incorporate women into our evolving U.S. democratic practices. Thus, feminist jurisprudence holds promise for providing not only a deep structural critique of legal practices, but also for finding new ways for Americans to talk about morality and fairness. Such talk can reach beyond the legal arena to shape national viewpoints on justice. But I also selected the law as a focus point because my first experience with political justice took place in legal terms.

Attending first grade at Montrose Avenue Elementary School was not as exciting as I had hoped it would be. That experience was made worse by the appearance of an excessive number of rules. Some of these rules were clearly sensible, but others seemed not only inefficient but unfair. One such rule was invented in the middle of my first grade year. *Students had to enter through the school door closest to their homes.* For me that was the east door, but my father always let me off at the west door, which was on the side facing my grandmother's house, which was located right across from the school. Often she would be sitting on her porch swing and would wave at me as we went by. My father would then watch me enter at the west door to be sure that I had arrived safely. If I walked around the building to the other entrance, he could not watch me enter. If he let me off at the east door, not only did I have to cross the street to enter the building, but I could not see my grandmother who lived on the other side. The rule seemed unfair and decreased my safety. After having taught in public school for five years, I still cannot imagine why this rule was so important to my teachers. Since my father was in law school, I asked him if this rule was a law. He said no, so I asked him to have the rule declared illegal since it exerted unnecessary control over me. The rule held, but in the process of pursuing this issue, I discovered that a six-year-old female could get some attention to her issues by utilizing the law as a moral authority to frame them. Litigation talk had inspired some careful listening by the adults in my world.

My second attempt to call upon the law was more effective. At age 33, I found myself in a divorce proceeding with a husband, who had found a younger woman and so decided to end our ten-year marriage. Although he promised always to look after my needs and had urged me to avoid the expense of an attorney, I decided that I wanted that promise in legal language. I was seeking three years of alimony to attend graduate school. Despite his promises to take care of me, six months after the divorce, he informed me that he could not afford to give me any more money, because he was worried that he might be laid off from his position as an airline pilot. This time the law proved more helpful; the legal system insisted that he keep his word. The law had offered me not only a forum for moral deliberation but gave it verbal force. In this case, verbal force was sufficient. Of course, such force depended on my ability to hire an attorney and my ex-husband's respect for the law. Our shared middle-class values made the legal discourse effective. But even this small example made it clear to me that the law reaches beyond individuals to shape the formulation of relationships. The law helped me and those around me consider what was a fair dissolution. It is this connection between fairness (justice) and relationships that makes legal conversations important for feminist politics.

The state, communities, organizations, corporations, and clubs are all shaped by the sorts of relationships persons have with one another. Public life orchestrates these relationships and politics makes them dynamic. For feminist politics to reform these relationships—in the state, communities, organizations, corporations, and clubs—requires close analysis of how such institutions have created gender bias practices. It is a vital and huge task. By limiting my analysis to the connection between the law and politics, I hope to focus this task on one dimension of how these relationships are structured. But feminist jurisprudence goes beyond what happens in courtrooms to shape what happens in the daily lives of persons within ear reach of legal talk. Although many citizens may never find themselves in court, the law shapes actions by providing models of what counts as acceptable and unacceptable behavior, that is, what is good and bad. Feminist politics becomes stronger when it can give public accounts of the values that shape feminist policy proposals. I hope by exploring feminist legal talk to make it easier for feminists and others to talk about gender justice by applying these accounts to a variety of situations.

WHY IS FEMINIST JURISPRUDENCE IMPORTANT?

Feminist jurisprudence works by linking legal discourse with feminist analyses.[1] Feminist jurisprudence seeks a new method of legal analysis unlike critical legal studies, which treats language as manipulation; unlike marxism, which treats definitions of justice as issues outside the law; and unlike liberalism, which treats justice as primarily a legal phenomenon. Feminist jurisprudence seeks new images and metaphors to politicize the law in order to secure justice for women and men. To politicize the law is to make it more responsive to the needs of public life; it is not to make it more responsive to the needs of those with status and/or wealth. Public life depends on citizens who can apply general principles and values to particular situations. If feminist jurisprudence can enable American citizens to talk about justice, to make fair decisions, and to negotiate the tension between particular situations and abstract cultural principles, it can improve public life.

While Americans hesitate to talk about justice, they/we are ready for such talk in relationship to legal matters. The structure of legal discourse helps create that ease in two ways. First, the American legal process recognizes the difficulty of making good decisions. It assumes that controversy over justice exists and so makes provision for at least two opposing positions to be fully presented. And it assumes the possibility of human error and so provides for appeals. Second, the law works by acknowledging a natural tension between particular situations and abstract principles.[2] Whereas legal codes offer abstract principles, courts examine particular cases. In turn, courts, through their rulings, create a body of legal precedents that serve as legal principles for interpreting the law. These rulings adjust, define, and thereby, to a degree, alter those "original" abstract principles. Legal proceedings value both the principles that guide their deliberations and the concrete situations that require judges and juries to reflect on the law by examining particular cases. Because political talk has focused primarily on abstract principles, the inclusion of particular cases in legal discourse is particularly important to feminists who have shown that daily concrete situations are vital for understanding women's situations.[3] Feminist jurisprudence can revitalize contemporary politics because of its focus on justice and its emphasis on the role of concrete examples in understanding social systems. Any new set of practices or theories will need to take account of women in reforming democracy in the United States. Therefore, feminist jurisprudence is an especially rich discourse for thinking about politics and how to do it well. While second-wave feminist activists were concerned that the law itself was a conservative force for patriarchy, the failure of the ERA and the even limited success of *Roe v. Wade* has helped to show how legal feminists create fundamental, even radical, social change.

Three types of legal powers serve as a background for examining the new connections feminists offer between law and politics. First, courts exercise power by allocating resources to litigants. Second, courts shape practices by establishing legal precedents. Once the courts have ruled in an area, citizens follow the practice to avoid litigation. Thus, the law reaches beyond a particular case to a set of practices. Third, the courts exercise power through the kinds of conversations that legal discourse helps establish in America. While the three areas are interwoven, it is this third area that I will examine to see how feminists can and do change legal discourse and thereby perform political work.

But legal discourse has played a contradictory role in the authority structure in the United States; feminists, like others, are both critical of legal power and rely on it. A feminist mantra chants dissatisfaction with the state and legal authority. Feminists have a long tradition of being suspicious of anyone at the "top," but in that suspicion, they share the concerns of the Founders who wanted a Bill of Rights, the separation of powers, and limitations on majority rule.[4] They feared kinglike authority and justified the consolidation of state power on the basis of protection. Not only did this offer a masculinist image of the state, but it created a minimalist public arena with little appreciation for political work. But feminists extend their/our suspicions with equal vigor to the private sphere—to corporations, who may fail to provide equal pay, fair hiring and firing; to organizations that may contain sexual harassment; and to families, who may fail to provide protection against domestic abuse, incest, rape, forced pregnancies, and forced abortions. By extending a critical eye not only to state power but also to authority in general, feminists have developed a critique of the "law and order" story and contemporary versions of liberalism that leave justice to the courts.

This critique does not go so far as to embrace anarchy—the elimination of all political authority—because feminists have found that it offers no collective strategies for eliminating racist-sexist behavior or for addressing other public wrongs. Marxist and socialist feminists who seek a stateless, classless society place authority in the hands of those who can move the historical dialectic forward.[5] While marxists and socialists explain patriarchy and racism, their political strategies sometimes are so global that they can be ineffective for undoing such problems in local settings. To fight such ills as racism, sexism, and heterosexism, American feminists often turn to the law: litigation, domestic violence legislation, the Equal Pay Act, and other legal mechanisms. The minimal success of such strategies has given support to feminist legal scholars who want to go beyond merely using the law as a tool for change. They seek changes in legal practices themselves. My focus is on how their rhetoric can be used both to facilitate legal changes and to reformulate the connection between justice and politics.

HOW CAN FEMINIST JURISPRUDENCE CONNECT JUSTICE AND POLITICS?

I begin the first chapter (chapter 2) with brief definitions of power, authority, justice, and citizenship. Drawing on my experience of feminist politics and political theory, I have designed these definitions to emphasize how all persons can and should be a part of public conversations. Sometimes, such public conversations will be smooth and amiable and so fit neatly into the structure of American public life and at other times the conversations shake that structure. I consider both sorts of conversations political to the degree that they attempt to create better public policies and practices.

Following these definitions, I examine how feminist jurisprudence offers new ways of speaking about the law and politics by analyzing the metaphors that these feminists employ. Metaphors offer insight into how a theory or story works and so analyses of metaphors show how basic concepts are put together.[6] By examining the key metaphors to learn how these feminists understand authority, I argue for replacing a set of old metaphors with new ones suggested by feminist jurisprudence discourse. Authority is important to feminist politics because it centers on how power is legitimated. While these old metaphors were perhaps appropriate for creating an authority with sufficient power for a group of dedicated men to found a nation, they no longer serve at this stage in the evolution of U.S. democracy, which now places women in positions of official public leadership. New metaphors can reform the symbols of authority and so change social-political practices. But new metaphors are not enough. In the next chapter, I examine how the law offers citizens ways of gathering information and making fair decisions. I examine how legal procedures and methods, which were designed to address men's needs, can be changed to deliver a greater measure of fairness to both women and men. Such reformulations enable the law to guide citizens toward better decisions in their everyday lives. But better decisions depend on citizens taking more active part in public life. In the third chapter on the law, I argue that it is important for citizens to use their political power to make reflective judgments. I offer four ways such judgments can enable citizens to become more effective in shaping the law and other cultural practices that serve as guidelines for everyday life situations. Emphasizing the politics of everyday life encourages discussions by all citizens about what needs to be done and how proposals for action create and/or fail to create just relationships.

These three chapters on the law emphasize how politics is interwoven with justice and how the law can help citizens talk about this connection as it appears in public courtrooms and in the everyday lives of women and men. For this connection to address the lives of both women and men requires some focus on women because from 1776 to 1920, women were excluded from many aspects of public life including the vote. Although women now vote, no woman has ever been president or vice-president; women regularly make up less than 10 percent of Congress, and few women serve as CEOs of corporations. Can feminist jurisprudence help citizens integrate women more fully into public life?

NOTES

1. For comments on this chapter, I wish to thank John Nelson, Tommy Burkett, Donna Childers, and Jenny Schenk.

2. For this general comment about the law, I thank John Nelson.

3. Carol Gilligan, *In a Different Voice: Psychological Theory and Women's Development* (Cambridge, Mass.: Harvard University Press, 1982); and Bettina Aptheker, *Tapestries of Life: Women's Work, Women's Consciousness, and the Meaning of Daily Experience* (Amherst: University of Massachusetts Press, 1989).

4. Zillah R. Eisenstein demonstrates how Locke utilized a critique of patriarchy to undo the state while failing to undo its existence in the family, *The Radical Future of Liberal Feminism* (New York: Longman, 1981).

5. For overviews, see Rosemarie Tong, *Feminist Thought: A Comprehensive Introduction* (Boulder, Colo.: Westview Press, 1989); and Alison M. Jaggar, *Feminist Politics and Human Nature* (Totowa, N.J.: Rowman & Allanheld, 1983).

6. For metaphorical analyses, see Eloise A. Buker, *Politics through a Looking-Glass: Understanding Political Cultures through a Structuralist Interpretation of Narratives*, (New York: Greenwood Press, 1987) and Paul Ricoeur, *The Rule of Metaphor: Multidisciplinary Studies of the Creation of Meaning in Language*, trans. Robert Czerny with Kathleen McLaughline and John Costello (Toronto, Canada: University of Toronto Press, 1977).

Chapter 2

Feminist Legal Discourse: Embodied Laws and Contested Authorities

To analyze the discourse of feminist jurisprudence, I draw on feminist political theory and my own political experiences to develop definitions of three basic concepts—power, authority, and citizenship. I use these concepts to highlight the political contributions of feminist legal scholars. I, then, examine the rhetorical moves in feminist jurisprudence to reveal how these feminists reconstruct the connection between politics and justice.[1] As I develop this analysis, I include suggestions about how their work can be used to build legal practices that make the law better able to address women's concerns. An important part of my concern is how the law offers citizens ways of talking about justice in everyday practices. That is, I continually ask how the law can empower citizens to act more effectively and more fairly in their everyday lives. Legal discourse is available to a broader segment of the population than is the legal system itself. Gaining access to the legal system requires funds and time. Gaining access to legal discourse is easier. Even those with limited financial resources can call on legal discourse to do political work that has real promise.

HOW CAN FEMINISM REDEFINE POWER, AUTHORITY, AND CITIZENSHIP?

Feminists, like others socialized into American liberalism, often use negative images of power that frame power in terms of control, oppression, and force. Accepting this age-old connection between power and corruption produces some unfortunate results. It encourages citizens to shy away from public political life in which power is explicitly exercised and creates a social contradiction because democratic republics depend on citizen involvement. This contradiction can be more intense for feminists because they see themselves as involved in politics.

Characterizing politics as unvirtuous, "dirty" activity can depoliticize women and may in part be responsible for the ways in which women shy away from calling themselves a "feminist." But, clearly, nothing happens without the exercise of some power. If women only see themselves as victims of social circumstances, they are less able to move to more powerful positions. This is not to say that oppression does not exist and that it can be merely denied. It is to say that power exercised on behalf of the right values is a *good* thing. Avoiding negative definitions of power and authority can help women and feminists become more fully involved in politics.[2] To equate powerlessness with virtue is dangerous for feminists because the exercise of power is necessary for social change.

New Feminist Definitions of Power

Nancy Hartsock addresses this contradiction concerning politics and power by developing a definition of power that goes beyond control and coercion to include such characteristics as "ability, capacity, and competence."[3] Relying on Hannah Arendt, Hartsock defines power as the energy to make things happen and so offers a positive definition of power: "Power is at once (1) the 'glue' that holds the community together, (2) the means by which a community is constituted, and even (3) the means by which immortality is attained and death overcome."[4]

According to Hartsock's analysis, as long as there is a group, community, or even coalition, there will be some power center that represents it, focuses its energy, provides a symbolic center, and establishes mechanisms for collective action. Giving "power" a positive image encourages feminists to acknowledge their own power and to support women who seek power. Hartsock's definition challenges the metaphor that compares politics to *dirty* business. The dirt metaphor discourages both women and men from participating in public matters and makes it too easy to characterize politicians as unscrupulous persons. While Hartsock is not arguing that feminists should no longer be critical of those in authority, she is encouraging citizens to understand the quest for power as honorable action based on a desire to perform respectable work.

Hartsock's analysis reveals that rejecting all hierarchies and forms of power can endanger feminist politics. For example, feminist organizations need to expect that members will quarrel, debate, and argue in order to become an effective group. Making their differences explicit can avoid unmindful struggles with one another. Executing projects involves members in some uneven allocation of tasks—that is, hierarchies. Because politics involves ruling and being ruled in turn.[5] It entails both empowerment and subordination. Since women and feminists have experienced greater degrees of subordination than of empowerment, it has been difficult for feminists to articulate the conditions under which women and feminists should defer to authority,[6] and because women have not yet gained equal political power, deference can have long-range consequences. On the other hand, citizens who continually challenge authority can undo the organizations, institutions, and/or states that serve them. Feminists are now in sufficient positions of power to dissolve some institutions and organizations, even our/their own. This is an important concern. Neither total challenge nor total deference works politically. Citizens need to continually decide what to critique and what to affirm in the process of exercising power.

While changes in the structure of power are important, feminists use Michel Foucault to offer a new definition of power that emphasizes that power is not a "thing" to be possessed.[7] This definition avoids negative images of power as a sum-zero-game and encourages women and men to understand power as a dimension that makes relationships work. Power as the energy between and/or among persons energizes and electrifies relationships so that they become more than the sum of their parts. Power makes relationships happen. This definition fits more readily into a feminist understanding of citizenship.

Redefining power in this way redefines political authority as a dimension of a relationship rather than an object some have and others lack. Such a definition empowers citizens by explaining how power circulates among persons to establish communities and relationships. By understanding power as a virtue that builds communities and makes relationships work, feminists can open the way for understanding politics as an activity that enriches the lives of all who participate in it. This makes it possible to understand politics not as a responsibility and burden, but as an activity in which individuals build a public life together based on virtues, values, and delights. This activity not only produces good will but it is good in itself because it enables persons to fulfill themselves as connected public persons who care about others. This care is not based merely on affection or kinships. Citizens care about others because they are "others" not like themselves but still part of themselves. Feminists who have used the term "other" to explain how women serve as permanent outsiders may well find this definition of citizenship particularly useful. If politics can bring together other outsiders—the different, the strange—then politics offers ways to connect with others on the basis of a shared humanity that is inclusive rather than exclusive. Such a politics builds community not only on unity but on differences that are to be respected, encouraged, and appreciated. With such a definition of politics, communities and organizations can build solidarities that go beyond affection and friendship. This erases the "they/we" dichotomy that arises out of inappropriate demands for others to be like us. It encourages members to reach a new level of existence by calling forth a collective being based on connecting with "others" who become part of "us."

Feminists' Interpretations of Authority and Citizenship

In democratic republics, governance is legitimated by granting authority to citizens, but that authority is not to be used simply to assert the immediate desires and/or will of even a majority of citizens. While citizens are to recognize the work of previous, even dead, citizens who have established political institutions and created organizational practices, they are to respond to the immediate concerns of their situations.[8] Today, nations and organizations lose legitimacy if they exclude women. No longer can democratic political authority rest only with male citizens.

Second-wave feminists criticized political authority by showing how the law favored men and how political authorities had created gender injustices. They put forth idealized visions of nonhierarchies in which all members would share power equally and support one another in order to avoid such abuses of power. But this nonhierarchy is dangerous because it encourages members to value the group's values and to suppress any desires that differ, or the group avoids collective action that brings differences to light. Even in social relationships some persons emerge to execute the wishes of the group. Everyone doing everything at once is a foolish model that demonstrates lack of trust rather than the presence of egalitarian relationships.

Part of the problem with second-wave understandings of authority comes from connecting hierarchy with patriarchy and egalitarianism with feminism. This dichotomy reifies an understanding of authority as a top-down structure with a pyramid chart that illuminates how power flows from the top to the others below. But such a chart misrepresents the dynamic quality of organizations. For example, American citizens often place the president at the apex of a pyramid, but at the same time, Americans affirm the "checks and balances" that counter such a fixed hierarchy. In organizations and nation-states, it may well be more accurate to describe the flow of power as a rotating or circulating process. At different times, a different component will roll to the top and serve as leader. For example, at the level of national government, sometimes the Senate exercises the primary authority over a situation, sometimes the House of Representatives, sometimes the media, sometimes the Supreme Court, and sometimes some staff members whose vision or issue articulates a consensus. While the process is fairly predictable, living organizations work by dynamic power relationships. Organizational and governmental powers are as much like a circle as they are like a pyramid.[9] The circle better articulates possibilities for democratic practices.

Similarly, in feminist organizations, leadership rotates as different members exercise their powers and talents to accomplish tasks. Rotating leadership need not destabilize the organization but instead can be part of the day-to-day operation in which members share power and responsibility. Power may move smoothly when it is shared in this rotational manner but becomes rough when people feel they need to grab and hold on to it. In trying to grab control, feminists create struggles over the rules, critique hierarchies, use personal relationships, negotiate in private settings, and debate in public forums. When an organization focuses solely on power, or when an organization ignores how it employs power, it is in danger of becoming dysfunctional. This circular image of power suggests that power functions best when it moves quietly from person to person.

When trust breaks down and power becomes *the* focus, the organization experiences an authority crisis.

Because some authority is necessary to keep a group cohesive and functional, some members' individual goals, wishes, desires, and dreams will fail to be realized. Failure to understand the fact that not all members will be satisfied can lead to disappointment, frustrations, and unproductive shouting matches among feminists. Second-wave feminists learned this lesson the hard way, as Jo Freeman's analysis of the tyranny of structurelessness reveals.[10] Then, a primary feminist question is not how to eliminate or neutralize authority; it is, "How shall authority be exercised so that hierarchies are flexible enough to sustain democratic practices and maintain the flow of power among members?" This still leaves citizens with the problem of deciding how authority is to be exercised and how much flexibility is desirable. The image of rotating hierarchies might be a way to synthesize the feminist critique of hierarchy with feminist desires to create new women-friendly institutions.

I have suggested that contingent hierarchies can help create women-friendly practices. Combining this notion of citizenship with a positive definition of power suggests that citizenship is not merely a responsibility. New versions of feminist citizenship explain citizenship as an activity that involves persons in becoming responsible for others and so evokes feminist models of care as a key way of understanding the work of citizenship.[11] First- and second-wave feminists demonstrated that becoming responsible for others makes persons into citizens. But I am suggesting that citizenship is a necessary part of becoming an adult woman who cares for others by participating in public life. These "others" are not necessarily friends and relatives but are individuals whose lives intersect in a public way as they attempt to work and live together. This sort of citizenship brings together persons who often do not have friendly feelings toward one another but who still have responsibilities to and for each other. While this assumes that communities owe individuals respect and have obligations to provide for their rights, citizenship is not so much about securing rights as it is about active participation in shaping the group's life together. Citizens have a responsibility to build good communities in the day-to-day aspects of their lives and communities need to make it possible for them to do this.

Modern liberalism emphasizes that citizens need to participate to make the group work. I am suggesting that citizenship is much more than an instrument for generating smooth or even just relationships. Humans need citizenship to develop themselves as persons. Public life with others (especially others who differ and so challenge each other), makes it possible for individuals to develop their full potential. The debates and conflicts that involve citizens in making their lives work together is a necessary condition for individuals to become full human beings. There is a part of each of us that requires connecting with others not just for affection but for the purposes of caring for and being cared for simply because we are.

My definition of citizenship does not limit it to nation-states but instead locates it in community and organizational structures designed to serve a variety of needs. Schools, banks, factories, cities, counties, and churches, for example, offer organizational structures within which opportunities for citizenship exist and which function better when participants are empowered to act as citizens by taking responsibility for making the organization work better. Because women in the United States have often been denied the opportunities of serving as full citizens, it may be easier for feminists to appreciate the value of citizenship as a personal opportunity and as a public virtue. The opportunity to act as a citizen enables individuals to grow by developing group identities that transform them into public persons. Thus, opportunities to act as a citizen often bring happiness and delight to individuals who learn to form bonds, not out of affection, but out of respect. In a classroom, this would be that all students and the teacher have a responsibility and an opportunity to make that classroom work. While they do not have the same or the same amount of responsibility, each contributes toward making the class work. The degree to which the class incorporates respect and justice is the degree to which the class becomes a community that works. Such political respect becomes possible when persons work together to make their organizational and community lives better.

My model of citizenship locates authority in the collective and emphasizes the role each person has in making an organization work. Emphasizing power as a circulating energy within an organization or institution places power with the collective rather than treating it as a *thing* possessed by the person at the top. So, for the legal system, this means that judges do not have THE power. Judges do not sit at the top of a fixed hierarchy, even though they render decisions. Those decisions come out of a chorus of voices and actions—some harmonious, some disharmonious—that includes the words of clients, the media, and attorneys, as well as other less direct cultural forces. Power emerges in the energy created by all the participants who come forward as players, as full citizens who are exercising their responsibilities to others. In this multiplicity of voices, the words of all the participants enact politics. To empower this multiplicity, citizens need to see themselves as active participants who shape public life.

HOW CAN FEMINIST LEGAL
DISCOURSE RESHAPE AMERICAN POLITICS?

While citizen participation makes the legal system a collaborative activity, words are vehicles for that activity. Anyone who has walked into a law library or utilized a legal database is aware of how the law is made through words. The court acts by speaking, and decisions are preserved through words. The distinction that Americans sometimes make between "real" action (the allocation of material resources) and talk does not work for the law where talk is action.[12] One of the courts' most important contributions to American politics is that they offer ways of talking about justice. Legal discourse shows that rhetoric is never empty but is filled with symbols that shape political life, mold expectations, and establish values. Because the law's actions take the form of words, its power easily moves from strictly legal circles to wider political ones. Hence, legal discourse—terms, conceits, rhetoric, grammar, and metaphors—reaches beyond the law to everyday conversations, and those everyday conversations in turn shape the law.[13] More "rights"—in the sense of more rightful practices—can be created through informal daily discussions about the law than through litigation and legislation. Turning to the rhetoric of feminist jurisprudence, I will examine how this discourse offers new ways of talking about American justice in order to make a new politics.

To show some of the contributions feminist jurisprudence has made to forming American political justice, I will begin by focusing on four images that appear within this discourse: (1) Father-Law, which serves to vest authority in men and in their heterosexual reproductive families; (2) male representations in which "man" attempts to represent humanity; (3) voice, which advocates hearing women's moral insights; and (4) contract, which structures personal intimate relationships as well as the relationships between citizens and the state. The first step is a critical reading of how Father-Law uses masculine imagery to limit political order to punishment and control. Second, an examination of how the law assumes a male body reveals how women are de-humanized. Third, in response to discoveries of how patriarchy shapes the law, feminists have developed a new voice to rebuild legal discourse. Fourth, as a part of that new gender-inclusive discourse, I propose replacing the contract image with a covenant analogy to articulate the connection between the citizen and the state and the connection between married and partnered persons in the family. The texts that I have selected for this analysis are part of an American feminist jurisprudence conversation that has come to the foreground since 1980. By reinterpreting these images, citizens can forge a new sense of the lawful and right, which promises to be more gender inclusive.

Father-Law and Mother-Compassion

The Father-Law image works metaphorically to link together three spheres: the private family (where "father" functions to stabilize and name the family), public social life (where laws represent paternal discipline), and the spiritual realm (where a "God-Father" presides). In each realm, the father image sits at the center to order things. Liberal popular ideology highly values this hierarchy and identifies law with order, articulated by the phrase, "law and order." This explains why neoconservatives assert the necessity of men in the household, for without a man, families appear to be out of order. Father-Law links the private and public realm by unifying them under a single male authority figure: Father, who appears in a variety of forms—economic caretaker, disciplinarian, enforcer, moral judge, protector, and head of the household.[14]

It is helpful to consider how the image of Father-Law implies a silent opposite, Mother-Out-Law, who gives comfort rather than punishment and whose compassion may come close to disrupting that order. While Father-Law provides a firm, steady hand throughout a citizen's life, Mother-Out-Law represents change and growth.[15] Mothers' guidance diminishes as children grow up; they outgrow her.[16] In contrast, Father-Law provides continuity as the life of the family as citizens move from family control to state control and beyond. What is politically dangerous about such images is the way they encode masculinity and femininity and so shape cultural responses to male and female citizens, who become life-size dolls playing out this mythic narrative that creates order by subordinating women and privatizing feminine qualities. Compassion should not be reduced to a childlike private female emotion while punishment is accorded adult male public status. The solution is not the elimination of all mythic allusions. The solution lies in replacing the metaphor equating masculinity with order with a new metaphor that imagines order in a gender-inclusive way. For example, such reductions make it hard for citizens even to imagine reducing crime except by punishment. But so far, jail crowding has not worked. Opening up new ways of thinking about law and order is important for addressing social problems. Connecting order with compassion and nurturance might suggest that programs for crime reduction begin by de-emphasizing materialism and redistributing material rewards, so that poor and rich citizens alike gain public affirmation for living simple, altruistic lives.

"Man" As Representative for WoMan

Notions of representative government became important with the birth of the modern state when governance moved from kings who ruled by divine right to presidents and prime ministers who rule with the authority of the governed. But from the birth of the modern state through the nineteenth century, citizens accepted that men represented the family, so that few considered it important even to grant women the vote. Men's bodies were used as the norm, and men's experiences shaped political, philosophical, and religious reflections. But the twentieth century has problematized "man" as a representation for all of humanity. However, remnants of male representation remain in the ways men's lives are made to explain "human" experience. Feminists like Catharine MacKinnon and Zillah Eisenstein show how the law has been built on the nature of "men" rather than the nature of humans.[17] Because of this male bias, when women are like men (the standard), women are able to operate as full "persons" before the law. But when women's lives differ from men's, women have trouble gaining just hearings.[18] Part of the problem is that the word "man" is used to refer to both women and men, yet at the same time is used to exclude the category "woman"—that is, women are to stay out of the "men's room." Despite feminist successes on this dimension, such usage still persists. This sneaky rhetorical move makes it appear as if women are just like men while simultaneously asserting the differences between the two. This rhetoric is especially dangerous if it is undetected.

Zillah Eisenstein in *The Female Body and the Law* analyzes the problem of male legal bias by analyzing the law from the perspective of the pregnant body.[19] She shows how the law treats pregnancy as a dis-ability, a dis-ease, which marks women as different—special, not normal, even sick. When the law attempts to treat pregnancy as if it were normal, the Supreme Court ends up claiming that denying medical benefits to pregnant persons is not sex discrimination because all pregnant *persons*—including pregnant men—are also denied benefits. "Person" appears to represent both women and men; but, in this case, it refers only to women. These gender ambiguities have made it easier to treat women unfairly. Because the law begins with the assumption that the male body represents all humans, it ends up placing "women" in double binds: for example, women must be like men to be human and different in order to be women. Eisenstein does not want to inscribe into the law a female body to replace the male body and she does not want to argue for treating women as "special" persons who are protected by the law. Providing medical care to pregnant persons is not granting a special privilege to "women" or to pregnant "persons." It is a normal and politically necessary thing to do. It is only by having a male body represent the human person that such an action can be labeled special, unusual, or deviant. Eisenstein argues for restructuring the law so that it can take account of the multiplicity of differences between men and women, including, but not limited to, pregnancy, and the differences among women, including class, race, and age. Legal equality cannot be based solely on similarity. While Eisenstein's examination of pregnancy provides a dramatic analysis of how the law ignores women, it is important to consider other ways in which the law fails to take account of women.

The case of battered wives offers another example of how males are used to represent all humans. First, the law expects women to leave abusive relationships and make themselves independent of the male batterer. However, women's socialization often involves developing commitments that encourage them to attempt repairing relationships, even at the sacrifice of their own safety. Furthermore, the law fails to recognize that the woman's leaving the relationship may escalate the man's anger and further endanger her. What Christine A. Littleton points out is how the law fails to take account of the woman's situation and treats her as if she were a man.[20] By assuming that equality means treating all persons the same, the political system permits male bodies and experiences to represent all humans. Eisenstein explains that "the silent male referent masks the hierarchy and inequality."[21] This "silent" male standard makes the law appear fair while perpetrating male bias.[22]

Remedying this situation does not call for developing a gender-free human representative. To remedy the situation, courts will need to become conscious of gender. Citing *State v. Wanrow*, Elizabeth Schneider shows how courts can use gender in their deliberations.[23] In this case, a Native American woman killed an intoxicated man, who she feared was about to molest her children. The court was asked if the action constituted self-defense or murder. The legal issue is whether a woman should be permitted to use greater force, a weapon, to defend herself against a man who is larger and stronger than she is. The court decided that her gender made it necessary for her to use a weapon to protect herself against his fists. This case shows how courts can take account of gender. Such considerations might also enable the law to treat men more fairly. For example, in child-custody cases men might be given more time to acquire expertise in child care before courts make the decision that the female is the better custodial parent. By considering the role gender plays in a case, courts can avoid decisions based on gender stereotypes or on the basis of women's similarity to, or difference from, men. Feminist legal discourse offers other ways to reform the law through the creation of new legal rhetoric.

Littleton shows how the legal system assumes a male body in physical assault cases.[24] Citing the case of a battered woman who shot and killed her mate, she explains that the law expected force to be met only with similar force. Even if the woman is smaller than the man—even if his fists might kill her while hers would not even slow him down—the law does not justify her use of a gun against his fists. By assuming that individuals are similar in physical strength, the law creates a bias against smaller *persons* often, but not only, women. Furthermore, this law assumes that persons are equally trained to defend themselves. This assumption creates a bias against many women and some men who cannot defend themselves with their fists.

Examining the law from feminist viewpoints can illuminate unfair assumptions in legal practice.[25] A more fair and precise law could easily give a person the right to defend himself or herself in such a way as to meet force with an adequate force to accomplish self-defense. Such a law might even take into account the original intent—to protect aggressors from excessive harm. Thus, women's situations can be used to locate and address unjust legal practices that affect both men and women.

Women's Voices and a New Political Rhetoric?

In the early years of the American republic, women were forbidden to speak in public, including in courtrooms. Remnants of this prohibition remain in such ideological slogans as "women's voices are shrill," as well as in sexist jokes that praise the "silent woman." Hence, it is not surprising that feminists use "voice" to represent female power. What may be more surprising is the way in which "voice" is employed to debate feminist positions. Feminists like Carol Gilligan who emphasize women as caregivers who differ from men, and feminists like

Catharine MacKinnon who emphasize women's similarities to men both call on the image of "voice."[26]

Evoking the voice metaphor in her title *In a Different Voice*, Carol Gilligan stirred up controversy among feminist legal analysts by arguing that women's moral codes are built on relationships rather than principles. Using Gilligan, feminist legal theorists work to feminize the law by infusing it with an ethic of care, a cooperative spirit, and a commitment to relationships. In legal contexts, this approach offers an alternative to rights-based language by asserting an expanded view of citizen responsibility and state activity that asks citizens and the state to provide for the economic and emotional well-being of all community members.[27] This takes the law beyond rights-based discourse, which has not served women as well as men. Rights protect the family from state intervention but women often need protection from situations within the family because it is in this so-called "safe haven" where women often experience abuse. In the care model, the state, neighbors, and friends bear some responsibility for protecting a woman they know or suspect to be abused and defenseless. Home life is scrutinized. This model addresses some of the problems raised by the battered-wife syndrome, since it is the wife or partner's isolation and defenselessness that leave her with only the option of a counter assault.[28] Gilligan's model expects citizens to act on behalf of the needs of others, but such action can also be considered interference.[29] The care model challenges the emphasis on individual liberty—"a man's home is his castle"—and sets aside the old adage "mind your own business," for the care and well-being of all citizens is everyone's business. Hints of this new model already appear in legal sanctions against spouse abuse and in legislation that prevents unfair discrimination on the basis of race, gender, and sexual orientation. Such regulations permit the state to take a proactive stand in struggling against the debilitating effects of sexism, racism, poverty, and other institutional practices that deprive citizens of a good life and the nation from benefitting from their talents. The care model invests the state and citizens with obligations that go beyond the old Roosevelt welfare state. In some regard, the care model is similar to a classical, conservative position because of its emphasis on citizen responsibility.

In contrast to this position, Catharine MacKinnon argues that women do not have a "different" voice but merely speak in a "higher register"[30]—a register that the law has difficulty hearing. She employs the voice metaphor to argue that the best legal-political strategy is to emphasize the similarities between men and women. Rather than advocating a care model that feminizes the law, MacKinnon calls for an unmodified feminism,[31] focused on power rather than on male/female differences. By using sexuality as a lens through which to view women's oppression, MacKinnon explains that patriarchy has reduced sexuality to domination, so that citizens—both men and women, both heterosexual and homosexual—can only imagine sex as domination, and so sex becomes an alienated activity in which persons are reduced to "fuckers" and "fuckees." To both women and men, femininity means subordination, and masculinity represents domination. In this situation, neither men nor women can experience genuine sexual pleasure or reach their full potential as masculine and feminine persons. It is not the difference between men and women that creates injustice but the way in which sex and domination have been gendered.

For example, MacKinnon's argument for abortion is not that women's pregnancy involves a situation very different from men's but that the problem with our understanding of pregnancy begins with avoiding the problem of how women get pregnant. The issue begins with sex not with pregnancy. She suggests that under some circumstances women, like men, should have the right to kill. MacKinnon suggests that it is women's femininity (images of powerlessness) that leads citizens to decide that killing persons in self-defense and in combat is acceptable while abortion is not.[32] Although some may think that abortion is different because it involves killing an "innocent" baby, modern warfare itself involves killing innocent babies as well as other noncombatants.

Gilligan wants to use women's voices to transform the moral code, whereas MacKinnon wants to use women's position to force the moral code to live up to its present promises and grant both women and men equality. Gilligan wants to change the way we think about relationships and moral codes, whereas MacKinnon seeks to eradicate the connection between domination and sexuality.[33] Neither Gilligan's nor MacKinnon's approach relies upon a case-by-case or client-by-client approach. For example, MacKinnon tells her feminist reader the story of a Euro-American woman, Linda Marchiano (Lovelace), the exploited porn star. But her legal energy is not directed toward representing Lovelace or her similarly situated sisters; instead, she focuses on a class action suit and argues that pornography constitutes slander against all women. The approach is political, not merely legal. MacKinnon's client is not a woman but all U.S. women.[34] She moves from an individual level to a political level to restructure the law rather than to seek redress for individual female clients. But, unfortunately, women's issues are more complex than those of any one client, and so representing all American women presents difficulties. Such an approach violates part of the power vested in clients—that is, their right to dismiss their attorneys. American women cannot express their dissatisfaction with MacKinnon by firing her. In this sense, her approach raises questions about who can "represent" American women[35] and appears to violate the feminist ethic that persons speak only for themselves. On the other hand, if no one is willing to speak on behalf of women, blacks, Native Americans, lesbians, the poor, and other out-of-power groups, their/our stories will not be told, and communities will suffer.

In some respects this debate is about what strategies will work. For Gilligan and her followers, the best strategy is to feminize the law by incorporating into it contemporary "traditional" women's values—especially an ethic of care. MacKinnon's strategy is to eliminate the oppression by using a feminist hermeneutic to redress wrongs and establish female-friendly precedents. Both sides of this debate are asking, "How can the law become responsive to both women and men?" The political question is "Should the symbol of the feminine be used to rewrite the law by infusing it with relational values, or should masculine bias be written out of legal texts?" Even though these two strategies represent clashing rhetorics, Zillah Eisenstein advocates using both of them.[36]

Drawing on Jacques Derrida, Drucilla Cornell suggests that feminist legal work should employ a "new choreography of sexual difference."[37] Suspicious of the idealization of Gilligan's female symbols, Cornell is likewise uncomfortable with MacKinnon's position as it is locked into a male/female struggle which reifies the masculine hierarchy and rejects the feminine.[38] Cornell seeks an alliance between feminism and deconstruction that promises to reframe sexual difference by taking advantage of feminine imagery.[39] Her way out of patriarchy and the similarity/difference dilemma is to circle through the feminine metaphors, being careful not to reject them but instead to employ mimesis to transform them. Her strategy is designed to articulate the feminine without displacing the masculine. It assumes the political possibility of bringing the feminine discourse to the foreground without discrediting masculine discourse. For example, patrilineal practices (including the naming of children through their father's line), imply the possibility of matrilineal practices (for example, naming children after their mothers). Replacing a matriarchy with a patriarchy simply privileges another part of the binary opposition. To employ a different strategy, Cornell brings the silent "female opposite" to the foreground and reforms social images by making the absent feminine image into a present possibility, not a necessity.[40] In doing this, she assumes that persons can image a layered self that contains both the masculine and the feminine. In a similar way, different ethnicities can retain differences while intermingling with "foreigners." In addition, Cornell undercuts the heterosexual-homosexual dichotomy that reduces the sex act to the object of desire—same sex, different sex. In accommodating these polarities, she invites feminists to build contingent feminine myths that make way for new performances of the female, new possibilities for ways of thinking of the feminine and new myths of sexuality that do not require a focus on the "man."[41]

Cornell argues that feminist politics needs all three strategies: (1) genealogical recovery of lost feminine images (Gilligan); (2) legal-political work (MacKinnon); and (3) contingent myth-making (Cornell).[42] She reminds her reader: "*The mistake is to think that we cannot engage in all three aspects of the project, and worse, that one excludes the other*."[43] The clash of feminist rhetorics can energize feminist politics without eliminating one of them.

Trading Contracts for Covenants and Relationships

Legal scholars and political analysts use a contract analogy to explain the relationship between citizens and the state and between husbands and wives in the family. To examine the political work performed by this analogy, I will begin with Carole Pateman's analysis of the history of the social contract, which explains why Father-Law stands for state authority. Pateman argues that the sexual contract is a part of a duality inherent in the "original" social contract, which establishes both the state and the family.[44] The social contract is formed by males giving up their natural power to the state in return for civil order and protection. Thus, males give birth to civil society.[45] This birth narrative has preempted other explanations of social origins (including science and religion), and thereby makes Father-Law the Father of Civilization. Pateman shows how this story fails to acknowledge that a citizen's freedom and autonomy rest on a prior sexual contract in which the woman surrenders her autonomy to a man in marriage. This agreement goes unnoticed because the nuclear family is understood as a natural phenomenon rather than a cultural one. Pateman explains that the notion of the freedom and autonomy of all persons does *not* underlie the social contract because it assumes a sexual contract in which the male gains sexual authority over a woman, which establishes him as a father who then can represent the family to create a civil society with other fathers. This is articulated as the husband's authority over *his* wife, but the process by which this happens is not an agreement, but a so-called natural act that needs no explanation.[46]

Furthermore, Pateman points out that social contract theorists use family and kinship, that is, blood relationships, as the basis for political community. But somehow these theorists fail to note that the family is founded not on blood relationships, but on the relationship between husband and wife—a marital agreement, understood in liberal societies as a contract.[47] Emphasizing paternal characteristics as natural authority symbols casts the husband as the "head" and the wife then becomes something like the "foot" of the household. Such a household forms a basic unit in the state:

> There are two implicit assumptions at work here. First, that husbands are civil masters because men ('fathers') have made the original social contract that brings civil law into being. . . . Second, there is only one way in which women, who have the same status as free and equal individuals in the state of nature as men, can be excluded from participation in the social contract.[48]

Once women are brought to submission by men, the social contract can be freely formed among men. Women do not contract to have men represent them politically as the head of the family. Thus, the social contract is a contract that is *not* built on freedom as a basic human condition. The social contract is in reality a social contract among men. It assumes a prior sexual contract in which wives subordinate themselves to their husbands. Only then does it become "reasonable" to see men forming community with one another on the basis of their status as masters of the household. Single women simply disappear. The social contract then implies that husbands provide protection to wives just as the state protects citizens. Thus, the consolidation of power for protection serves as a primary motivation for forming the family and the state.

Civil society is built by males bonding with each other. Female bonding becomes either a matter of necessity—for example, women cooking in the kitchen or quilting—or an unnatural act—for example, gossips who collect to do harm, or worse yet, press for gender equity. It is not then surprising that nineteenth and twentieth century America produces women's organizations as auxiliaries to men's. *Uncle* Sam embodies the state in ways that *Aunt* Sally cannot; she cannot enter into the social contract and trade her sovereign power for state protection because she has already given it to her husband (or she must keep it for her potential husband).

In time the contract analogy is used to explain all relationships, including marriage. Unfortunately, as Pateman explains, "the contractarian conception of social life implies that there is contract 'all the way down': social life is nothing more than contracts between individuals."[49] Besides the male bias in this social/marital contract, there are two other major problems with it. First, it assumes voluntary and limited commitments in the construct of the state and family relationships. Second, it understands such relationships in terms of exchanges among members. Citizenship goes beyond exchanging freedom for security, and marriages are not really an exchange of child-rearing services for protection. Marriage and other intimate partnerships (including gay and lesbian couples, and families formed on the basis of nonsexual bonds) involve life-altering commitments that cannot be represented as a set of exchanges.[50] Neither citizens in a state nor persons in a family can imagine all of the things that will be required of them to fulfill such a "contract." Nor can they anticipate what wonderful and/or destructive actions a partner to the contract will commit. Even in the case of a heterosexual marriage contract, consent is complex, and "vows" cannot clearly specify the types of actions, sacrifices, or rewards that will be forthcoming over a lifetime—or even over the course of a few years.

Legally, a contract implies that both parties are aware of the conditions of the agreement. No one entering into a marriage or other form of intimate family commitment or into citizenship in a state knows what the relationship holds. In the case of marriage or citizenship, parties cannot be so informed and unpredictable and impossible demands may emerge. In this sense, neither citizenship nor family formation is merely a voluntary contract; they entail life-altering commitments based on faith in the relationship. The analogy of the state and marriage as contracts obscures the commitments and demands involved in them.

Marriage and other intimate family bonds constitute agreements about a type of relationship that, unlike a contract, fails to specify particular duties and services. Promising to love someone for the rest of your life is a far too abstract notion to serve as an agreement.[51] The solution is not to specify the conditions of the marriage, nor is it to force persons to keep their promises. In marriage, two parties do not agree to particular behaviors or acts; they agree to a state of being.

Divorce is not a violation of the original agreement but instead a recognition that the state of being is over. In similar ways, contract imagery distorts the relationship between the state and citizens. The relationship between the citizens and the state is not constituted by a set of duties and obligations but by a way of being. Furthermore, shifting cultural values have made the marriage-contract analogy even less workable. Lifelong commitments to another person have become less common and divorces more frequent. Divorce is so frequent that it is now "no one's fault" when such a "contract" is broken. Since business and other private contracts do not so readily assume no-fault language, this new language further strains the contract analogy.

Finding a replacement for the contract analogy is not easy, but the term "covenant" might work. An advantage, as well as a disadvantage, to this term is its Western roots. According to Daniel Elazar:

> A covenant is a morally informed agreement or pact based upon voluntary consent, established by mutual oaths or promises, involving or witnessed by some transcendent higher authority, between peoples or parties, having independent status, equal in connection with the purposes of the pact, that provides for joint action or obligation to achieve defined ends (limited or comprehensive) under conditions of mutual respect, which protect the individual integrity of all the parties to it.[52]

He continues to explain that covenants establish "bodies" that are both "political and social."[53] Going beyond mere legal obligations, a covenant "provides the basis for the institutionalization of that relationship."[54] Unlike a contract, which is a private agreement, a covenant is a public political act that forms a new relationship.

An advantage of the "covenant" image is its emphasis on the politics of the relationship and the institutionalization of a set of practices designed to support the integrity of the parties to it. The covenant image avoids the problem of exchange and focuses on the responsibilities that each party has to contribute continually to the relationship. It treats the relationship as an unfolding process rather than a series of discrete exchanges. In biblical discourse, a covenant represents an "unconditional agreement" that does not depend on the performance of the parties; it is a bonded relationship. In contrast, a contract represents a "conditional agreement" that obligates parties to perform narrow and specific actions and does not imply a complex bonding.[55] Because covenant images have roots in Old Testament biblical discourse, secular feminists may well be uncomfortable with them.

However, Jesse Jackson has secularized the symbol of the covenant between God and his/her people by using the rainbow to represent the unity of a citizenry and the diversity of the cultures of those citizens. Bill Clinton employed the covenant language to counter the neoconservative "contract with America." "Covenant" seems to be acquiring a meaning that takes it beyond religious discourse, while retaining the notion of moral commitment. But neoconservatives have formed a group, the Promise Keepers, who also endeavor to capitalize on the "covenant." They argue for two kinds of marriages—one which would be like a contract and another which is more permanent, called a "covenant marriage." However, this neoconservative definition differs from the Old Testament one outlined by Elazar, the one referred to by Jesse Jackson and Bill Clinton. The difference is important. The neoconservative viewpoint defines the problem as men failing to fulfill their part of the agreement. The problem lies in understanding relationships in terms of contracts or promises.

The term "covenant" suggests that participation in the relationship is an end in itself that involves the entire fabric of a person's life. Such a relationship is not simply an instrumental action with limited purposes. Covenant imagery might reconceptualize intimate family ties as complex, holistic situations that are institutionalized on the basis of mutual care, support, and pleasure, rather than as exchanges that function to accomplish economic interests such as rearing children, providing care for workers, and offering safe recreational sex.

But a covenant is not necessarily binding for life, so describing marriage as a covenant does not imply that there will be no divorce; it does imply that divorce entails public and private concerns that go beyond the division of community property and child custody. This change does imply that citizens have a moral responsibility to create institutional practices that support such intimate relationships and protect the integrity of participating parties, even in the instances where the marriage is broken. Protecting those whose family ties are broken is important practically as well because what happens to such individuals affects the economic and political well-being of the state. The problems that poor female-headed families face is a social responsibility that needs to be addressed not by the man who left "her" but by citizens who have an obligation for caring for one another—for valuing family life.

In many ways, the role of wife or the caregiving partner is already understood as a covenant, even though the role of the husband is not. Wives are expected to give up their careers, restructure their work life outside the home, and make other sacrifices to build the marriage relationship. Husbands are less often expected to take on these life-altering moves. The contract image suggests that wives do this in exchange for economic security. That is an unrealistic characterization. It is only at the point of marriage dissolution that marriage is cast as an economic exchange. However, a divorcing husband, who often provided economic resources, can readily take the resources of his career and labor from the marriage. In contrast, her economic contributions in rearing children and providing care are less easily transferred to another setting. Her work disappears; her sacrifices mean nothing in other contexts. Wives and other homemakers who give up careers, educational opportunities, promotions, public service, hobbies, and more to support and follow their partner as "voluntary" workers make life-altering sacrifices during the marriage tenure. Even temporary economic support that enables a partner to prepare for a career is inadequate. In some instances wives are able to negotiate divorce settlements that compensate them as partners in the business. The United States military provides for long-term wives (those who "served" ten years or more) to receive a portion of a spouse's retirement benefits. Such recognition of wives' economic compensation is reserved for special cases. Understanding marriage as a *covenant* rather than a *contract* may clarify the types of commitments and sacrifices that women and some men make as homemakers. Agreeing to be a homemaker would not then constitute a silent agreement to endure future poverty or substandard living conditions.

The covenant language offers new ways of talking about family relationships. Employing the covenant language to displace the business analogy reconstructs marriage as an organic life commitment. The commitment does not prevent divorces or even make them more difficult to obtain; it constructs relationships as personal life-altering situations that go beyond economic partnerships. Failure to take account of the total impact of intimate commitments like marriage on individuals creates unjust resolutions of those relationships. Taking fuller account of the personal sacrifices involved in marriage can help reduce the negative effects of divorce. An important aspect of this is recasting the family from an economic unit designed to care for children to a social unit designed to provide settings for mutual caregiving.

Furthermore, the covenant image might enable citizens to appreciate the public contributions made by a wide variety of intimate family relationships, including gay/lesbian families who collectively provide care for large numbers of citizens. Such care benefits companies, individuals, and states.[56] Recognizing this public good might help eliminate some forms of heterosexism as well as encouraging all citizens to appreciate how intimate relationships contribute to the well-being of persons and the collective well-being of the state. Avoiding the problem of making women the sole caregivers and degrading men's ability to care could reaffirm family values—that is, the care families give in intimate settings.

For public life to value families will involve some general policy changes. First, family members need released time from work to properly fulfill these responsibilities in times of greater needs. Economic sanctions that prevent adults from fulfilling these needs should be curtailed just as the government prevents economic sanctions against those called to serve in the armed services. The Family and Medical Leave Act begins to address these concerns. Certainly, tax relief needs to be given to all types of families that offer care to needy members. While commercial establishments are reimbursed for such care, families are often not. This needs to change. Second, private corporations, public corporations, and government can recognize the skill involved in family care and credit such activities as work experience. Unpaid work can enable individuals to develop skills that are hard to acquire in the paid workforce. Skills such as self-sacrifice, generosity, dedication to others, and unselfishness can be discouraged in the workforce and yet such skills are vitally needed on the job. For example, men and women who learn to express their emotions in intimate care situations at home may be better colleagues at work. Men who care for young children may become more attended to the nonverbal communication in the workplace and so more responsive to the needs of coworkers. While workers are offered an array of workshops that teach interpersonal skills, it might just be that encouraging those skills to flourish at home might be the bosses' best plan to make the workplace better. Making workers more content by reducing the tension between home and work certainly would be a benefit in itself. Family situations provide opportunities for developing skills in such complex management tasks as priority setting, working with others, problem solving, goal analysis, negotiation, and organizing the work of others. Learning to care for someone is not only important to individuals and societies, it builds a set of habits that makes persons work better and the quality of these habits can be assessed. Résumés could include such family contributions, just as they include work done in the military. Including family work as work redefines work in a way that credits and supports the individuals who perform such tasks. Treating adult family relationships as covenants that support community and the state can enable employers to develop new practices that see commitments to the family not as competition with business, not as the same as business, but as support for business. Like serving in the military or acquiring an education, time spent contributing to family life builds good persons, who will be good employees. Doing good for others is a vital part of developing human character.

Abandoning the social contract in the case of the state might offer similar benefits for citizens. Elazar argues that the social contract is more like a pact or covenant than a contract because its character is public and reciprocal.[57] Understanding the state as more than the means for gaining protection, citizens might see the state as a good in itself because it offers citizens the opportunities to form a public life together. Politics is not a necessary "evil"; it is a good, healthy part of human life. Understanding this can facilitate and sustain public life.

The covenant analogy suggests that citizens are not autonomous terminal points for exchanges but instead interact to become a constitutional entity.[58] Elazar, in commenting on the postmodern covenant theologians, describes the understanding of a religious covenant between God and the people of Israel as "rejecting an overemphasis on human rationality or human subjugation."[59] To secularize this relationship, I suggest that political covenants can redraw boundaries that enable citizens to become parts of a variety of collective selves, including communities. Citizens, like family members, live connected lives.

CAN FEMINIST CITIZENS RECONSTRUCT POWER, AUTHORITY, AND CITIZENSHIP?

I have used feminist legal-political discourse to show how reconstructing American popular understandings of power, authority, and citizenship can enable citizens to reform public commitments and reconstruct state responsibilities. But my understanding of citizenship goes beyond participation in state matters to include public relationships in organizations, corporations, and communities. To reflect on how these new definitions work together to create new political possibilities, I will draw on the classroom for examples. Since almost all citizens have classroom experience, since it is likely that those reading this text might at this very moment find themselves in classrooms, and since I have spent my life working in classrooms, the classroom offers a place for testing these insights in everyday life situations.

By offering a positive definition of power, feminists encourage women to enter public life and to delight in their own ability to exercise power. In the classroom setting this means that each person, all students, and the teacher(s) have power. While power is not necessarily evenly distributed, power is a positive energy. By understanding citizenship as a part of becoming a full human being, individuals can develop and express themselves as they build a public life with others. For example, everyone in a classroom then has the responsibility for it. Classes are not "ivory towers" separate from society but locales for experiencing it.

By understanding hierarchies as temporary authority structures, citizens can appreciate the services hierarchies provide without worshiping them. Classrooms that rely on group-work already create temporary hierarchies to accomplish tasks. While teachers exercise more continuous authority, is this not a necessary part of making a class work? Is it not good that books are ordered and the syllabus prepared before class begins? In classrooms, is power an energy that circulates among members rather than a thing possessed by one or a few? Transforming notions of power, authority, and citizenship provide creative ways of reforming organizations and communities, including legislatures, churches, families, schools, communities, towns, and clubs. Does this work in the classroom? How is authority shared? Can all persons present be citizens?

Does a critical discussion of the four metaphors—Father-Law, "man" as representative of humans, voice, and covenant—enable citizens to reform families and the state? If Father-Law is divested as the primary symbol for authority and "man" can no longer represent humanity, can social order be revitalized to include not just discipline but also compassion, and not just males but also women? Does this figure of Father-Law appear in many different forms? Is it in classrooms? Does displacing Father-Law and "man" make politics more possible? Can Cornell's strategy of using both similarity and difference empower women's voices and make all social bonds more just? What happens if those in a class reflect on how they are both similar to, and different from, each other? If relationships are recast from contract to covenant, does this better enable citizens to connect with each other? Does it enable citizens to exercise more integrity in such relationships? What happens if students in a class think of themselves as involved in a covenant with one another? What happens in the classroom if students think of their relationships to the state and to their families in this way? What happens if the teacher thinks of his or her relationships to students as a covenant? At the national level of political life, feminists can use the law to support these new understandings. Explaining how law depends on language to create social change, feminist legal scholars invite citizens to see changes in legal discourse as new ways for making just decisions in their everyday lives. By critically analyzing Father-Law, male representations of humanity, feminist images of voice, and contract imagery, citizens can move toward legal practices that include women. But feminist jurisprudence does not merely offer some new principles for redefining the connections between the law and politics. This connects issues of justice to the everyday lives of citizens and suggests that the responsibility for making justice happen lies with each citizen who can seize the power of language to alter the world. While such changes may seem minor, they add up to make a difference. The next step in understanding the insights feminist jurisprudence offers American citizens involves examining feminist strategies for reframing legal practice. By reforming legal practices, feminists can also illustrate how citizens can develop gender-inclusive methods for making fair decisions.

NOTES

1. For examples of the use of rhetoric for philosophical and political analysis, see Paul Ricoeur, *The Rule of Metaphor: Multi-disciplinary Studies of the Creation of Meaning in Language,* trans. Robert Czerny with Kathleen McLaughline and John Costello (Toronto, Canada: University of Toronto Press, 1977); Michael J. Shapiro, *Reading the Postmodern Polity: Political Theory As Textual Practice* (Minneapolis: University of Minnesota Press, 1992); George Lakoff and Mark Johnson, *Metaphors We Live By* (Chicago: University of Chicago Press, 1980); and William E. Connolly, *Politics and Ambiguity* (Madison: University of Wisconsin Press, 1987).

2. For example, Kathleen Jones criticizes MacKinnon and Dworkin for rejecting authority altogether. Kathleen B. Jones, *Compassionate Authority: Democracy and the Representation of Women* (New York: Routledge, 1993), 7.

3. Nancy C. M. Hartsock, *Money, Sex, and Power: Toward a Feminist Historical Materialism* (Boston: Northeastern University Press, 1983), 225.

4. Hartsock, *Money, Sex, and Power*, 218.

5. Aristotle, *Politics*, Book I, lines 15–17, in *The Basic Works of Aristotle*, ed. Richard McKeon (New York: Random House, 1941), 1127.

6. Jones articulates the politics of these tensions in *Compassionate Authority*.

7. Jana Sawicki, *Disciplining Foucault: Feminism, Power, and the Body* (New York: Routledge, 1991) and for a less sympathetic summary, see Robin West, *Caring for Justice* (New York: New York University Press, 1997), 259–264.

8. For a discussion of the citizenship as a struggle between institutions and citizen action, see Roberto Alejandro, *Hermeneutics, Citizenship, and the Public Sphere* (Albany: State University of New York Press, 1993).

9. For this observation about the pyramid circle metaphor, I thank Jenny Schenk, student at Denison University, summer 1996.

10. Jo Freeman, *The Politics of Women's Liberation: A Case Study of an Emerging Social Movement and Its Relation to the Policy Process* (New York: Longman, 1975).

11. Ruth Lister, *Citizenship: Feminist Perspectives* (New York: New York University Press, 1997), 168–204.

12. For arguments about the connections among law, language, and patterns in everyday discourse, see Stanley Fish, *Doing What Comes Naturally: Change, Rhetoric, and the Practice of Theory in Literary and Legal Studies* (Durham, N.C.: Duke University Press, 1989); Robin West, *Narrative, Authority, and Law* (Ann Arbor: University of Michigan Press, 1993); and James Boyd White, *Heracles' Bow: Essays on the Rhetoric and Poetics of the Law* (Madison: University of Wisconsin Press, 1985).

13. For arguments about the connections between law, language, and patterns in everyday discourse, see Fish, *Doing What Comes Naturally*; and West, *Narrative, Authority, and Law*.

14. Because Americans assume that a father heads the household, when a female heads the household, citizens must use a special term—"female-headed household." While the U.S. government uses parallel terms "female-headed household" and "male-headed household," the comparatively fewer numbers of the latter makes the second term sound strange.

15. The basis of meaning developed on the principle of oppositions develops within semiotic language theory; see the work of Ferdinand de Saussure, *Course in General Linguistics*, eds. Charles Bally and Albert Sechehaye with Albert Riedlinger, trans. Roy Harris (LaSalle, Ill.: Open Court, 1983). In *Maternal Thinking: Toward a Politics of Peace* (Boston: Beacon Press, 1989), Sara Ruddick argues that motherhood can be used as a way of reconstructing notions of citizenship and moral responsibility.

16. For the ways in which motherhood symbolizes death in modern Western culture, see Sherry B. Ortner, "Is Female to Male as Nature Is to Culture?" in *Woman, Culture, and Society*, eds. Michelle Zimbalist Rosaldo and Louise Lamphere (Stanford, Calif.: Stanford University Press, 1974), 67–87.

17. Catharine A. MacKinnon, *Feminism Unmodified: Discourses on Life and Law* (Cambridge, Mass.: Harvard University Press, 1987); and Zillah R. Eisenstein, *The Female Body and the Law* (Berkeley: University of California Press, 1988).

18. In *Feminism Unmodified*, MacKinnon uses the image of standard to make this point and in *The Female Body and the Law*, Eisenstein develops a particular analysis of this male bias.

19. Eisenstein, *The Female Body and the Law*.

20. Christine A. Littleton, "Women's Experience and the Problem of Transition: Perspectives on Male Battering of Women," *The University of Chicago Legal Forum* 25 (1989): 23–57 and Elizabeth M. Schneider, "Describing and Changing: Women's Self-Defense Work and the Problem of Expert Testimony on Battering," *Women's Rights Law Reporter* 9, (fall 1986): 193–222.

21. Eisenstein, *The Female Body and the Law*, 222.

22. In *The Female Body and the Law*, Eisenstein uses "silence" as an image to represent this male bias.

23. Schneider, "Describing and Changing," 195–222.

24. Christine A. Littleton, "Women's Experience and the Problem of Transition: Perspectives on Male Battering of Women," *The University of Chicago Legal Forum* 25 (1989): 23–57.

25. In examining parental leave policy, Wendy Williams suggests a similar model that begins with women's need to have leave for child care but quickly illuminates the ways in which men need such policies as well. See Wendy Williams, "Equality's Riddle: Pregnancy and the Equal Treatment/Special Treatment Debate," *New York University Review of Law & Social Change* 13 (1984–85): 325–31. Ida B. Wells suggests a similar strategy in using the situation of black Americans to discover ways in which the political system is unfair to both blacks and whites. See Ida B. Wells-Barnett, *Crusade for Justice: The Autobiography of Ida B. Wells*, ed. Alfreda M. Duster (Chicago: University of Chicago Press, 1970), 3–75.

26. Frances E. Olsen, ed. Section 7, "Women's Voices," *Feminist Legal Theory I: Foundations and Outlooks* (New York: New York University Press, 1995), 143–223.

27. For an examination of this notion of citizenship, see Joan Tronto, *Moral Boundaries: A Political Argument for an Ethic of Care* (New York: Routledge, 1993).

28. This is the point made by Tillie Olsen's short story "Tell Me A Riddle," in which the neighbors begin to see how they were partly culpable for failing to help the abused wife.

29. In *Moral Boundaries*, Tronto addresses this problem.

30. Catharine A. MacKinnon, "Difference and Dominance: On Sex Discrimination," in *Feminist Legal Theory: Readings in Law and Gender*, eds. Katharine T. Bartlett and Rosanne Kennedy (Boulder, Colo.: Westview Press, 1991), 82.

31. For a discussion of the distinction between modified and unmodified feminism, see Drucilla Cornell, *Beyond Accommodation: Ethical Feminism, Deconstruction, and the Law* (New York: Routledge, 1991), 119–41.

32. MacKinnon, *Feminism Unmodified.*

33. I want to thank Kevin Hoyes for conversations about MacKinnon that helped to clarify her work (fall 1996).

34. This shift in the representation of an individual versus a group comes from two sources. First, MacKinnon utilizes a class action approach to take on pornography. Second, the text *Representing Women: Law, Literature, and Feminism*, eds. Susan Sage Heinzelman, Zipporah Batshaw Wiseman (Durham, N.C.: Duke University Press, 1994), suggests a double meaning for the word "represent" even though the notion of the feminist attorney as a person who represents her client, the group called "woman," is not explicitly developed.

35. For a discussion of definition of representations and the way in which feminists have problematized the issue of who can speak for whom, see Martha Minow, "From Class Action to 'Miss Saigon': The Concept of Representation in the Law," in *Representing Women*, 8–43.

36. Eisenstein, *The Female Body and the Law*, 191–224.

37. Cornell, *Beyond Accommodation*, 63.

38. Cornell, *Beyond Accommodation*, 132.

39. Cornell, *Beyond Accommodation*, 79–118.

40. This strategy relies upon a semiotic linguistic theory that explains that language works by creating meaning through a series of oppositions; therefore, the term male becomes meaningful in relationship to its linguistic opposite, female.

41. Cornell, *Beyond Accommodation*, 147–64, especially 164.

42. Cornell, *Beyond Accommodation*, 170–71.

43. Cornell, *Beyond Accommodation*, 171 (italics in original text).

44. Carole Pateman, *The Sexual Contract* (Stanford, Calif.: Stanford University Press, 1988).

45. Pateman.

46. Pateman, 23.

47. Pateman, 27.

48. Pateman, 48.

49. Pateman, 59.

50. The term "family" refers to persons who live together, share their economic resources, and make commitments to care for one another. This term includes gay and lesbian couples, adult mother-daughter, sister-brother, sister-sister relationships, some deliberate communities who live in family groups, as well as any other number of persons who decide to establish a household on the basis of affections that go beyond mere housing necessities.

51. The Promise Keepers attempt to recapture a predivorce era, but they too misunderstand marriage and construct it as an agreement, a promise rather than a life-altering commitment.

52. Daniel J. Elazar, *Covenant & Polity in Biblical Israel: Biblical Foundations & Jewish Expressions* (New Brunswick, N.J.: Transaction Publishers, 1995), 22–23.

53. Elazar, 23.

54. Elazar, 24.

55. Charles S. McCoy, "Creation and Covenant: A Comprehensive Vision for Environmental Ethics," in *Covenant for a New Creation: Ethics, Religion and Public Policy*, eds. Carol S. Robb and Carl J. Casebolt (Maryknoll, N. Y.: Orbis Books, 1991), 214–15, 224–25.

56. The current difficulty of providing adequate care for orphans, the elderly, and the mentally handicapped illustrates the problems of state-funded care.

57. Elazar, 31.

58. Elazar, 28–51.

59. Elazar, 434.

Chapter 3

Reconstructing Legal Discourse: Feminist Possibilities

It is important that everyday life decisions be made in a fair and just way. Because citizens are used to turning to legal discourse for justice, this discourse can invite citizens to think beyond narrow self-interests and utilitarian strategies for satisfying those interests. For this same reason, I turn to legal methods to find ways to make decisions fair. Legal discourse, like other professional discourses, works by relying on methods that shape systematic understandings, which, in turn, make decisions possible. I chose this focus on methods to emphasize that fair decisions depend on procedures for gathering evidence and reflecting on it. While present U.S. legal methods evolved out of a male-centered history, I show how each of these methods can be redesigned to include the other half of the population and become gender inclusive. Then, I will turn to four strategies that feminists offer for transforming legal procedures so that citizens can make fuller use of the court as a public political institution that can bring justice and politics together. This has implications for use in making everyday decisions more fair.

HOW CAN LEGAL METHODS BECOME GENDER INCLUSIVE?

Five legal methods are particularly important for understanding the ways in which gender bias enters into legal decisions. First, I examine the problem of intent as a primary lens for interpreting the meaning of actions. Second, I explore how precedent serves as an unsteady guide for legal ethics. Third, I examine how legal processes work by relying on both adversarial and cooperative discourses. Fourth, I explore how masculine legal discourses silence women. Fifth, I examine how understandings of racism and sexism as intersecting categories liberate legal discourse from unjust restrictions. Feminist citizens can reform these methods to create more just ways of making legal decisions. These reformulated legal methods are useful in making everyday life decisions more fair.

Understanding Actions in Terms of Intentions

American popular discourse relies on intent as a basic way of understanding an action. When someone's actions don't make sense, citizens ask, "What did you mean to do?"—that is, "What did you intend to do?" If responses reveal harmless intentions, forgiveness can be ready at hand. "Oh, you didn't intend to step on my foot, OK." But even harmless intentions are not as harmless as they appear. This becomes clear by looking at how "intention" functions in legal procedures.

The concept of "intent" has been used to narrow Supreme Court power and expand congressional powers. While legal theorists attempt to use the concept of "intent" to resolve legal ambiguities, it has failed to fix interpretations because the original framers did not all agree. Their intents differed. For example, some framers wanted to eliminate slavery, and some did not. Furthermore, reaching into the mind to gain an "intent" is difficult and may reveal a multiplicity of interlocking intents that point toward different interpretations. When American citizens seek the founders' intent, they often project onto them versions of a lost paradise where there was harmonious consensus. Even in our current situations, legislators and other types of writers have difficulty revealing "the" single intent that motivated their actions. Anchoring a fixed interpretation of the law by finding out what the framer or writer thought he or she was doing does not yield a single answer. But the writer's intent is not the only problem involved in using intent as a focus for legal interpretation.

MacKinnon explains how legal emphases on the intent of an individual's actions produce discrimination against women and minorities.[1] Clearly, some legal scholars search for the original U.S. constitution framers' intentions to assert a conservative agenda especially in regard to race and sex issues. The framer's original intentions were not free from racism and sexism.

By emphasizing intent as if it were an individual, creative act of a single writer, courts have failed to take account of how cultures form intents and how citizens simply use them.[2] Although a single individual might not intend to discriminate against blacks, the pattern of discrimination exists unless citizens intentionally remove it. Intents are not neutral but infused with cultural habits, some of which are not good. Because it has been a general American practice, both past and present, to discriminate against women, people of color, the elderly, and other such persons, citizens can continue to do so quite easily without any special intent. Unfair discrimination comes naturally.[3] Because the law presently works by focusing on the actions or faults of individuals, cultural norms go unscrutinized. Investing the past with special access to moral rectitude may prevent good decisions rather than promote them.

While intention is important in assigning individual blame and handing out punishments, a focus on intentions can actually support irresponsible citizenship. It does so in two ways. First, it permits citizens to excuse harmful behavior by claiming good intentions and provides indirect aid to those who do intend such harm. This sort of passive citizenship is especially harmful. Second, it encourages citizens to remain ignorant of problems so that they can maintain their innocence. An example from the politics of racism in the Northwest illustrates how the good intention excuse promotes racism.

In the 1980s the neo-Nazis wanted to establish their headquarters in Coeur d'Alene, Idaho. Not only was it a beautiful scenic spot but there were few people of color and so they thought this was an ideal place for their white supremacist activities. They expected support from other whites in the region and began a campaign of cross-burning, harassing so-called "mixed" race couples, forcing Jews to leave town, and beating blacks and Asians. Their intents were self-consciously racist and they created propaganda and held rallies to promote their racist agenda. It was easy for citizens in the region to oppose them and to differentiate themselves from these "bad" people.

The Northwest Coalition Against Malicious Harassment, formed to respond to the neo-Nazi presence, decided to use this occasion to not only address the problems of overt racism but to use it to point out the unintentional acts of racism that composed community life in the Northwest. Discussion and public rallies were held to talk about racism. Referring to the neo-Nazi racism as *fancy* racism, Robert Cahill explained that neo-Nazi actions work politically to hide *plain* everyday racism, which may well be unintentional. These everyday racist actions involve a complex list of activities that include not giving people of color fair access to jobs, housing, educational opportunities, social rewards, and other necessities. While each racist act in itself may be minor, collectively such acts create a network of denigrations that deprive people of color of full citizenship. White supremacist activities can be used to assure other citizens that such so-called minor acts are not really racist. At the same time such minor acts serve as silent encouragement for neo-Nazi acts.[4] *Plain everyday racism* supports *fancy racism* and *fancy racism* hides the harm of *plain racism*. Whether a citizen intends to promote racism or sexism does not change the harm that such actions inflict.

Obviously, penalties for instances of intentional harm should be more severe, but it is important that citizens find ways to identify and reduce the incidence of unintentional harm as well. Citizens need to take responsibility for such harmful actions, even those that are unintended. Accidental racism and sexism, like vehicle accidents, create social harm and require public scrutiny.

Relying on intent in matters concerning racism, sexism, and other social biases can excuse citizens and thereby encourage them to remain ignorant of such practices. Remaining "innocent" permits citizens to be free of "bad" intentions. Such "strategic innocence"[5] or "strategic ignorance" sustains racism and sexism. It also silences critiques of them by claiming that "there was no harm intended." The cry that so-and-so is not a racist can cut off conversations about socially inscribed racist practices.

By examining the actual consequences of an action, the law can begin to discourage race and gender discrimination as well as other similarly dysfunctional practices like those that support upper-middle class privileges and heterosexual privileges. This move away from intention replaces the old aphorism "ignorance of the law is no excuse" with a new one: "ignorance of the consequences is no excuse." Just as boat owners must watch out for the wake of their boat, and just as car drivers must watch out so that persons are not hurt by their driving, citizens need to learn how to watch out for the effects of their acts, including racist/sexist acts as well as other practices that disenfranchise citizens by virtue of an identity rather than their behavior.

In the United States, citizens have some measure of responsibility for the "accidents" that result from the careless conduct of their lives. In the case of drunk driving, citizens have redefined responsibility to make the drunk driver and those who serve him/her responsible for harm. This shift required a firm political commitment to revamp the laws and legal discourse. Similarly, citizens could be held accountable for the harmful prejudices that kill life opportunities for some groups of citizens and thereby harm all of us. Some of this has already been done through laws that make corporations responsible for unfair actions within their company that involve sexual or racial harassment. Holding citizens responsible for acts of racism and sexism recognizes the public nature of such actions. Reforming legal discourse asks citizens to exercise greater care so that unintended acts of racism or sexism do not bring about harm. While totally disregarding intentions would produce its own unfairness, it is now important to make citizens responsible for the harm their racist and sexist actions produce. The absence of bad intentions is not enough to excuse such social harms. But what is important here is that citizens take collective action to address them rather than merely finding some individual to punish.

Precedent As an Unsteady Guide

A second practice that privileges men over women is the law's reliance upon precedent.[6] In the earlier years of the republic, women often were not even allowed to testify in court; the court system has developed from a male-centered perspective. It might seem, then, that precedent is hopelessly mired in patriarchy. However, a feminist hermeneutic can reread some of these earlier precedents and offer alternative constructions of male-female relationships. For example, prior to 1973 the military had constructed men as breadwinners and women as dependents by denying servicewomen access to the same benefits as servicemen. *Frontiero v. Richardson* represents a feminist hermeneutic that treats both men and women as potential breadwinners and insists that male dependents of military personnel receive similar benefits. Shifting economic responsibility from the husband to both the husband and wife frees men and women to choose the role of breadwinner rather than having it assigned. Other cases reconstitute women's roles and responsibilities. *Roe v. Wade* changes women's responsibility in abortion by taking it away from the state in the first trimester. So court cases re-form women's roles. While courts rely on precedent, even for the most conservative precedent requires reflection on current cultural equivalents. This is true for all sorts of practices, including gender issues. For example, freedom of speech works differently in the press than in radio, television, or the Internet. Precedent can serve only as an unsteady guide to justice because historical changes make old practices no longer viable.

Adversarial and Cooperative Legal Discourse

The law has a tradition of providing a structure in which adversaries can vigorously present their case to permit the truth to emerge. Relying on the advantages of distance and opposition, the legal system attempts to gain truth by emphasizing competition and conflict; the law establishes two opposing sides—the prosecution and the defense (the plaintiff and the defendant). Something akin to Shakespeare's "the truth will out," this approach can give men an edge because women are socialized to privilege cooperation over competition.[7] Some lawyers want to solve the difficulty by feminizing the law's representation to bring its cooperative elements to the foreground.[8] As I mentioned earlier, cases are more often settled through negotiations that depend on a cooperative spirit. Certainly, moves toward mediation capitalize on these elements. Hence, such stereotypic feminine qualities as persuasion, cooperation, sensitivity, and expressiveness are key to successful litigation. Viewing the legal system as a forum for negotiation and mediation highlights how the law can serve as a social institution for resolving conflict rather than exacerbating it. If the law is a resource for resolving ethical difficulties, then citizens may avoid using it simply as a tool for revenge and punishment. Good attorneys work with opposing council to find solutions. America might become less litigious if citizens could approach legal matters with a more cooperative spirit.

Masculine Cultural Practices and Legally Silent Women

A fourth way in which the law fails citizens is by silencing women. In part, this comes about because courts assume that legal practices are free of cultural limits and citizens assume that society is basically neutral and fair. It is not without social significance that Lady Justice is not robed in American dress. But Western cultural assumptions give less credence to women's testimony because they/we are presumed to be hysterical, prone to exaggeration, and too sensitive. Such assumptions show how the phallocentric underpinnings of American culture can permeate even feminist jurisprudence. By recognizing the possibility of such cultural bias, feminist jurisprudence leads the way for understanding how cultural assumptions prevent women from getting a fair *hearing*. MacKinnon makes the point dramatically and succinctly:

> No law silences women. This has not been necessary, for women are previously silenced in society—by sexual abuse, by not being heard, by not being believed, by poverty, by illiteracy, by a language that provides only unspeakable vocabulary for their most formative traumas, by a publishing industry that virtually guarantees that if they ever find a voice it leaves no trace in the world.[9]

Kristin Bumiller uses rape to show how the law attempts to silence women's experiences. The law has focused its attention on the victim's consent or lack of consent in constituting an action as rape. So in the absence of evidence of refusal (such as a physical struggle or verbal screams), the court assumes the victim's consent. Thus, the court fails to take account of the fact that a woman might sense that even a refusal would further endanger her life by increasing her injuries. Bumiller refers to the case in which a woman left a party with a man she trusted. He led her into a gang rape setup. She decided that active resistance would only increase her injuries but the court had a hard time hearing this part of her experience.[10] The court was unable to take account of the victim's situation because of its prior commitment to constituting the difference between sex and rape in terms of the victim's consent.[11] It could not take account of how consent and coercion work differently for males and females.

By reinterpreting issues of consent and by employing a reasonable woman standard, the court can redefine power relationships so that it can recognize situations in which power is structured in an unequal way. This means that the court considers gender in reflecting on what counts as consent and coercion. For example, the court takes account of power differences in sexual harassment. Sexual harassment involves understanding the way in which a harasser uses power and authority to sexualize an interaction to gain an advantage. The issue is not simply whether the harmed party consented; it is whether the initiator misused authority to gain sexual advantage.[12] Society attempts to set aside issues of consent in some circumstances—that is, minors cannot consent to adults, those unconscious cannot give consent, and the mentally ill cannot give consent except under some circumstances. Just as robbery is not "shopping by other means," rape is not sex by other means. Cultural experiences shape how men and women interpret coercion and consent. Those in authority need to take account of how their actions may involve coercion, even if they did not intend that result.

Feminists have helped legal theorists to understand how "sex" has been used as a subterfuge for committing violence. Assault committed under the name of "sex" is still assault. And assault is not simply a crime against an individual but it disrupts public life. Men fear the possibility of false accusations and may worry that their presence will frighten a woman; women fear that men will harm them. Assault threatens public security. Courts need to take account of the cultural practices within which women experience rape threats, just as they need to understand the prison conditions within which men experience rape threats. By taking account of power differences within cultural contexts, courts can take account of a wider range of experiences.

Race and Gender As Intersecting Categories

The silence of black women presents a dramatic case of how the law can ignore situations involving the intersection of race and gender. Kimberlé Williams Crenshaw refers to a General Motors case to show how the court restricted the testimony of black women who were forced to choose between race or gender in providing statistics on discrimination.[13] Since black women constitute a small minority, comparable statistics could not be constructed. The only other option was for black women to categorize themselves as either blacks *or* women. Because the white male category is itself a silent presence in the law, white men are often treated as individuals, while blacks, women, and others are treated as representatives of a category type, in this case a single category type. While Tom may be Tom Smith, Mari Hashimoto is a Japanese-American and/or a female who will have to work hard to become Mari Hashimoto.[14] And even if she succeeds in one venue, she may well have to prove herself again in others. The court is hard of hearing when Ms. Hashimoto speaks. Littleton shows how legal discourse can be reconstructed so that it can stop forcing women's experiences into masculinized legal categories.[15]

The Anita Hill hearings offer an example of how this might work politically. Although some may think that Anita Hill and feminism lost because Clarence Thomas was appointed to the court, I do not. Anita Hill's testimony changed the way sexual harassment is understood by the American public. Shortly before the hearings, I walked into a political science department office to overhear eight faculty members joking about sexual harassment. Sexual harassment is no longer dismissed as a joke. Anita Hill has helped citizens hear women speak about sexual harassment. Corporations pay attention to it, and citizens no longer dismiss it as silly. Certainly, feminists including Anita Hill worked to make this change happen. But others did background work that made feminists more able to respond to the situation when it took place. Many feminist attorneys, including Catharine MacKinnon, had written about sexual harassment and litigation had already been successful in articulating the issues in sexual harassment. Feminists had also debated sexual harassment and the ways in which it could be used against women, especially lesbians. Drawing on the work of Ida B. Wells, black feminists have been especially alert to the problem of false accusations in cases like rape.

These sorts of preparations are important so that when a national situation arises, the arguments have been worked out in a number of different ways. But being prepared means being able to reflect on the situations of both a harassed victim and an unjustly accused individual. Citizens now have some understanding of how sexual harassment harms entire communities, corporations, and governments, as well as individuals.

HOW CAN FEMINIST STRATEGIES
ENHANCE LEGAL DISCOURSE?

While reforming legal methods to make them gender inclusive is important, such reforms have a mundane incremental quality. Feminist jurisprudence has more to give American citizens. That gift lies in part in its ability to empower citizens by making them more responsive. Conservatives link responsibility and rights to emphasize obligations. But what the neoconservative agenda misses is that responsibility directed toward rules and principles is not enough. Both radicals and conservatives know that political responsibilities require being responsive for other people's needs in the context of a set of principles and values. Responsibility depends on citizens being responsive to each other. Drawing from feminist jurisprudence, I will offer four strategies that can enable citizens to become more politically responsive. The first is asking women questions. Questions encourage dialogue and assume that the individuals in a situation have something to say to each other. Such interrogations work to the degree that questioners and respondents engage each other honestly to discover new qualities about each other. The second strategy is employing feminist practical reason, which can encourage citizens to consider the variety of standpoints each brings to analyses. Feminist practical reason appreciates that reason does not lead to THE one right answer but that its purpose is to solve a particular problem. Consciousness raising offers a third strategy for citizens to help each other analyze situations and name problems.[16] But the sixties feminist consciousness raising has become the nineties storytelling. My fourth strategy, storytelling, encourages citizens to respond to each other by enabling them, for a moment, to enter into each other's worlds.

Asking Questions and Politicizing Legal Discourse

Questions, as a way of interacting with others, have a long history in the West. Certainly, it includes the Socratic dialogues, biblical narratives, and Enlightenment empiricism as well as postmodern notions of interrogation. Anyone with a television knows courtroom discourse moves forward via questions and responses. But feminist interrogations have a different telos in that there is less interest in interrogating and exposing guilty persons and more interest in undoing harmful social practices. In the spirit of this telos, Adrienne Rich and Michelle Rosaldo urge feminists to question the questions.[17] Heather Ruth

Wishik argues that feminist legal scholars should question everything.[18] Bartlett proposes asking the "woman question" and using it to raise questions about other excluded groups.[19]

Feminist interrogations focus on women's situations and so change questions. Questions concerning rape move from "Did the victim consent?" to "Did the perpetrator use coercion?" The Bumiller tale about the woman who was trapped into a gang-rape situation at a party serves as one example.[20] Feminist jurisprudence facilitated this shift by showing how cultural contexts structure coercion into a situation. Feminists invite readers to cross-examine society. By asking the courts to take account of these cultural factors, feminist jurisprudence can take citizens beyond a narrow concern for rights. In other words, the Court can serve as a political institution that helps citizens create habits of more just interaction.[21] Making such social-political matters legal concerns asks courts to protect citizens by doing more than just punishing individuals. Certainly, rapists should be punished but it is equally important that courts find ways to show how society supports rape through the denigration of women, the sexualization of domination, and the glorification of sexual conquests. Courts need to be able to indict unjust social practices. I have suggested that such questions can critically review social structures that support racism, sexism, and other denigrating practices. Feminist attorneys, clients, and witnesses can bring such matters into legal conversations. But feminist interrogations need to move beyond asking questions to developing new ways of arriving at solutions.

Feminist Practical Reason

Katharine Bartlett synthesizes feminist theory with Amelie Rorty's model of practical reason to create feminist practical reason. It has three qualities: (1) it is reflective about its own partiality and aware of the "moral and political choices" implicated in its position;[22] (2) it integrates emotion and reason; and (3) it moves to open up new situations rather than to limit them.[23] All three work by keeping in focus concrete situations and political values. For example, citizens in school settings are far too often confronted with the problem of the female student who is sexually harassed by a male teacher or professor. Reflectivity asks these citizens to be aware that investigating such a charge itself has political consequences and that such investigations are often always partial. The complete facts cannot be known. Evidence needs to be reviewed so that questions can encourage participants and witnesses to tell a richer narrative about what happened but those reviewing the situation need to be ready to take in new information. Calling upon Sylvia Law's work, Anne E. Freedman explains that "non-conforming evidence" can often be treated as a mistake.[24] Considering that the court's decisions evolve from facts that are socially conditioned and from eyewitness testimonies that will tend to confirm what is socially expected and not to "see" what is socially unusual,[25] it is vital that an account of social context be included in legal arguments so that evidence can be properly evaluated. Even so, it may be still difficult for witnesses to believe their own eyes and for the jury and judge to believe their own ears.

The legal system urges a presumption of innocence. Should citizens employ this presumption or should they lean toward believing the female student because of the vulnerability of her position? Reflectivity asks citizens to critically consider this issue. Certainly, such a situation can create empathetic responses by those who have been harassed as well as those who have had emotional sexual attachments for persons in superior positions and/or inferior positions. Acknowledging these emotions in oneself is an important part of employing feminist practical reason. Third, seeking solutions that avoid future occurrences is as important as gaining retribution for injured parties. If the problem is false accusation, that needs to be prevented and structures that support it eliminated. If the problem is sexual harassment, school practices need to be reviewed—teachers may need to become more aware of their own coercive power and how they can respond to it in their colleagues. Equally important is responding to the pain of the individuals in the situation and providing them with support that comes out of honest reflections on their situation. Punishing guilty perpetrators and/or lying accusers is not enough. Those engaged in the process need to be ready and able to create a new situation that is less supportive of harmful acts.

Each case can add new insight into cultural practices. A case-by-case reform strategy avoids overwhelming participants and so encourages critical reflections on how cultural norms may institutionalize sexism, racism, class, and other biases against groups of persons. Practical feminist reason asks that those reviewing situations assume a modest posture that acknowledges their own partiality is shaped by past experiences, acknowledge the role reason and emotion play in their own reflections, and be ready to receive new information.

From Consciousness Raising to Storytelling

Consciousness raising has been an explicit feminist method of analysis since the 1960s. CR can create conversations that reveal personal experiences, articulate social patterns, and develop strategies for transforming the world.[26] Bartlett characterizes CR as a process involving a team approach, moving forward through trial and error via commitments to risk-taking, vulnerability, and honesty.[27] Leslie Bender explains, "Feminist consciousness-raising creates knowledge by exploring common experiences and patterns that emerge from shared tellings of life events."[28] Relying upon group process, CR stresses personal disclosures over privacy. Personal disclosure contrasts with traditional legal methods, which withhold information to gain advantage. Witnesses are encouraged not to volunteer additional information in cross-examination, and clients are advised against even discussing trivial details of a case. CR calls on a cooperative rather than adversarial approach toward solving problems.

Showing how CR can involve more than simple narrations, Bender suggests that corporations who are responsible for workers' injuries should be directly involved in rendering personal care to the injured parties. Corporate managers might provide personal transportation for medical care, serve in burn care centers, or work with the injured in other ways. She believes that such service would alter the consciousness of managers.[29] Of course, some injured workers might not welcome help from managers who had either directly or indirectly been responsible for their injuries. Injured workers might not even want help from managers from other companies. Is Bender's approach a way to transform corporate American consciousness? Is it a naive dream? Is it just hard to imagine because citizens stereotype the legal process as adversarial?

The politics of feminist consciousness raising depends on each party being ready to transform themselves as they transform others. Such transformations entail risk and depend on trust. For this reason among others, consciousness raising has elicited considerable criticism.[30] Mari Matsuda solves this tension by calling for a dual consciousness that blends liberal rights-based arguments with radical arguments. Pointing to the Japanese reparations as an example, she defines consciousness raising in terms of acquiring a multilayered consciousness rather than a single "correct" mind set. [31] Giving Japanese Americans an apology and financial compensation are small tokens that do not erase the effects of the wrongs done, but a dual consciousness can embrace the way in which this apology marks a new national commitment.

A dual consciousness is necessary to reframe the term "consciousness raising," because it implies a hierarchy in which some have got it right once and for all and others have got it wrong. While a single-minded CR can create political solidarity with those "who have got it," it also creates rigidity and arrogance. Feminist legal conversations are replacing the metaphor of consciousness raising with that of storytelling. Vicki Shultz uses the latter in the title of her article "Telling Stories about Women and Work: Judicial Interpretations of Sex Segregation in the Workplace in Title VII Cases Raising the Lack of Interest Argument," and Robin West titles one of her books *Narrative, Authority, and Law*.[32] Taking conversations beyond narrow legal definitions of rights, storytellers encourage listeners to reflect on issues rather than just examine rules. In this way storytelling promotes moral discussions without moralizing.

Stories for the Personal and the Political

Patricia Williams uses narratives to examine legal arguments and to reveal her own personal responses to them by talking about her experiences as a law professor.[33] Her narrative rings true because she has the courage to take her reader into her confidence. Revealing the negative comments in her student's evaluation of her teaching, she openly discusses her struggles to perform as an academic.[34] While in some ways storytelling may appear as a neutral genre, Williams shows that it is not. Only those actually willing to reveal themselves to others can tell a good story.

Because narratives can communicate basic philosophical truths, legal scholars have become quite interested in this genre.[35] Certainly, narrative forms fit with legal discourse, for each case is in itself a set of at least two competing narratives and Supreme Court opinions can be read as legal narratives with their own set of characters, conflicts, and conflict resolutions. But narrative is especially helpful in speaking about race and gender issues because of the ways in which narratives invite readers to suspend judgments until they have heard the whole *story*. This allows readers to listen to painful details. Patricia Williams is especially effective in developing ways of telling the story that enable a reader to hear the whole tale without resorting to creating only villains and victims.[36] Employing the metaphor of storytelling can encourage clients, attorneys, and courtroom auditors to develop an understanding of the situation that values each person's experience while realizing that decisions come about through only partial viewpoints and so are contingent.

SO, CAN DECISIONS BE MADE FAIRLY?

The purpose of legal methods is to guide decisions so that they will be fair. The law is especially helpful to those whose interests are dissimilar and/or who have a history of antagonism toward one another. Unfortunately, no legal method offers a pristine, clean way of reaching perfect decisions since all methods contain both the virtues and the vices of the social environments that create them. By paying attention to how women are treated, feminist legal scholars point out how aspects of these methods create unfair decisions by favoring men. Identifying five of these methods, I offer ways in which these methods can be reformed to yield more fair decisions in legal situations. Because Americans depend on the law as a guide to everyday decisions, these reforms are important for remedying bias in larger political contexts. First, actions need to be understood in terms of both the actor's intentions and the consequences of those actions. Emphasizing intent allows citizens to remain ignorant of cultural ills and to perpetrate them under the guise of strategic innocence. Cultural and legal scrutiny must take account of the consequences of action to avoid the continual repeat of accidental acts of racism, sexism, and other socially harmful denigrations. Citizens need to take on the responsibility of making decisions that avoid racist, sexist results. Second, participants in legal matters need to be aware of the dangers of relying on precedents, which may reiterate past social harms. History and legal precedent serve as unsteady guides for those seeking just decisions. Third, citizens need to be aware of the ways in which cooperative as well as adversarial discourse contributes to good legal resolutions. Similarly, arriving at political resolutions to wider problems depends on stereotypic feminine cooperative skills as much as it does on stereotypic masculine adversarial skills. Fourth, legal scholars and citizens need to recognize how the law can silence women by doing nothing at all. Reexamining issues like consent and reason help illuminate how these concepts can be reconstructed to take account of the situations of both women and men. Fifth, considerations of the intersection of race and gender enable courts and citizens to reflect more clearly on how to eliminate such denigrations and the harms they produce especially when they are compounded.

While these reformulations are important, feminist jurisprudence makes an important contribution by offering new methods for legal decision making. First, feminists encourage reflective citizens to question the questions. Taking a wider critical view of situations, feminists can reframe issues so that previous bias habits can be illuminated and avoided. Second, feminists develop a way of using practical reason that acknowledges the partiality of all positions, the intersection of emotions and reason in assessments of all situations, and the necessity for opening up new ways of approaching old problems like sexual harassment that take account of the ways perpetrators can silence victims as well as the possibility for false reporting. New ways of talking can avoid old unproductive alienations. Third, feminist jurisprudence shows how moving from consciousness raising to storytelling enables feminist legal scholars as well as other citizens to hear the emotional and analytical details of an event, to develop empathy with the participants in an event, and to respond more fully to the complexities of the particular historical and cultural components of the event.

Replacing CR with storytelling encourages feminists to talk with one another about their similarities and differences. Beginning with personal narratives can move onto political commentaries. They convey not only situations but the emotional quality of those situations. Stories have a contextualized base that focuses on the particulars of a situation. In this sense the legal system is a forum for storytelling. Some stories are told more fully outside the courtroom in other media, but, nevertheless, the court system draws attention to the issues that frame the tale. The O. J. Simpson case might illustrate this. I respect the jury's decision about his innocence. I think it important to realize that those not in the courtroom did not hear the evidence and that media reports are not substitutions for courtroom attendance.

But the media have been helpful in using this case to alert the public to a number of important social issues and I would like to test the powers of these legal methods to see if they can illuminate the political issues in this case. The case illuminates the intersection between race and gender issues and the conflicting responses of black women reveal some of the complexities involved in this intersection. The case highlighted the seriousness of wife abuse. Using the case as a starting point, the media called on feminists to discuss how such abuse works, including the pattern of escalation. Making such discussions a central public concern is a victory for America as long as citizens realize that this is a general social problem rather than a discussion of what happened in the Simpson case. Feminist practical reason encourages all citizens to reflect on their own experiences of wife abuse and the emotional quality of such situations without forgetting the long tradition of punishing successful black men through false accusations. Certainly, the case also illuminated how racism and sexism come into play in the legal system. The Simpson case was told in a dramatic way in a variety of forms by television and other media. If these stories can be read as tales about problems in American society, citizens can use the story to become reflective about key moral issues.

But winning and losing cases, old-style macho values, is not the primary political issue. And while the media merit some scrutiny, they are not our primary political watchdogs. The primary watchdogs are critical citizens. What is vital politically is finding ways to explore the complex moral issues that frame such situations in American public life. Courts can offer a place to begin to frame these issues. Citizens need to find ways of telling the stories, exploring the narratives, and reflecting on how they are morally telling. Politically, morals and ethics are important, not simply to form codes, but to inform the day-to-day decisions citizens make in choosing how to act. This choice depends on making judgments. But judgment has been especially difficult in American public life. I will next argue that by making judgments explicit, feminists can reveal the ethical insights that inform their positions and avoid the so-called amoral, false-neutrality constructed by utilitarian models of public life.

NOTES

1. Catharine A. MacKinnon, *Feminism Unmodified: Discourses on Life and Law* (Cambridge, Mass.: Harvard University Press, 1987), 63–64.

2. Stanley Fish, among others, demonstrates how intent is culturally shaped in *Doing What Comes Naturally: Change, Rhetoric, and the Practice of Theory in Literary and Legal Studies* (Durham, N. C.: Duke University Press, 1989).

3. Fish makes this point in *Doing What Comes Naturally*.

4. This analysis of plain and fancy racism was developed by Robert Cahill as a part of his political work with the Northwest Coalition Against Malicious Harassment, which used the presence of the neo-Nazis in northern Idaho to develop understandings of everyday racism and to develop anti-racist strategies in the Northwest. See his unpublished essay, "Plain and Fancy Racism in North America" and a published summary of it in David Schuman and Dick Olufs, *Diversity on Campus* (Boston: Allyn & Bacon, 1995), 175–80.

5. A term invented by Robert Cahill (Spokane, Wash., 1989) to describe the practice of race discrimination that embraces racial ignorance in order to preserve a pattern of discriminatory practices.

6. Catharine A. MacKinnon, *Toward a Feminist Theory of the State* (Cambridge, Mass.: Harvard University Press, 1989), 238.

7. Carol Gilligan, *In a Different Voice: Psychological Theory and Women's Development* (Cambridge, Mass.: Harvard University Press, 1982).

8. For example, see Carrie Menkel-Meadow, "Portia in a Different Voice: Speculation on a Woman's Lawyering Process," *Berkeley Women's Law Journal* 1 (fall 1985): 39–63.

9. MacKinnon, *Toward a Feminist Theory of the State*, 239.

10. Kristin Bumiller, "Rape as a Legal Symbol: An Essay on Sexual Violence and Racism," *University of Miami Law Review* 42 (1987): 78–82.

11. Bumiller, 81.

12. For a discussion of this problematic from the viewpoint of a feminist accused of sexual harassment, see Jane Gallop, *Feminist Accused of Sexual Harassment* (Durham, N.C.: Duke University Press, 1997).

13. Kimberlé Williams Crenshaw, "Demarginalizing the Intersection of Race and Sex: A Black Feminist Critique of Antidiscrimination Doctrine, Feminist Theory, and Antiracist Politics," in *Feminist Legal Theory: Readings in Law and Gender*, eds. Katharine T. Bartlett and Rosanne Kennedy (Boulder, Colo.: Westview Press, 1991), 57–80, reprinted from *The University of Chicago Legal Forum* 25 (1989): 139–67.

14. White men are beginning to experience some of the injustices associated with such labeling, as power reversals in the women's movement and the black movement sometimes unjustly target white men for special scrutiny and discrimination.

15. Christine A. Littleton, "Women's Experience and the Problem of Transition: Perspectives on Male Battering of Women," *The University of Chicago Legal Forum* 25 (1989): 23–57.

16. Katharine T. Bartlett identifies woman questions, feminist practical reason and consciousness raising as three important legal methods in "Feminist Legal Methods," *Harvard Law Review* 103 (1990): 829–88, especially 836–37.

17. Michelle Z. Rosaldo, "Moral/Analytic Dilemmas Posed by the Intersection of Feminism and Social Science," in *Interpretive Social Science: A Second Look*, eds. Paul Rabinow and William M. Sullivan (Berkeley: University of California Press, 1987), 280–301, especially 286–89.

18. Heather Ruth Wishik, "To Question Everything: The Inquiries of Feminist Jurisprudence," *Berkeley Women's Law Journal* 1 (1986): 64–77, especially 64–65.

19. Bartlett, "Feminist Legal Methods," 847–49.

20. Bumiller, "Rape as a Legal Symbol," 75–91 and Bartlett, "Feminist Legal Methods," 842.

21. In American politics, the Supreme Court has been considered a major political institution along with Congress and the presidency but popular conceptions of the Supreme Court has given it more limited purposes.

22. Bartlett, "Feminist Legal Methods," 857.

23. Bartlett, "Feminist Legal Methods," 857.

24. Ann E. Freedman, "Feminist Legal Method in Action: Challenging Racism, Sexism and Homophobia in Law School," *Georgia Law Review* 24 (1990): 866, citing Ann Scales, "The Emergence of Feminist Jurisprudence: An Essay," *Yale Law Journal* 95 (1986): 1402.

25. Freedman, "Feminist Legal Method in Action."

26. For an emphasis on dialogue, see Ruth Colker, "Feminist Litigation: An Oxymoron?—A Study of the Briefs Filed in *William L. Webster v. Reproductive Health Services*," *Harvard Women's Law Journal* 13 (1990): 137–88.

27. Bartlett, "Feminist Legal Methods," 864–65.

28. Leslie Bender, "A Lawyer's Primer on Feminist Theory and Tort," *Journal of Legal Education* 38 (1988): 9.

29. Leslie Bender, "Changing the Values in Tort Law," *Tulsa Law Journal* 25 (1990): 767–73.

30. MacKinnon has been criticized for her model of consciousness raising because it assumes that all women are alike. See, for example, Angela Harris, "Review Essay: Categorical Discourse and Dominance Theory," *Berkeley Women's Law Journal* 5 (1989–90): 181–96.

31. Mari Matsuda, "Looking to the Bottom: Critical Legal Studies and Reparations," *Harvard Civil Rights and Civil Liberties Law Review* 22 (1987): 323–99; and Angela P. Harris reinforces this multiple consciousness in her article "Race and Essentialism in Feminist Legal Theory," *Stanford Law Review* 42 (1990): 615–16.

32. Vicki Shultz, "Telling Stories about Women and Work: Judicial Interpretations of Sex Segregation in the Workplace in Title VII Cases Raising the Lack of Interest Argument," in *Feminist Legal Theory*, eds. Bartlett, Kennedy, 124–55; and Robin West, *Narrative, Authority, and Law* (Ann Arbor: University of Michigan Press, 1993).

33. Patricia J. Williams, *The Alchemy of Race and Rights* (Cambridge, Mass.: Harvard University Press, 1991).

34. Williams, *The Alchemy of Race and Rights*, 95–97.

35. Peter Brooks and Paul Gewirtz, eds. *Law's Stories: Narrative and Rhetoric in the Law* (New Haven, Conn.: Yale University Press, 1996).

36. Patricia J. Williams, *The Alchemy of Race and Rights* and *The Rooster's Egg* (Cambridge, Mass.: Harvard University Press, 1995).

Chapter 4

Judgments and Politics: Citizens and Justice in Everyday Life

"Don't judge others — Don't be judgmental — You can't legislate morality" serve as slogans to silence public discussions of moral issues and to affirm American rugged individualism in the spirit of live and let live. Building on a minimalist view of governance, this spirit delegitimates ethical conversations about public life. While these slogans appear to enforce tolerance by encouraging citizens to accept others rather than judge them, the slogans pretend that public law does not affirm certain values over others. Such an amoral pretense does more to promote status quo politics than it does to encourage tolerance. I have argued in that the law needs to be reformed in order to replace masculinist exclusive practices with gender-inclusive ones. This involves new metaphors, including new ways of thinking about relationships as commitments like covenants rather than contracts, and I have suggested that reforming legal methods will lead to more fair decisions. These reforms depend on citizens seeing themselves as political actors whose work is creating justice. This means citizens see themselves as responsible for making judgments about what ethical matters in both the legal system and in everyday life.

Refraining from judgment is not only an unproductive goal, it is an unobtainable one. Every purposeful action requires some judgment about what to do — some decisions that choose this action over that one. So perhaps the prohibition on judgment is about judging others and not one's own actions. But even this seems impossible because almost every purposeful action involves judgments about others. If I decide to assign a class a reading, I have made a judgment about the level of the readings, the interest of students, and my colleagues' assessment of the worth of such readings. If I decide to have an abortion, I make judgments about the moral right of such action, the involvement of others in it, and the professional medical persons to be included. Judgments about one's own actions are intertwined with judgments about others. But maybe these judgments are only about competency and not about moral ethical matters and so the prohibition on judgment is about making moral pronouncements about others. Such compartmentalizations fail. Judgment about competency includes judgments about honesty, forthrightness, humility, self-reflection, and fairness. I certainly would be hesitant to select a doctor who did not bring all of those qualities to bear in his or her work, and I would feel the same way about teachers. In fact, all work requires these basics. My selection of a doctor is not only guided by assessment of the state and its licensing procedures as well as other public institutions designed to ensure health. Such judgments depend on legislation and are never merely private matters. Action and morality are interwoven and private moral decisions depend on public political judgments. But then why is there such a public outcry against making judgments?

Such prohibitions have both religious and secular roots. Christian religions teach followers to "judge not, lest they be so judged"—that is, to leave judgments to God. While popularized versions of this may encourage tolerance for others, the theological import cautions followers to leave eternal and final judgments to God. Theologically, followers are not admonished to make no moral judgments; but instead to make them provisional. Persons, and even groups, are liable to sin and err. Furthermore, even if right, such judgments have only contingent, transitory authority, not eternal authority. Calling on a different explanation, scientific authority has also discouraged making judgments by claiming merely to be making observations. Positivistic scientists warned against personal judgments that permitted values or ethics to influence descriptions. Thus, both Christians and positivists give judgment a "bad" name. Scientific neutrality, religious practices, and citizens' fear of one another have conspired to discourage American citizens from "making" judgments. This dogma is so strong that despite the fact that actions cannot be taken without some form of judgment, citizens, even scholars, cry out that they are making no judgments.[1] Some, often conservatives, admit to making some judgments but minimize them by claiming to judge only the actions, not persons. The taboo against making judgments is so strong that even politicians find themselves explaining that they only do what they *have* to do. There are few judgment calls.

This failure to acknowledge the role of judgment in everyday life has made it difficult to talk about politics—to talk about how we can live well together—because such talk requires citizens to make judgments about present actions, past deeds, and future possibilities. Whenever such discussions do arise morality is equated with sexual behavior. "Good" presidents lead sexually acceptable lives. It seems that the only virtue left for public officials is chastity. Citizens who think feminists are primarily interested in the sex lives of officials misunderstand "the personal is political," as the "personal is sexual." Feminists study sexual politics to reveal how power is gendered, not to discover who is sleeping with whom. Reducing morality to sex even makes it difficult for citizens to reflect privately on their own moral commitments. Telling citizens that making judgments is uncivil has created a dangerous neutrality that obscures how decisions are made. I want to encourage citizens to make judgments about ethical matters that compose public life because political justice depends on citizens making justice happen. While it needs to happen in the legal system, it is equally important that citizens act to create justice in their/our everyday lives.

HOW DOES JUSTICE DEPEND ON CITIZENS?

The court system is the one institution where talk about judgments still works. This may help explain the popularity of television dramas and novels about the legal system. It is possible that citizens hunger for such public discussions, and talk of rights comes close to providing a discourse about "morality." While churches are no longer viable, science has lost its innocence, Congress is greedy, the presidency is smudged, and attorneys are morally questionable, the legal system retains a kind of pristine goodness. Even the convicted innocent will become fugitives, who can finally exonerate themselves. Such judgments make the system sacred and give it the aura of a political guardian angel. Courts serve as the nation's conscience. Using the court system as a model, I will argue that making judgments explicit can make American public life more just, more honest, and more fun. Becoming less fearful of making judgments, citizens can more fully respond to the challenges that racism, sexism, heterosexism, and other social ills offer and they can become more at ease in public life. Thus, politics can be more engaging, more fun, and more just.

I will propose four changes in the legal processes that help make judgments more reflective and more fair. Just habits are not primarily about the regulation of sexual behavior. They are about how citizens support or fail to support each other in nurturing the best in every person and the best in the collective of persons that compose public life. These four changes offer a new way of understanding how the court system serves the politics of everyday life and they offer ways citizens can act to make justice happen. In the everyday practices of their lives, all citizens can and do wear the judges' robes. And like judges they represent social values. Judges put on their robes and dress themselves in ways that display their commitment as representatives of the state. Each citizen can don a metaphorical black robe that reminds the wearer of the responsibility each citizen has for creating fair practices and just systems.

FOUR STEPS TOWARD MAKING JUDGMENTS FAIR

Drawing on feminist jurisprudence, I show how the legal system can replace neutrality as an ideal with reflectivity to gain a more honest account of how judgments are made. Second, I outline how the legal system can integrate emotion and reason into its public deliberations. Third, I show how court decisions are shaped by the actions of all participants, not just by judges and/or juries. Fourth, I explain how courts can serve as a public forum that scrutinizes cultural codes as well as individual behavior. Moving beyond the scrutiny of individuals, legal judgments can review social behavior and cultural habits. If legal discourse can incorporate these four strategies for reintrepreting the court as a political institution, then courts can render more fair decisions and citizens can look to the court for how to make better decisions in their everyday lives. The first step is replacing the virtue of neutrality, which represents blind judgment, with the virtue of reflectivity.

Lady Justice's Blindfold and Avoiding the Lie of Neutrality

Lady Justice's blindfold has symbolized the court's desires to render unbiased judgments—that is, the disregard of social differences (blindness to social factors) in applying the law. But more current understandings of social differences show citizens that such blinders serve as a poor metaphor for rendering objective decisions. With the introduction of philosophical hermeneutics and ethnomethodology, many social analysts claim that neutrality makes social understanding impossible.[2] But neutrality is also undesirable, for if achieved, any analyses or action performed from this viewpoint would be irrelevant to society. Judgments make sense to the degree that they are framed within the concerns of a particular social historical context.[3] The Archimedean point—which represents distance, disinterest, and disconnection—does not yield a meaningful view of society and serves as a poor location for the judge's bench.

Turning away from early Enlightenment emphases on neutrality brings citizens closer to classic Greek notions that emphasize the connection between social theory and action.[4] Praxis explains this connection as a dialectic in which theory is shaped out of social experiences and social experiences are viewed through the lens of theory. Good social analysis means continually being open to the dialectical changes that this tension produces. However, openness does not mean beginning an analysis with a blank slate (that is, no prejudice) because some pre-judgment position makes analysis possible. Reflection emerges by critically examining the pre-judgments that frame the inquiry and the new insights produced by inquiry.[5]

Such reflectivity encourages citizens to know their own cultures and histories, to learn about themselves as they learn about others.[6] The praxis turn is especially important for analyses of gender and race because of the ways in which historical practices have inscribed racism and sexism into a range of social habits and theories. Both habits and theories need to change to address such issues. For example, liberal theories about abstract humanity hide the ways in which such images of humanity are male and Eurocentric. Mistaking some cultural norms for universal characteristics of human nature, Western culture has often devalued women and people of color.[7] These racist and sexist norms and theories will occur with less regularity if citizens can abandon the false belief that some humans can assume a neutral stance.

Once citizens have this post-Enlightenment understanding of knowledge, Lady Justice's blindfold and scales serve as poor symbols of fairness.[8] Lady Justice not only needs to remove her blindfold in order to see the world more clearly, but "she" also needs to stop suggesting that rendering justice is like weighing apples. The scales may have been helpful at the height of modernity, which prided itself on developing pristine truths untouched by human hands, but new epistemologies, old Greek ones, and new technologies suggest that the scales are a poor symbol of good judgment. Balancing and weighing are no longer useful metaphors. Certainly, treating all persons exactly alike fails to take account of how persons' situations make them different. When man sits on one side of the scale and woman on the other, the scales are not balanced because society weighs men more heavily. A similar argument can be made for legal contests between the rich and the poor. Demonstrating how blindness to gender creates unjust actions, feminists offer new understanding of the connection between values and analyses.

I am arguing that becoming aware of what values shape particular situations will render better judgments. Employing a radical hermeneutics, which encourages examinations of the historical and cultural contexts of previous legal practices, I want to establish a dual authority for political life that reconciles past values with current ones. Legal hermeneutics defines the courts as active interpreters of the law within the context of precedent, statutes, and history. While relying on tradition, judgments are about immediate situations.[9] Recognizing this dual authority can enable legal reviews that treat precedents as both guides *for* and the products *of* a historical tradition. Although this hermeneutical approach to the law has received considerable attention in other areas, it has less often been employed to address racism and sexism. By using a suspicious feminist hermeneutic that regards how the past has been shaped by patriarchal practices as well as by wise, fair decisions, feminists can cast suspicion on both the past and the present.[10] Of course, past traditions must include women's traditions as well as men's. A feminist legal hermeneutic can learn from the past while critically reviewing it in the light of present values, specifically the rejection of racism, sexism, heterosexism, and class privilege.

Thus, Lady Justice might be better represented as a storyteller who enables people's experiences to be heard[11] than as a blindfolded mannikin holding scales. The storytelling image is a central one in feminist conversations.[12] Anne B. Goldstein compares lawyering with novel writing, claiming that "Litigation is a storytelling contest,"[13] and Kathryn Abrams in the same text argues that: "Paradigm-shifting narratives, as well as other kinds of narratives, help alter our conception of the normative by offering a new image of what is necessary to effect legal change."[14] Abrams explains how stories can alert the public to problems that can be addressed by litigation and legislation.[15] Storytelling is not political because it presents emotions and so may unduly persuade listeners. Storytelling is helpful politically by enabling citizens to enter into new situations and empathize with others—especially others who differ from them. Stories can create closer political communities while permitting opportunities for the articulation of differences. Because stories enable citizens to see society differently, storytelling is a powerful tool in motivating political action and transforming public life. Furthermore, it is nonviolent, simple, and inexpensive. Lady Justice might take off her blindfold, set aside her scales, take a seat, open up a book with one hand and with the other hand beckon citizens to come forward and listen to the legal stories she reads to them and the stories those legal tales encourage them to tell each other.

Considering legal discussions as forums for telling public stories can help citizens understand how the law can serve as a cultural guide. American courts have been good at exposing individual wrongs but have been less useful in understanding wrongful social practices. If citizens understand the court as a setting for social stories, the courts might be able to serve broader normative functions without broadening the legal powers of the court. To enable courts to do this would involve encouraging citizens to listen to the court differently. The emphasis would shift from listening to the court *for* a set of rules to listening to the court *as* a set of social practices. For example, citizens could interpret the O. J. Simpson case as a story about how racism and sexism create unfair situations in America. Instead of listening to court proceedings to find out if Simpson murdered his wife, citizens could listen to court proceedings to find out about the tensions involved in such social problems. The more important question is not, "Did he do it?" but "What does this tell us about ourselves?" Hermeneutical listening can encourage citizens to be reflective about their own social situations and the laws that structure those social situations. Legal conversations can offer opportunities for examining the intersection between past values (which laws affirm) and the present concerns that a legal case brings to light.

Incorporating Both Emotion and Reason

While some detachment in legal judgment is important, it is equally important to use empathy and engagement. Emotion, like reason, needs to be subject to discipline and deliberation. Hot emotions and cold, cool reasons are not opposites in judgment processes, because good judgments rely on both reason and emotion.[16] Asking persons to cast aside emotions is not only impossible but may encourage emotions to run silently wild. Becoming reflective about emotions asks juries, judges, and citizens to use their emotions to empathize with *both* sides of the case. Empathy and tears are not to be reserved for "victims"; empathy should be a part of the response to all litigants.

Personal injury cases serve as one example. Such cases often elicit painful dramatic tales of individual tragedies; defendant attorneys often find themselves at a disadvantage, for the tale may unfold with the corporate giant Goliath injuring a poor innocent David or Sarah. Furthermore, the American tendency to cheer for underdogs can put corporations at a disadvantage. If all participants in the legal process can understand their emotions, better judgments can be rendered. It is unrecognized emotions that are more likely to have undue influence. Thus, making emotions part of legal deliberations can infuse the process with greater reflectivity, insight and compassion,[17] because legal judgments involve thinking about situations that never quite fit the rules and persons never neatly conform to categories. That is why courts proceed by reflection rather than by relying on computer programs to make decisions. A just response to a situation involves a complex blend of reason and emotion.

Experience

Some popular American stories imply that justice requires citizens to cast aside previous experiences and that will make them open and fair. In jury selection, such visions of neutrality create problems, particularly in well-publicized cases. Because almost everyone has had some experience with the "facts" of the case, jury service is left to those who seldom read newspapers, watch television, or listen to the radio. In other words, this ideal carried to its logical end point recruits only the most disinterested, alienated citizens to set in judgment. But even this sort of neutrality can be difficult to obtain. For example, in cases that involve gender issues, all jury members have previous experiences as gendered members of society. Searching for the gender-neutral party is difficult. Can only hermaphrodites serve in cases involving gender? But hermaphrodites frequently have lived part of their lives as male or female, and so even they might not qualify. The same is true of race/ethnicities; we have all lived as persons with particular cultural heritages. Is experience a detriment to good judgment?

Knowing a person has been raped or knowing a person has been the victim of a robbery does not indicate how such a person will view a particular case that deals with those issues. Clearly, social science research demonstrates the difficulty of predicting the behavior of individuals as well as groups. Although some companies gain financial success by jury prediction, it is possible that rather than telling attorneys whom to select, they alert attorneys to the ramifications of a number of different types of arguments. Attorneys might be better served by simply consulting with firms who can bring relevant psychological issues to their attention. Perhaps attorneys may not want to present themselves as in need of that sort of help. Thus crystal ball social science[18] may simply bring psychological factors to the attention of attorneys.

Acknowledging the role previous experiences have in shaping all decisions might empower both judge and juries to become more reflective about how they are responding to information. The point is not to eliminate experience but to use it in ways that enable the present situation to receive a full evaluation. Calling on experience can render sounder social judgments. Those who are aware of their own prejudice against attorneys are better at making judgments about them. Those who have experience at using analysis and/or empathy in interpreting facts will want to bring those skills to bear on making decisions. Not only does this avoid the impossible pretense that the jury can keep all previous events of their lives at bay while making decisions, but it urges jurists and citizens (who make judgments in other settings) to be mindful that their own experiences work to produce a fair decision.

Cultural Contexts and Pre-Judgments

Becoming reflective about cultural contexts does not focus on some narrow confessions of bias. The focus is broader than individual bias. The legal system emerges within a biased cultural context that needs critical examination. While maintaining the presumption of innocence of individuals, courts need to treat social environments with suspicion.[19] If courts assume society is innocent of prejudices, then the burden of proof rests with individuals who must prove biases exist in society. By assuming gendered and racialized biases, courts can respond more accurately to social problems. While the presumption of innocence for the accused is vital, the presumption that society is innocent is not. A suspicious approach to social practices can enable courts to address broader social needs.

Reflection depends on critical reviews of cultural norms; it requires actions that remedy situations for its completion. But such actions values reformation over retribution. A reflective spirit seeks deep and genuine reform. While such a spirit might decrease an individual woman's ability to gain a large settlement, it might benefit women in general by enabling the court to scrutinize gender bias more thoroughly and to serve as a public forum for changing it. Often women and people of color explain that a primary purpose of lawsuits is to curb bias practices; thus, they might find greater satisfaction with outcomes that alter practices rather than simply punish offenders. Courts could focus on the review of social circumstances that lead to legal infractions. For feminists, such reflection introduces historical and cultural factors. Undoubtedly such factors will be used to excuse certain actions, but even such excusing can be helpful in indicting social practices—even if it lets some individuals "off" because the culture "made them do it." Greater good may be accomplished in social change than in punishing an individual. Court time might be better served by airing social ills than by rewarding or punishing litigants.

However, this reflective approach depends on all who work within the legal system taking time to consider the social effects of their actions. Attorneys already speak about social factors in briefs and in opening and closing arguments. Being more self-conscious about the way social factors shape questions might enable attorneys to become more aware of how their questions also have social impact. Clients can be encouraged to reflect on how their decisions will affect persons in similar situations. Expert witnesses can be encouraged to explain cultural patterns even though the opinions of experts differ. What is important is that sociopolitical considerations become an explicit concern for all participants in legal processes. In this regard, even the *EEOC v. Sears, Roebuck & Co.* can be understood as a positive contribution to feminist politics.[20] Because there was expert feminist testimony on both sides, the Sears case demonstrates that feminist analyses offer complex and opposing voices. The Sears case shows that feminist experts, like medical experts, do not offer one model that settles issues but instead enable rich reflections on gender. Such feminist differences can deepen political conversations. In the long run this enriches feminist analyses, even though in the short run the Sears decision did not benefit the female litigants. The point here is that the more feminist analyses come to the foreground, the better able citizens will be at reflection on gender issues. Although it is sad that the women who experienced discrimination at the hands of Sears were not compensated for their loss, the case helped the women's movement because it gave public voice to these issues and gained voice for feminist analyses. Similarly, Dworkin and MacKinnon's work on pornography has lost in court but won attention in American politics.

WHAT CAN FEMINISTS TEACH CITIZENS ABOUT MAKING RESPONSIBLE JUDGMENTS?

American citizens have made such a fetish out of the statement "judge not" that they may have fooled themselves into thinking that they make no judgments. But every day, citizens act on the basis of a host of judgments about what is right and wrong. Even refraining from action has political and moral consequences. For example, the failure to report sexual harassment shapes power relationships and subsequent social environments. Reporting it does as well. However tentatively citizens may understand such judgments, actions and decisions not to act proceed from making judgments.

Feminist jurisprudence shows that it is important to take responsibility for the actions that compose life by becoming more aware of how persons make judgments and by developing public conversations about justice. Feminist jurisprudence can revitalize the courts as a force for justice by enabling citizens to understand how the courts work as a political institution that does not merely reward and punish individuals but explores the distinction between right and wrong. The courts offer a public forum for deliberation about social values. Rather than passively watching the court maintain order by merely finding the guilty and doing legitimate violence to them,[21] citizens can listen to courtroom activity to scrutinize social practices. Citizens can then act to make justice more possible.[22]

The problem with the courts is not that they are ignored or that their rulings are not enforced but that the story told about them is insufficient to describe the work they can do for citizens. The new story renders reflective judgments by making four changes in current popular understandings of legal deliberations. This new form of legal deliberation can guide courts and citizens toward more fair decisions in the politics of everyday life.

First, court participants need to reject the pose of neutrality and replace it with a hermeneutical understanding that both appreciates traditions and critically scrutinizes them in the light of the ways they may perpetuate racism, sexism, and other long-standing social ills. Second, court participants need to discipline themselves by employing empathy and emotions as well as reason in reaching judgments. Third, experience needs to play an explicit role in authorizing jurists to utilize their own expertise along with legal tradition in making judgments. Fourth, court participants need to take account of cultural practices in their discourse so that their models of society include not only the actions and responsibility of individuals but also the way in which cultural practices shape situations to offer citizens guidelines for ethical behavior. Thus, feminist jurisprudence invites courts to bring into full view how emotion, cultural values, empathy, and experience shape judgment processes and to offer citizens not merely codes of conduct but models of how to make just decisions in the context of the daily life of each citizen. Thus, the courts are not only a source of justice but a resource for demonstrating how to obtain justice in other contexts. The court as a government institution can teach her citizens to make fair judgments and to recognize the important role of judgment in the lives of all citizens.

NOTES

1. Even Teresa L. Ebert, who employs a postmarxist analysis to nudge feminist theory away from postmodernism, is unable to argue for judgment and settles for explanation. See *Ludic Feminism and After: Postmodernism, Desire, and Labor in Late Capitalism* (Ann Arbor: University of Michigan Press, 1996), 12.

2. For a discussion of philosophical hermeneutics, see Paul Ricoeur, *Hermeneutics and the Human Sciences: Essays on Language, Action, and Interpretation*, trans. and ed., John B. Thompson (New York: Cambridge University Press, 1981), and Hans-Georg Gadamer, *Truth and Method*, trans. Garrett Barden and John Cumming (New York: The Seabury Press, 1975).

3. Eloise A. Buker, "Feminist Social Theory and Hermeneutics: An Empowering Dialectic?" *Social Epistemology* 4 (1990): 23–39.

4. For general discussions of the ways in which classical Greek thinkers, especially Aristotle, contribute to current foci on the connection between social theory and judgment, see Richard J. Bernstein, *The New Constellation: The Ethical-Political Horizons of Modernity/Postmodernity* (Cambridge, Mass.: MIT Press, 1992), especially 23–29; and Hans-Georg Gadamer, *Reason in the Age of Science*, trans. Frederick G. Lawrence (Cambridge, Mass.: MIT Press, 1981), 88–138.

5. See Gadamer, *Truth and Method* and *Reason in the Age of Science*, and for a social science interpretation of this epistemology Buker, "Feminist Social Theory and Hermeneutics."

6. For an argument showing the connection between *prohairesis*, judgment, the law, and the realization of the good in social practices, see Hans-Georg Gadamer, *Reason in the Age of Science*, 90–97.

7. For examples, see Sandra Harding, *The Science Question in Feminism* (Ithaca, N.Y.: Cornell University Press, 1986); *Is Science Multicultural?: Postcolonialisms, Feminisms, and Epistemologies* (Bloomington: Indiana University Press, 1998); and Donna Haraway, *Primate Visions: Gender, Race, and Nature in the World of Modern Science* (New York: Routledge, 1989).

8. For a discussion of this figure from the perspective of feminist jurisprudence, see Eloise A. Buker, "Lady Justice: Power and Image in Feminist Jurisprudence," *Vermont Law Review* 15 (1990): 69–87.

9. Eloise A. Buker, "Feminist Social Theory and Hermeneutics."

10. Feminists do not merely present alternatives but offer visions that build upon past feminist work and traditions.

11. This understanding of communication assumes a semiotic theory of language that is consistent with hermeneutics. For discussions of the politics of this communicative process, see Eloise A. Buker, *Politics through a Looking-Glass* (New York: Greenwood Press, 1987); and for an application of semiotics to the law, see James Boyd White, *Heracles' Bow: Essays on the Rhetoric and Poetics of the Law* (Madison: University of Wisconsin Press, 1985).

12. For discussions of storytelling and feminist analysis, see Robert L. Hayman, Jr., Nancy Levit, eds., *Jurisprudence: Contemporary Readings, Problems, and Narratives* (St. Paul, Minn.: West Publishing Co, 1995), 297–322; Eloise A. Buker, "Storytelling Power: Personal Narrative and Political Analysis," *Women & Politics* 7 (fall 1987): 29–46; and Robin West, *Narrative, Authority, and Law* (Ann Arbor: University of Michigan Press, 1993).

13. Anne B. Goldstein, "Representing the Lesbian in Law and Literature," in *Representing Women: Law, Literature, and Feminism*, eds. Susan Sage Heinzelman, Zipporah Batshaw Wiseman (Durham, N.C.: Duke University Press, 1994), 357.

14. Kathryn Abrams, "The Narrative and the Normative in Legal Scholarship," in *Representing Women*, 52.

15. Abrams, 52.

16. Alison M. Jaggar, "Love and Knowledge: Emotion in Feminist Epistemology," in *Gender/Body/Knowledge: Feminist Reconstructions of Being and Knowing*, eds. Alison M. Jaggar and Susan R. Bordo (New Brunswick, N.J.: Rutgers University Press, 1989), 145–71; and for a commentary that does not include feminism, see *Understanding and Social Inquiry*, eds. Fred R. Dallmayr and Thomas A. McCarthy (Notre Dame, Ind.: University of Notre Dame Press, 1977).

17. In "The Difference in Women's Hedonic Lives: A Phenomenological Critique of Feminist Legal Theory," in *Feminist Legal Theory 1: Foundations and Outlooks*, ed. Frances E. Olsen (New York: New York University Press, 1995), 426–29, Robin West argues that it is important to tell about women's pain. For an argument on the connection between compassion and politics, see Kathleen B. Jones, *Compassionate Authority: Democracy and the Representation of Women* (New York: Routledge, 1993).

18. The crystal ball metaphor suggests my rejection of the ability of social scientists to predict human behavior. Arguments to support my viewpoint can be found in the work of Richard Bernstein, Richard Rorty, Charles Taylor, Michael J. Shapiro, William Connolly, Laurel Richardson, Glifford Geertz, and others who argue for an empirical, not a positivistic, model of social science.

19. This is different from treating sex as a "suspicious category."

20. Edited from *EEOC v. Sears, Roebuck & Co.,* 628 F. Supp, 1264 (N.D. Ill. 1986), *EEOC v. Sears, Roebuck & Co.* 839 F.2d 302 (7th Cir., 1988); and Alice Kessler-Harris, "Equal Opportunity Commission v. Sears, Roebuck & Company: A Personal Account," in *Applications of Feminist Legal Theory to Women's Lives: Sex, Violence, Work, and Reproduction,* ed. D. Kelly Weisberg (Philadelphia: Temple University Press, 1996), 571–610.

21. I use the term "violence" here to refer not only to physical punishment but also to the general understanding of how violence is a part of judgment itself. This view is articulated by Jacques Derrida, "Violence and Metaphysics: An Essay on the Thought of Emmanual Levinas," *Writing and Difference,* Alan Bass, trans. (Chicago, Ill.: The University of Chicago Press, 1978), 79–153; and utilized by Stanley Fish to talk about the law, see Stanley Fish, *Doing What Comes Naturally: Change, Rhetoric, and the Practice of Theory in Literary and Legal Studies* (Durham, N.C.: Duke University Press, 1989), 503–24.

22. For example, men and women regularly receive unequal pay for similar jobs. The Equal Pay Act has been circumvented by a complex of social practices that have made it difficult for this act to eliminate such injustices. Comparable worth emerged as a way of combating that circumvention. If the court were able to assign blame not simply to a single company for engaging in unequal pay practices but also to a social context, it might be easier to successfully litigate against companies and end sexual discrimination. Stopping unjust practices is the goal of much litigation. Often, parties involved want the practice stopped more than they want to punish the company. However, punishing the company under the present system seems to be the only way to warn other companies to stop. But is it? Is it possible that the court could acknowledge the ways in which it serves as a body that sits in judgment not only on individual parties but also on social practices? Could the court make public acclamations about social injustices even if it did not punish someone?

Part II

❖   ❖   ❖

Feminist Scientific Conversations: Truth and Politics

My examination of feminist jurisprudence focused on politics and justice. In this part, I will concentrate on the connection between politics and truth—that is, between social practices and epistemological claims.[1] Modernity has constructed two modes of knowing as polar opposites—reason, which is represented by detachment, and emotion, which suggests some attachment to the subject under review. Emotional knowledge is called intuitive; reason is deductive. Intuitions, connections, and sentiments have been located in the arts and humanities while deductive, objective, distant modes of knowledge have been associated with the sciences. Modern universities have reinforced this dichotomy by separating the sciences and the humanities. This distinction lines up science with objective truth and the humanities with subjective emotions. But at the same time the interdisciplinary nature of epistemological work challenges this separation. Feminists join this challenge, pointing out that representations of reason have been masculinized and those of emotion feminized. Integrating scientific discourse with public matters requires that citizens undo the rigidities in the dichotomy that gets played out with reason-truth-science on one side and emotion-politics-humanities on the other.

My first experience with this polarity between the arts and sciences came about when I was in graduate school in English literature at the University of California at Davis. My epistemological loyalties were easy to sort out. I was a "literature person," and science was the other side—the strange, foreign, unliberated camp. I could set the tension aside. But in 1973, a taste of living in Taiwan and an old longing for political science led me again to begin graduate school at the University of Hawaii, Department of Political Science. Here, I suddenly had become "the odd, unliberated one," who claimed to be *a* scientist. Already estranged from society by my female body, I wanted to fit in, to be right, to find the truth, even to embody the truth. But even though the department had empirical scientific commitments, it had collectively encountered Thomas Kuhn, Michel Foucault, Jürgen Habermas, Eric Voegelin, and other critics of positivism. Many faculty were integrating empirical methods with interpretive strategies from the humanities. The science part of political science had changed even before I could actually get myself into its ranks.

While this change had begun to crack open my own rigid commitments to the science/humanities dichotomy, I was determined to become a scientist first and then learn the critique. But this approach just didn't work. Two things happened to me. First, as I learned empirical research design, I saw the connections between knowledge and politics. Slowly, I began to understand how scientific observation depended on imagination. Gradually, I figured out that a value orientation to science was not a failure, but a necessity. I saw how my old literary world could be, even must be, a part of my new world. Second, I did field work in Hawaii and so was able to study with Native Hawaiians.[2] As I became comfortable in the community, I heard Hawaiians speak about rocks and sharks as "teachers"—as *amakua*, or special guardians. At first, this way of speaking about natural objects seemed to me to be some creative form of pantheism, or perhaps totemism.[3] It violated my own beliefs about science and how the truth was to be learned. Later, I realized that this way of talking was built on careful systematic observation: it represented a scientific analysis that did not depend on the Western nature/culture, human/nonhuman distinctions. This approach represented the intersection of culture and nature in a less human-centered form. Considering rocks as teachers anticipates that careful observations will yield cosmological information as well as physical information.

At first, I thought my old image of the war between science and the humanities was just a personal mistake born out of my own prejudices. But graduation brought me to a new mainland environment and a political science faculty less interested in evoking the symbolism of science and more interested in interdisciplinary conversations. These interdisciplinary conversations with those in the so-called hard sciences reconfigured me once again as a "stranger"—a not-so-competent, even pseudoscientist. In conversations about science, being female has not always been an advantage nor has being an academic feminist. So why was I so interested in talking to scientists, as if I were one of them? Why did truth seem to rest on my ability to persuade others that I was really a political scientist? Did I just want to invoke the power that the label "science" offered? Or was I just a feminist bent on rescuing women from the ills of science? After some false starts, I became more comfortable with myself as a scientist. I learned to tell others, but more importantly to tell myself, how I could ascribe to the truth claims of both empiricism and post-structuralism. As more folks like me entered political sciences, the intensity of the debate about the one and only way to do science—positivism—receded. Empirical science emerged as one method among many.

Meanwhile, many feminist scientists were offering new ways of doing science that not only avoided unsustainable claims to value free science, but also presented a more self-conscious model of the scientist as a political worker—that is, as one who tries to make the community better by working not only on behalf of truth, but also on behalf of justice. Groups like the Physicians for Social Responsibility also were engaged in connecting science and social justice concerns. For many, the separation of science from humanistic matters had become tedious, and for many academics the excitement of interdisciplinary work was in itself engaging. For feminists, interdisciplinary work made the attempt to undo sexism more effective. For example, drawing from both the humanities and the social sciences, five feminist psychologists worked together to compose a qualitative project that paid attention to women, metaphor, and empirical observations. Their book, *Women's Ways of Knowing,* provided a new way of talking about the truth and epistemological diversity.[4]

WHY CONNECT SCIENTIFIC TRUTH WITH POLITICAL ISSUES?

Because science offers information about life and death matters and because it provides a strategy for gaining the truth, it plays a key role in American public life. Science has come to serve as a primary discourse for defining humanity, life, death, health, and sex; it affects eating habits, physical expectations, exercise, health, ecology, economy, defense, and more. U.S. citizens turn to science not only for information but also for methods of gaining such information. In fact, those in the social sciences have admired scientific methods developed by the natural and physical sciences so that they have looked to them for direction. More recently, historians and others in the humanities have turned to empirical methods. Scientific discourse has made possible life choices that before were not even imagined, and so citizens have come to respect science for its ability to provide reliable, dependable, objective—that is truthful—information. Citizens credit science for the prosperity of the United States and the longevity of its citizens.

Since the Enlightenment, science has promised the truth in the form of objective information about how human bodies can be kept safe and healthy. Because the modern state promises to keep citizens safe and because citizens need the truth to make good decisions, public conversations place a high value on scientific information. Increasingly, the state has wanted to know about safe food, safe sexual intercourse, safe environmental conditions—all of which scientific discourse addresses. Just as the state has relied on science for weapons to secure citizens against "foreign" threats, it has come to rely on science for information to protect citizens in the new post–cold war era. But scientific authorities disagree; science does not offer guarantees. Protection has not been totally forthcoming. Citizens continue to die; some even experience early deaths. Malpractice suits have become more common. Economics and social pressures shape medical practice and research. Health care costs escalate and burden middle-class Americans; too many working-class citizens cannot even get health care. So, in the latter part of the twentieth century, scientific discourse has not only been a central force in American public life, but it has also become an object of critical reflection. Since the Enlightenment, tales of masculine objectivity and feminine subjectivity have haunted conversations about science; discussions of "the hard" and "the soft" sciences contain not-so-subtle allusions to a gendered hierarchy.[5]

Feminist scientists and other scholars have criticized science at the level of everyday practices as well as at the level of methodologies. At the epistemological level, the critiques have included negative reviews of both absolute objectivity (which claims a neutral singular articulation of THE truth) and absolute subjectivity (which claims that truth is as varied as the persons who opine it). Rejecting both positions, feminists are now ready to suggest that the truth lies in some compromise between neutral objectivity and radical relativism. Many feminists embrace a contextualized understanding of truth that recognizes the interdependence of knowledge and social life[6] and that makes authoritative truth claims based on the findings of a community of scholars, who respect the limits that the natural physical world places on humans as well as the limits of cultural circumstances. These epistemological conversations within scientific discourse have made science more open to academic feminist reflection and have encouraged feminist scientists to discuss the philosophy of science.

WHY IS SCIENTIFIC TRUTH IMPORTANT TO FEMINISTS?

Modern ideologies have used scientific discourse to justify women's subordination. Because scientific authority has such force in American public life, it is important for feminists to explore how these ideologies have used scientific discourse to explain women's political subordination. Sometimes female subordination is explained as an evolutionary survival mechanism that will disappear as societies develop. Others explain women's subordination as an optimum condition for human reproduction and so part of the cost of species survival. Others explain that women have their spheres, which are important, although not politically important. These ideological uses of science have made some young women wary of science careers, have created difficulties for female scientists, have made some feminist scholars suspicious of scientific thought, and have made many citizens forego investigations of gender difference in deference to the "laws" of nature. Three primary features of modern scientific discourse make it vulnerable to misuse by modern ideologies whose goals are female subordination.

First, scientific discourse constructs and polices the application of the term "woman" and its companion category, "man."[7] Because sex categorization is foundational for American citizens, sex is an essentialized, reified individual characteristic—that is, sex is fixed for life. It is, then, no surprise that Olympic Games call upon scientific-medical practitioners when in doubt about a participant's sex. Because sex/gender, like race/ethnicity, can be used as an external mark for categorizing citizens, the sex/gender category has created an elaborate array of codes of behaviors attached to these external "physical" signs. Furthermore, all sorts of values and talents are allocated to individuals under the rubric of "masculine" and "feminine."[8] Citizens employ a complex set of costuming practices and gestures to announce their gender, even to strangers. Everyone seems to need to know the gender of those with whom they interact, even for a moment. Even riding an elevator requires knowledge about the gender of fellow passengers. At birth, the medical doctor not only announces this lifelong identity marker but also may orchestrate the reconstruction of the newborn to remove sex ambiguities.[9] Changing sex requires interaction with scientific authorities. Scientific discourse differentiates females from males and constructs this distinction as a physical lifelong, difficult-to-change, difference. Once you are female you're "it" for life. Scientific discourse is important because it has been used as *the* discourse that determines who and what counts as female.

Second, scientific discourse is used by ideologues to represent sex differences in terms of reproduction. Modern ideologies frame this representation so as to make man the standard human and woman a special kind of human. They explain that women differ from men because they bear children. This distinction is signified by emphasizing certain female characteristics—external genitalia and breasts. Even though external genitalia and breasts serve other functions and even though all women do not bear children, this emphasis on women's role in reproduction has created a mythic structure that defines womanhood in relationship to children. This mythic structure has become so pronounced in modernity that women who cannot conceive often feel that they are not really "women."[10] At the same time, during the nineteenth and early twentieth centuries, the supervision of birth has moved from women's hands through midwifery to medical-scientific hands that control the machinery and economy of reproduction.[11] Linking this medical definition of "woman" with psychological social discourses, modern ideologies embrace the "fact" that reproduction restricts women's ability to participate in public life—paid work and politics. The ideologies explain that women give up full participation in public life in exchange for the privilege of bearing and rearing children. But even those who do have children will spend a small portion of their years in bearing and rearing children. From even a conservative view, assuming that women take on the primary responsibility for rearing children, a woman who can vote at 18 and who has two children by age 24 would have her children in school by the time she was 30. If she lived to 76, she would have 46 years to work in politics. Thus, 83 percent of her adult life could be devoted to politics. Reproduction need not control or restrict women's entire lives. Yet defining "women" in terms of childbearing shapes social responses even to women who do not bear children. Such ideologies restrict females rather than help families.

Because twentieth-century capitalism needed secondary workers, its beneficiaries found this definition of woman helpful. However, current capitalist practices depend on full-time female workers. While neoconservatives might want to change the ratio between middle-class birthrates and working-class birthrates (which has significance for them in terms of impact on the ratio between whites and people of color), this ideological commitment has less power in a new world order in which whites are a minority population, whose self-interest lies in protecting minority rights. Just as citizens came to discard flat-earth theory, which restricted modern explorations, citizens are beginning to discard such impractical and unrealistic theories about women. To respond to these ideologies, feminists need to be able to use modern scientific thought to address these attempts to reduce womanhood to reproduction.

Third, modern ideologies symbolize the truth with gendered imagery from scientific discourse. Masculine imagery is used to depict the objectivity of the so-called "hard" sciences that depend on clarity, while feminine imagery is used to represent notions of subjectivity that offer so-called soft, less predictable, more unreliable, *viewpoints*.[12] Objectivity represents clarity, reason, certainty, and agreement, while subjectivity represents confusion, emotions, uncertainties, and disagreements. Feminine imagery links up with subjective ways of knowing just as masculine imagery links up with objectivity and rationality.[13] Cultural narratives that propagate these binary oppositions have become familiar aspects of common everyday ideologies—women : men :: private : public :: nature : culture :: connected : distant :: hard : soft :: reason : emotion :: head : heart :: objectivity : subjectivity. These gendered images make it appear such oppositions result from natural laws in which each sex possesses its own specialized ways of knowing. Although this sexualized epistemology does not stand up under critical review, ideologically it functions to explain how it is that women are so suited for the private realm where emotions are needed. Not only does such stereotyping limit both women and men, but it also confines expressions of reason to public life and expressions of emotion to private life. It supports the old dream that reason will create orderly productivity in public life and that private life will supply all emotional needs. Thus, such gendered compartmentalizations can create unrealistic expectations for family life, for public life, and for real-life women and men. The dream that the truth can be found in unemotional representations of objectivity has some undesirable side effects.

As scientists have become more open to discussions about scientific cosmologies, feminist scholars outside science have become more receptive to empiricism. The old dichotomies between objectivity and subjectivity, sciences and humanities, and women and men, no longer serve, and so it is a good time for feminist scholars to speak about new epistemologies that link the humanities and sciences to reframe the connection between politics and truth.

HOW DO FEMINIST SCIENTISTS
CONNECT POLITICS AND TRUTH?

While the separation of science from politics has enabled certain kinds of projects to go forward under the heading of "pure" science, it has also held science back. Abandoning this separatist strategy not only requires relinquishing some of the mystique of science—its magical, pristine, godlike qualities (most real scientists are happy to rid themselves of such heroic status)—but also means becoming more involved in the mundane struggles of public values. Scientific separatism has also "protected" scientists from intellectual conversations about the interaction of physical, psychological, and cultural phenomena. While such separatism has focused scientific work and created solidarity among scientists, a wide range of scientists (including Edmund Wilson, Carl Sagan, environmentalists, feminist scientists) has sought broader-based, even public, conversations.

The separation of science from politics is sustained in part by granting objectivity to science and subjectivity to politics. "Distance" works as the official metaphor for objective truth claims. Objective truth—based on distance, neutrality, disassociation, and deductive reason—is the polar opposite of subjective truth—based on connections, relationships, empathy, and inductive reasoning. This positivist objectivism presents the scientist as no more than a careful secretary who records what the world dictates to him or her. The secretary model of science suggests that imagination, desire, and language can be controlled by scientific method and that the bold reality of the physical world will prevail over human concerns. In contrast, radical relativism depicts science as an activity in which the lone scientist can make up any world he or she chooses without regard to any physical limits. Manipulating the arbitrary qualities of language and symbols, the scientist becomes free to make the world whatever he or she wishes it to be. Truth is limited only by imagination and desire. But truth involves the investigation of real physical phenomena within the context of theories dependent on a social imagination. Both radical positivism and social construction miss the mark. The claim that science is merely a social product rejects the way in which the physical world makes demands on humans and shapes observations, and the claim that the natural physical world determines human nature rejects the fact that scientists make choices. Those choices involve political values. Because feminist scholars emphasize connections, feminist scientists are less taken by the separation of nature from society. Sidestepping value-free science and individuated relativism, feminist scientists often find the polarization of nature and culture problematic. Scientists are neither superhuman recorders nor supercreative inventors. Observation requires imagination, and imagination requires the discipline provided by physical phenomena and the methods that bring them into view.

To show how feminists connect truth and politics, I focus this analysis on feminist scholars who work in the area of the philosophy of science.[14] I have selected texts that directly explore the relationship between science and society rather than texts that focus on particular problems within science or on the treatment of female scientists. In chapter 5, I begin this analysis of feminist science by examining three metaphors used in feminist scientific discourse. These metaphors can be used to reformulate the connection between scientific truth and gender politics. Going beyond mere critiques of absolute objectivity and subjectivity, each metaphor shows how citizens can address the crisis produced by the loss of faith in absolute objectivity to establish a new understanding of scientific truth.[15] This new understanding shows how citizens can use the truth to do the political work of building better societies. In chapter 6, I explore how understanding science as storytelling can enable citizens to read science more accurately, and can empower scientists to describe their work more precisely. Good politics depends not only on the talents and moral integrity of scientists but also on the ability of citizens to read science without either idolizing scientists or rejecting them. Speaking about science as storytelling makes better readings possible. In chapter 6, I argue that scientific rigor requires more than merely accurate descriptions of real world events and careful readings of them. It requires reflection on the ethical dimensions of scientific discourse. The scientist is a citizen who has contributions to make to the community and things to learn from it. In this sense, I argue that all scientists are political scientists who can make valuable contributions to public life. In chapter 7, I present a six-step model for developing a reflective approach to science. This approach is designed to make science not only reflective about the connections between science and politics but also reflective about how scientific discourse is gendered. I propose six steps that scientists and citizens can take so that scientific truth can be used in developing social policies that respect both the goals of scientists and the democratic values of broad-based citizen participation.

NOTES

1. For comments on this section on science, I wish to thank Kaye Rasnake, Laurel Richardson, Rita Snyder, Lee Swedberg, and Jennifer Skillicorn, a women's studies major at Denison University.

2. Native Hawaiians are the indigenous people of the islands; this term does not refer to residents of the state of Hawaii.

3. Eloise A. Buker, *Politics through a Looking-Glass: Understanding Political Cultures through a Structuralist Interpretation of Narratives* (New York: Greenwood Press, 1987).

4. Mary Field Belenky, et al., *Women's Ways of Knowing: The Development of Self, Voice, and Mind* (New York: Basic Books, 1986), which uses qualitative empirical methods for analysis.

5. For an overview of this history, see Evelyn Fox Keller, *Reflections on Gender and Science* (New Haven: Yale University Press, 1985), 75–94; and Evelyn Fox Keller, "Feminism and Science," in *Sex and Scientific Inquiry*, eds. Sandra Harding and Jean F. O'Barr (Chicago: The University of Chicago Press, 1987), 233–46.

6. Mary E. Hawkesworth, "Knowers, Knowing, Known: Feminist Theory and Claims of Truth," *Signs* 14 (1989): 533–57.

7. Constructing a complementary female category in relationship to a male category itself in some ways reiterates a heterosexual social structure. For this observation, I thank Jennifer Skillicorn, women's studies major at Denison University.

8. For a discussion of the connection between biological sex differences and politics, see Glendon A. Schubert, *Sexual Politics and Political Feminism* (Greenwich, Conn.: JAI Press, 1991).

9. For explanations about this process, see Anne Fausto-Sterling, *Myths of Gender: Biological Theories about Women and Men* (New York: Basic Books, 1985), 77–85.

10. Fay Faraday, *Can Poststructuralist Theory Help Us Discover a Feminist Method for Creating Laws?: A Case Study on the Debate about New Reproductive Technologies* (Ottawa, Canada: National Association of Women and the Law, 1992), 22–27; and Denison Women's Collective, "Iconography of Motherhood," *Frontiers* (1999) forthcoming.

11. For an analysis of the twentieth-century midwifery among black women, see Valerie Lee, *Granny Midwives and Black Women Writers: Double-Dutched Readings* (New York: Routledge, 1996).

12. For an analysis of the tension between objectivity and subjectivity, see Richard J. Bernstein, *Beyond Objectivism and Relativism: Science, Hermeneutics, and Praxis* (Philadelphia: University of Pennsylvania Press, 1983); and for discussions of male objectivity and female subjectivity in science, see Keller, *Reflections on Gender and Science*, 3–15, 67–126.

13. For analyses of the gendered nature of this dichotomy, see the work of Evelyn Fox Keller, Sandra Harding, Anne Fausto-Sterling, and Donna Haraway.

14. In gender analyses, I include the sex-gender system. Even the biological category of sex is shaped by social meanings, so the sex/gender distinction is problematic.

15. Jürgen Habermas has both analyzed this crisis in *Legitimation Crisis*, trans. Thomas McCarthy (Boston: Beacon Press, 1975), and in *Knowledge and Human Interest*, trans. Jeremy J. Shapiro (Boston: Beacon Press, 1971).

Chapter 5

Feminist Scientific Discourse: Knowing Metaphors and Images

To examine the connections between science and society, Evelyn Fox Keller analyzes contemporary biology by examining how biologists use metaphors. In her opening example, she explains that the 1970s scientific study of the encounter between the human egg and the sperm recalls the Sleeping Beauty myth in that the sperm finds and awakens the egg. While it *made sense* to explain reproduction in this way in a historical period that accepted the image of the active male and the passive female, this sleeping egg tale no longer works. As gender images have changed, contemporary biological discourse has changed as well, and the discourse now characterizes the interaction of the egg and the sperm in egalitarian language. Keller quotes from a molecular biology text that describes "'the process by which egg and sperm find each other and fuse.'"[1] Her point is not that the former description of the egg and sperm is wrong, but instead that social images and scientific explanations work together to create meanings. The metaphor that she evokes for this analysis is "border crossing," and the border she sees herself crossing is that between humanities and science.[2] Even though her work makes it clear how science uses metaphors to describe interactions, what she leaves unsaid is that this border crossing involves politics.

Feminist scientists have developed two strategies to respond to gender bias. The first is to use empiricism to eliminate sexist observations by developing scientific research designs that test dubious observations and correct errors. Without making any change in scientific method and/or epistemological claims, these scientists have eradicated many sexist observational biases. For example, Jeanne Altmann, editor of *Animal Behavior*, asked questions that encouraged sociobiologists who described some animal behavior as "rape" to question those descriptions and to challenge the premise that rape is a "natural" act. Haraway makes it clear that Altmann's questions did not work by replacing men's viewpoints with women's viewpoints but instead worked by destabilizing scientific analysis to open it for critical review.[3] The politics of such destabilization is far reaching because if rape is natural, the failure to eradicate it in humans may be more easily accepted. The scientific problem comes about because of the ways gendered social behavior (male rape of females) can frame biological observations. Feminism also helped scientists reconstruct the role of female orgasm in primate[4] social survival by showing how female primates can be seen as "coy" (and in control) rather than "passive" (controlled) in mate selection.[5] With more research, it became increasingly apparent that human stereotypes of males and females had been projected onto animals. Data were collected and evaluated in a spirit of confirming the stereotypes rather than testing the null hypothesis. However, Jeanne Altmann and Sarah Hrdy maintained that authentic observation was possible and constructed alternative interpretations of animal behavior that demonstrated the power and vitality of female animals.[6] While such observational problems are easier to see in animal research, this gender work serves as the basis for further exploration of how the scientific method itself may be intimately connected to cultural practices.

The second approach in analyzing gender and science is to reframe scientific epistemology to recognize that scientific discourse depends on the interaction between science and society. This approach examines the scientific method itself to explore how the method itself is shaped by social factors. Because I wish to explore this connection between science and cultural practices, I will emphasize feminist scientific discourse that focuses on methodology. Assuming that scientific methods will continue to evolve and change, these feminists embrace a new model of science that emphasizes the standpoint of observations and the context-dependent nature of theories. They argue that observations depend on theories developed within a social linguistic context, which makes them meaningful. This second approach explains that cultural, historical values infiltrate scientific work at every point of inquiry—the formulation of questions, hypothesis development, the designation of independent and dependent variables, the operationalization of variables, and the articulation of findings. What I find especially valuable about this second approach is the ways in which it can be useful in understanding how truth works. Without dispensing with the truth, this approach offers a new understanding of truth that avoids the arrogance of a god's-eye view—or even a man's-eye view—of the world. Abandoning the desire to be supermen or superwomen who know the truth finally once and for all, feminist scientists show that truth is not arbitrary and error exists. These scholars help reconceptualize the multiplicity of the ways by which citizens can gain reliable knowledge about the world in order to act in it.[7]

Because metaphors are especially useful in understanding the conceptual world view that scientists compose, I will examine three metaphors that appear in the work of these feminist scientists. I will show how replacing three old metaphors with new ones enables feminists to offer citizens a new understanding of how truth works: (1) feminist scientists replace the metaphor of the *mirror* (which described scientific knowledge as a duplication of the physical world) with the image of science as *construction*; (2) feminists replace the metaphor of *vision* (a key metaphor for knowledge) with *standpoint*; and (3) feminists replace the metaphor of *grounding* theory with that of working in a *field*. These three metaphorical moves show how feminist scientific discourse offers a new understanding of the connection between truth and public life.

FROM MIRRORS TO CONSTRUCTION SITES

For the first part of the twentieth century, the mirror served as a productive metaphor for explaining how empirical science worked to *reflect*—that is, *copy*—the natural world. However, the more scientists claimed that they produced representations of the real, natural, unmediated world, the more philosophers discovered that values had distorted viewpoints. The mirror image of science depended on a correspondence theory of truth that asserted a one-to-one direct connection between the world "out there" and representations of it. In the context of the critique of positivism, the old value-free claims (that had been part of the formation for this mirror metaphor) are no longer viable. With the publication of Richard Rorty's *Philosophy and the Mirror of Nature*, the basic metaphor was problematized.[8] A correspondence theory of truth that proved itself by accurate predictions failed to capture "Mother" nature.

This correspondence theory of truth had presented science with two problems. First, because the complexities of the natural world could not be matched by the relative simplicity of word and symbol systems, science seemed to be engaged in an impossible quest. How could words or even formulas be made to fully articulate the complexities of even a narrow part of the physical world? For social scientists, the quest seemed to be more than merely an impossibility. Those who create models of the world, whether linguistic or mathematical representations, must by necessity pick and choose areas for emphasis and leave the remainder uncopied, unreflected, and invisible. Inevitably, cultural circumstances shape such selections. So U.S. mirrors, like all mirrors, have distinctive slants on the world and fail to offer genuinely neutral god's-eye reflections of the world. The second problem created by a correspondence theory of truth is that it does not take account of the way culture and cultural symbols shape scientific discourse. Historically, no matter how intently scientists attempted to develop a pristine language free of cultural bias, cultural norms found their way into scientific narratives. For all its ambitions to rescue science from its cultural and historical context, scientific methodology proved inadequate to the task. The correspondence theory of truth could no longer stand as cherished dogma.

Feminist scientists had a special point to make in this critique of science as a mirror because of the ways this mirror distorted males and females. The issue arose most dramatically in the context of animal research. Feminist scientists argued that it was not that science mirrors the natural world, but rather that the natural world had been constructed to mirror the social world. Scientists equipped with modern everyday language (especially English) and the everyday habits of culture (especially American and British cultures) observed animals whose behavior seemed surprisingly similar to that of humans in these cultures. For example, male animals dominated female animals. The reason for this similarity was that these scientists unwittingly *constructed* their observations of animals on the basis of their own social and often ideological experiences. Such biased observation even appears in observing cells.[9] Feminist scientific questions illuminated unspoken assumptions and gave support to the hypothesis that scientists had projected their own social images onto their research observations. Having formulated such hypotheses, feminist scientists began to substantiate them. Looking for human female stereotypes in animal research opened up a wealth of new hypotheses designed to rid science of patriarchal components. Feminist scientists used empirical research methods to expose gender bias in earlier research projects. Without abandoning empirical science, they showed the connections between science and social experiences.

But even before Rorty's book, feminists had been critical of the epistemological implications of the mirror metaphor. Donna Haraway notes that Linda Fedigan had wanted to use the word "mirror" in the title of her book, but it was later published under the title *Primate Paradigms: Sex Roles and Social Bonds*. Haraway points out that "paradigm" has a more scientific sound, but "mirrors" contains a more fundamental critique:

> "mirrors" would have emphasized the process of historically located human researchers actively polishing reflective surfaces that returned the images of their own societies and bodies in their pictures of the animal other.[10]

Put more crudely, scientists expected the male primates that they observed to be aggressive and to dominate females, and then those scientists used these observations as data to support claims that male primates, including male humans, are naturally dominant. The political implication of their research was that human females should be satisfied with secondary citizenship status; men should run things as nature dictates. Haraway talks about turning this mirror around to enable scientists to become reflective about their own activity; she asks scientists to become philosophically reflective about their work.

More commonly, feminist scientists replace the mirror image with one of science as a construction project in which the scientist builds theories. Rejecting the image of passive descriptions, feminists rely on the construction metaphor to depict the scientist as one who is making something. This construction metaphor suggests that research reports are created objects and thus, in part, reflect their *makers'* images of the world. The mirror image is replaced with the image of the scientist as a construction worker who is making a "model" of the world. The social "construction of knowledge" becomes a key way of talking about scientific theory.[11] The construction metaphor creates a different relationship between the world and scientists and suggests that truth is not found by reproducing the "real" world in scientific language but instead is found by using scientific language to interpret the world for human purposes. This construction metaphor emphasizes a modern, human-centered approach to truth. Once this approach is accepted, it is easier for feminist scientists to explore how patriarchal biases have found their way into the human production of knowledge and to eliminate some biases. While this approach may enable scientists to become more responsible for their own actions, it does not offer a neutral value-free analysis. Because the world is not described as it "really" is but as it is from a human perspective, such descriptions continue to evolve and change as humans change.[12]

FROM OBSERVER TO CITIZEN

This epistemological shift from understanding science as a mirror to understanding it as a construction site, has three important public policy implications. First, abandoning the godlike, separatist viewpoint, implicit in the mirror image, makes it more possible for citizens and scientists to work together to solve problems. Scientists are no longer positioning themselves as above and beyond real world concerns and real world struggles. Second, it opens the way for citizens to integrate a variety of ways of knowing in developing reliable information about the world. Science is one of many fields that can inform public life. Other academic fields that represent different ways of knowing, such as art, history, sociology, and literature, can be integrated with science in developing public policy analyses. Thus, citizens who need the truth in order to make decisions will need to gather knowledge from various paradigms or disciplines to get a fuller understanding of a situation.

For example, in the case of abortion, science cannot tell citizens when life begins because the answer to that question depends not only on scientific evidence but also on what is meant by "life" within a particular cultural and historical setting. Because our cultural context lacks agreement on this issue, science cannot merely describe when life begins without taking up one or another political viewpoint on abortion. If science says that life begins at conception, the pro-lifers win; if science says that life begins at the point of fetal viability (independence from the mother's support system), the pro-choicers win. Abortion policies develop not only by taking account of scientific knowledge about fetal development but also by considering other types of knowledge, including social values—individuality and self-determination, the sacredness of human existence, health, economic survival, psychological pressures, law and order, and social control. Science alone cannot tell citizens what to do about abortion. Citizens, thus, need to call upon analyses informed by a range of academic disciplines and ways of knowing in order to use the truth as a basis for forming abortion policies.

The third policy implication of the construction site metaphor involves a revision of scientific authority that better supports democratic conversations about public life. In the premodern era, political authority lay in the divine right of kings, and in modernity natural law and science assert public authority. In the modern era, science has promised to protect and prolong human life, and nature has become a new savior, who offers rules for a harmonious, safe life for all humans. By late modernity, the critique of absolute and scientific objectivity opened up the way for a more diversified model of experts who organize knowledge in consultation with each other. The critique of objectivity fits well with the slow democratization of American society. This new authority is more democratic because it endows a community of scholars and citizens with the responsibility for the social order.[13] It rejects scientific engineering as a hegemonic activity without rejecting scientific expertise as an important part of policy development. In this context, bell hooks's and Cornell West's call for public intellectuals becomes especially appropriate.[14]

This shift away from the scientific elite to a community of scholars anticipates a multiplicity of disciplines and persons becoming involved in gaining the truth about life situations.[15] Judith Cook and Mary Margaret Fonow show how these issues promote connections between democratic values and scientific knowledge. They argue that consciousness raising is a necessary aspect of scientific knowledge.[16] While the term "consciousness raising" evokes a hierarchy of value judgments leading to a perfect apex (the raised consciousness), it can also be used to understand Sandra Harding's notion of a strong objectivity.[17] I prefer to call this process *critical objectivity* to emphasize the need for interrogations of a variety of positions. Feminists use the terms consciousness raising, strong objectivity, and critical objectivity without claiming a know-nothing relativism, which would negate all knowledge claims. Scientists do not have to choose between absolute objectivity and know-nothing relativism. I do not employ the term "critical objectivity" to claim absolute knowledge, but instead use it to make a distinction between truth and falsehood, the good and the ill, and correctness and error. In this case, falsehood and truth are distinctions made in the context of the limits of a society. Critical objectivity requires access to a multiplicity of disciplines, viewpoints, and values to correct cultural biases in analyses. These biases can occur in the choice of areas for inquiry, the formation of research questions, selecting variables, the development of key concepts and their operationalization, observations, the reporting of observations, etc. The claim here is not that critique corrects science once and for all, but that it offers a critical edge that is itself limited by a particular cultural/historical context.

THE POLITICS IN "EYEING" DATA AND "TAKING" A STAND

The mirror metaphor is supported by a more fundamental metaphor that explains knowledge in terms of vision. The common expression "I see," meaning "I know," exemplifies the popular use of this vision metaphor, and Colin Murray Turbayne in *The Myth of Metaphor* shows how the vision metaphor has shaped scientific inquiry.[18] The vision metaphor depicts scientists as beings with a god's eye, Mt. Olympus view of the physical world. While this vision or "viewpoint" metaphor is certainly not missing from feminist science, its meaning has changed. Vision permits the observer to maintain distance and puts space between the observer and the object of observation. But some feminists replace this image of the distant, uninvolved, systematic observer with the image of a systematic participant-observer, who, unable to obtain the Archimedean point from which to see all, understands that they see only *because* they have obtained a point from which to view *some* aspects of the world. Everything cannot be seen all at once.

Taking this vision metaphor one step further, Judith A. Cook and Mary Margaret Fonow argue that feminist academics, among others, need to acquire "double vision" in order to see themselves as both privileged and oppressed and thereby to take account of the multiple power relationships each woman inhabits.[19] This image suggests two political moves. First, it encourages coalition building by undercutting the search for the most oppressed group to serve as privileged seers. Reducing the tensions among women—academic women and working-class women, white and black women, Native American and African-American women, straight and lesbian women, and others—enables women to put their full energy behind fighting patriarchy. Second, the concept of "double vision" avoids the problem of the "professional" victim who, wallowing in her or his own oppression, dares not acknowledge her or his own power. While the professional victim may experience satisfaction in self-righteousness, she or he is caught in a trap that requires choosing between self-righteous purity and effective action. Double vision can assist feminists in "seeing" both their powerlessness and their power. The mirror metaphor positioned the scientist as one who held the mirror up so that others could see the world. Double vision suggests that the scientist's own face as well as other aspects of the world appear in the mirror.

While "double vision" pluralizes the concept of viewpoint, it retains the concept of distance as a part of the knowledge enterprise. World views can be made from a great distance, even from outer space. While Fonow does not call on postmodern discourse to make her arguments, Haraway focuses on how such viewpoints are restricted and partial. She explains:

The moral is simple: only partial perspective promises objective vision. . . . Feminist objectivity is about limited location and situated knowledge, not about transcendence and splitting of subject and object. It allows us to become answerable for what we learn how to see.[20]

Many feminist scientists argue that knowledge requires connections with the object of study rather than distance from it, so it makes sense to move from vision metaphors to the "feminist standpoint" metaphor. This metaphor, developed by Nancy Hartsock, makes three important political points about observations.[21] First, the word "standpoint" emphasizes that each observer is a participant who sees the world from a partial, partisan, gendered "position." Second, the "standpoint" metaphor suggests that scientists take a stand in their work, and so should see their work as taking a political stand that can improve public life. Third, the "standpoint" metaphor emphasizes the concrete and particular character of observations, rather than their abstract universal lawlike characteristics. This focus on concrete detail invites scientists to consider how experience shapes their projects and encourages them to become reflective about the values that frame those projects.

Harding shows how feminist standpoints link experience to scientific truth by explaining how observations are partial and value laden. She argues that scientific rigor requires analysts to take account of social locations and histories.[22] In the concluding two chapters of *Whose Science? Whose Knowledge?* Harding works out the connection between experience and knowledge by arguing that personal experiences are important but that standpoints can be taken by those who lack personal experiences—that is, men can take women's standpoints; heterosexual women can think from the position of lesbian women.[23] For Harding, standpoint does not represent an essentialist position because anyone can take up any standpoint. While life experiences make some standpoints easier than others, standpoint is not determined by fixed identities. Experiences can be gleaned through study. It may be easier for those who are not privileged to understand dominant standpoints than it is for those in positions of power to understand marginalized viewpoints. For example, blacks can take white standpoints and may need to do so as a part of negotiating everyday life. But through diligent study, those in positions of privilege can work to understand underprivileged standpoints: that is, whites can take a black standpoint; men can take a woman's standpoint; and straights can take gay-lesbian standpoints. Standpoint is not formed by bodily marks, but by life experiences, including study.

However, I do not mean to imply that persons who have lived as whites can speak *for* blacks or that persons who have lived as men can speak *for* women. I do mean that persons who have lived as whites can speak *about* blacks and that persons who have lived as men can speak *about* women, just as persons who have lived as women can speak about men.[24] But simply acquiring information about a social position may not be enough to assume a standpoint because standpoint also implies that the analyst would in some way share the fate of the group whose position is assumed. Can men share women's political fate? Does this sort of stake in public life change the type of analyses that men perform? These questions remain tangled in the debate between objectivity and subjectivity.

Harding does not go on to explain in detail how to resolve these issues, even though she is aware of a certain amount of feminist resistance to her view of standpoint and its relationships to lived experience.[25] Her position permits those in power to analyze the experiences of those out of power. While her position creates some problems for advocates, the alternative—restricting analyses of blacks to blacks and of women to women—reinscribes essentialist notions of these identities. Such essentialist notions would make knowledge dependent on such physical features as sex/race characterizations rather than actual cultural experiences. Recognizing both the limit and power of life experiences as a part of scientific inquiry can enable the recognition of such identities without reifying them.

Sara Ruddick, who develops the epistemological standpoint of motherhood, explains that men, too, can take such a position.[26] Patricia Hill Collins is somewhat less clear about whether Euro-Americans can develop African-American analyses. She emphasizes social experience as a fundamental aspect of social analysis that calls into question the ability of Euro-Americans to acquire Afro-American experiences. However, she avoids addressing the case of those whose lives may be lived in part as Euro-Americans and in part as Afro-Americans or whose identities may be framed by both cultures. Since fewer persons have lived as both women and men, this is less of an issue in reflecting on a "woman's standpoint."[27] The term "feminist standpoint" constructs the analyst's as a self-conscious choice.

For Harding, standpoint is a "starting point" for analysis and not a conclusion. She points out that standpoint theories support a democratic politics that thrives on pluralities and differences.[28] Standpoint theory encourages involving a wide variety of people in public conversations. The point is not to reduce analyses to the identity of the analyst but to empower the analyst to include aspects of the self in the analysis—to put "I" into the discourse of science. Identities do not determine an epistemological standpoint. The point is for the analyst to become reflective about social experiences that shape assumptions and observations. This point underscores a second political one. The politics of "standpoint" suggests that all analysts take a stand in order to make an observation because all observations are based on theoretical and cultural assumptions. These assumptions have social consequences. Recognizing that all observation involves a standpoint—that is, taking a stand—can help scientists to become reflective about the social and political implications of the research process. The "feminist standpoint" has served feminist political scientists so well that a special edition of *Women & Politics* has been devoted to reflections on it.[29]

MOVING FROM "GROUNDED" THEORY TO FIELDS

A third metaphor that connects science and society is "grounding." This image fits well with the political implications of the "standpoint" image, in that "One takes a stand and stands one's ground." Land, territory, turf, and ground often symbolize politics because geography both literally and metaphorically marks state boundaries. Nations that grant citizenship on the basis of place of birth exemplify the centrality of geographic imagery. Feminists use "grounding" to emphasize that theories need to develop out of concrete situations. They work from the "ground" up, from particular to general. Grounded theories take account of "real" life situations and offer abstractions informed by those situations. For example, the stories of racism told by Ida B. Wells give citizens particular images of racism and, hence, "ground" those images with details.[30] Theories about how citizens can fight national racist policies have been developed out of Wells's reports. Fiction can also serve to ground theory. Rape is abstract, but Alice Walker's tale of Celie articulates an example of rape in such a way that the reader can understand the dynamics of rape, can empathize with victims, and can imagine ways of altering such situations.[31] Details that are set into a narrative enable readers to understand them in personal terms and thereby inspire action.

Second-wave feminists argued for the importance of the concrete over the abstract and encouraged theory to find its "grounding" in social experience and in arguing for praxis—the connection between theory and social action. For example, Nancy Cott evokes the "grounding" metaphor in *The Grounding of Modern Feminism*.[32] Emphasizing the concrete aspects of existence highlights women's experiences and the material conditions of their lives. The "grounding" image stabilizes explanations by linking them to the material conditions of social life, and this link to materialism fits well with both scientific empiricism and marxism. Connecting beliefs (abstractly held models, values, principles) and social experiences (events in one's day-to-day life), Harding uses this metaphor to draw from Hilary Rose's work to explain that "a feminist epistemology must be grounded in the practices of the women's movement."[33] Harding's argument is that the foundation for science is not a method that attempts to transcend society, but rather social experiences that can make science reflective about its own values.

Harding demonstrates the way social life shapes science. Before World War II, science operated like a handicraft, based on simple divisions of labor and low capital investment. A single scientist in a lonely laboratory worked by himself to produce insights. In the latter part of the twentieth century science operated like a factory,[34] depending on large-scale capital investment and complex divisions of labor.[35] The factory image not only explains the scientific production of knowledge but also has influenced scientist's views of the world, which in turn have influenced citizens. For example, a mechanistic image of nature is transferred onto women in the analysis of women's bodies, which become factories for production—the production of babies. Harding uses Emily Martin's analysis to document the way in which menopause has been constructed by medical texts as "failed production" rather than as a natural life process.[36] According to Harding, the factorylike production of science has produced factorylike observations. Furthermore, Martin shows that these factory images have shaped the ways that middle-class mothers tell their daughters about menses.[37] Large-scale factory production has shaped how science works and how scientists explained the workings of the female human body. But the postmodern era finds these explanations no longer meaningful.

Harding praises Hilary Rose, who advocates blending subjectivity with objectivity. This blend is symbolized by representing science as work that requires connecting the "brain, hand and heart."[38] Connecting brains, hands, and hearts means that science is no longer depicted as separate from human existence but is considered as part of that existence. Flexing her biceps, Harding signals to her audience that "strong" objectivity avoids weakness.[39] For her, the critique of positivism and the introduction of a less grandiose version of objectivity do not diminish the authority of scientific truth, but strengthen it. Acknowledging the connection between social life and science makes science more rigorous.[40]

In order to make science more creative and reflective, Harding suggests that science might be better thought of as an art—like sculpturing[41]—than like factory work. The artists know themselves to be making something and are proud of their roles in the process. Unlike scientists, they do not try to keep themselves out of the creative process. But it is important to note that all of these images—grounding, sculpture, factory product—have a material basis. Harding does not suggest that science can be arbitrarily shaped in any direction. Material circumstances limit scientific inquiry; cultural understandings limit science; methodologies place limits on science. Such limits make science meaningful. Moving from a modern emphasis on materialism to postmodern emphases on linguistic moves, Haraway introduces a different metaphor that highlights all three of these limits.

RECORDED EXPERIMENTS AND FIELD RESEARCH

Replacing the metaphor of "grounding" with the metaphor of "foregrounding," Haraway shifts attention from the object observed to the observer. The grounding metaphor suggests that the researcher has grasped a foundational reality, while the foregrounding metaphor suggests that the researcher has decided to pay attention to a particular aspect of reality. Things do not automatically foreground themselves, nor do they come with labels that require them to be foregrounded. Therefore, scientists make decisions in the course of their research. Of course, these decisions have consequences for the project and its political import. For example, in describing the work of Fedigan, Haraway explains that Fedigan's early strategy was "foregrounding female animals,"[42] while her later strategy "foregrounded the yawning gaps between theorizing and empirical demonstration."[43] Foregrounding a phenomenon gives it power, importance, and prestige. The "foregrounding" metaphor enables Haraway to show scientists how to talk about self-conscious moves that acknowledge their judgments and the political work that those judgments perform.

Haraway's "foregrounding" metaphor describes scientific work, but for her own research, she uses the term "field," which works not because of its connections to the "ground" but because of its double meaning. This double meaning reminds her reader that research is done in the "field."[44] Primatology field research is especially important because of its central role in gathering data, and because of the special challenges it brings to researchers, who may track animals across difficult terrains. But Haraway also uses the "field" metaphor to explain how researchers are all already in a "field" (a cultural and physical environment as well as an academic discipline), even when they are not self-consciously involved in field research. Such cultural environments shape the research project. All researchers are already in a field.

Haraway's understanding of standpoint differs from social constructionists, who suggest building theory from the "ground" up, "constructing" it. Their emphasis on social human activity creates a clear distinction between human needs and natural forces, while Haraway's field metaphor involves the intersection between nature and culture. The field metaphor evokes phenomenology to suggest that theory comes from imaginative play. Laurel Richardson uses such imaginative play in her sociological autobiography, *Fields of Play: Constructing an Academic Life.*[45] "Field" and "foregrounding" bring the researchers into view as actors who are making decisions, as does the constructionist image. But in the field imagery, the scientist is more like a bricoleur than a builder.[46] The bricoleur makes use of what someone else provides. In this case the other might be nature, history, and/or a cosmological spirit. This bricoleur image makes room for mystery as part of the epistemological project. Science is not so much quasi-experimental research designs, which fail to control for some factors, as it is a way of receiving information in the midst of complex commitments and messy circumstances. All laboratories, even those housed in university laboratories, are in some "field," with all the messy conditions that a field evokes—metaphorical dirt, weeds, insects, and rain. This mess both annoys scientists and enriches them. While many scientists are aware of this dirt and mess, those who use scientific information may not be. As many scientists already realize, taking note of the messy conditions that produce research as well as the research results does not defile science, but makes it more honest and so more effective.

FROM TELLING STORIES TO READING THE WORLD

Making a similar point about interpretation, Haraway introduces the metaphor of scientific work as "reading the world." She explains that she *reads* primatology as *science fiction* and so challenges the boundary between fact and fiction. Making a similar philosophical point, Paul Ricoeur argues that science is fiction. By this, he does not mean that science is untrue or the product of mere fantasy. He reminds his readers that the word "fiction" comes from *facere*, which means to make or remake.[47] Clifford Geertz makes a similar point in arguing that anthropological work should be signed just as paintings are signed.[48] All three, Haraway, Ricoeur, and Geertz, show that scientific analyses can be understood as the product of human imagination. By this, they are suggesting that fiction, even literary fiction, articulates true-life circumstances. To call science "fiction" is not to suggest that it is "untrue" but, instead, to suggest that truth depends on imagination.[49] Human imagination is finite because it takes place in the context of life in the world and so like material circumstances it, too, is limited.

Haraway invites her readers to read her text as stories that they rewrite "in the act of reading them."[50] This recommendation shifts the emphasis from scientists as builders of theory and knowledge, to scientists as interpreters of the world. The key relationship changes from that between the scientist and the research project to that between the scientist and her or his audience who receives the interpretation. But Haraway's readers are also in a field—a cultural historical environment—where they both receive and observe her text. This connection between the scientist and her/his reader depends on a semiotic theory of language that explains how meaning depends as much on the reader as the writer[51]—that is, the truth and accuracy of science requires not only thoughtful, careful scientists, but also thoughtful, careful readers.

While both Harding and Haraway talk about science as a narrative, Harding characterizes science as a true story, while Haraway emphasizes the fictional aspects of scientific narratives—science fiction. Haraway emphasizes the multiplicity of interpretations that science makes possible. What Harding and Haraway have in common with many other feminists is their emphasis on the way in which scientific knowledge depends on communication between scientists and other citizens. Science is not so much a discovery project conducted on the "frontiers" of knowledge, as it is a conversation that takes place within a culture.

NOTES

1. Evelyn Fox Keller, *Refiguring Life: Metaphors of Twentieth-Century Biology* (New York: Columbia University Press, 1995), xii, and the quotation is from Bruce Alberts, et al., *Molecular Biology of the Cell*, 2d. ed. (New York: Garland, 1989), 868.

2. Keller, *Refiguring Life*, xviii–xix.

3. Donna Haraway, *Primate Visions: Gender, Race, and Nature in the World of Modern Science* (New York: Routledge, 1989), 310–11.

4. For the active role of primate female orgasms in evolutionary theory, see Sarah Blaffer Hrdy, "Empathy, Polyandry, and the Myth of the Coy Female," in *Feminist Approaches to Science*, ed. Ruth Bleier (New York: Pergamon Press, 1986), 119–46; and for the politics of primate female orgasms, see Haraway, *Primate Visions*, 355–67.

5. Hrdy, "Empathy, Polyandry, and the Myth of the Coy Female," 119–46.

6. Haraway, *Primate Visions*, 355–67.

7. For example, Mary Field Belenky, Blythe McVicker Clinchy, Nancy Rule Gold-berger, Jill Mattuck Tarule, *Women's Ways of Knowing: The Development of Self, Voice, and Mind* (New York: Basic Books, 1986) is a collaborative study that blends empirical-objective methods with phenomenological subjective analyses that take account of how women explain their own process of learning.

8. Richard Rorty, *Philosophy and the Mirror of Nature* (Princeton, N.J.: Princeton University Press, 1979), and Richard Rorty, *Objectivity, Relativism, and Truth* (New York: Cambridge University Press, 1991).

9. For an analysis of the gendered image of cells, see Bonnie B. Spanier, "Gender and Ideology in Science: A Study of Molecular Biology," *National Women's Studies Association Journal* 3 (spring 1991): 167–98.

10. Haraway, *Primate Visions*, 318.

11. The metaphor of "construction" creates an epistemology that contrasts with a natural law epistemology that relies on the metaphor of "discovery."

12. Those who take this position argue that scientific knowledge is dependent on human social circumstances and the language that supports communication among persons within such circumstances. As social meanings change, human viewpoints are articulated in new and different ways that change scientific description.

13. For a discussion of feminist empirical methods that supports collaborative research, see Shulamit Reinharz with Lynn Davidman, *Feminist Methods in Social Research* (New York: Oxford University Press, 1992); and for a discussion of the importance of critical dialogue in the construction of the community of scholars, see Helen E. Longino, "Subjects, Power, and Knowledge: Description and Prescription in Feminist Philosophies of Science," in *Feminism & Science*, eds. Evelyn Fox Keller and Helen E. Longino (New York: Oxford University Press, 1996), 270–78.

14. bell hooks and Cornell West, *Breaking Bread: Insurgent Black Intellectual Life* (Boston: South End Press, 1991).

15. For an argument on the role of pluralism in science, see Helen E. Longino, "Subjects, Power, and Knowledge," 274–77.

16. Judith A. Cook and Mary Margaret Fonow, "Knowledge and Women's Interests: Issues of Epistemology and Methodology in Feminist Sociological Research," *Sociological Inquiry* 56 (winter 1986): 2–29.

17. Sandra Harding, *Whose Science? Whose Knowledge?: Thinking from Women's Lives* (Ithaca, N.Y.: Cornell University Press, 1991).

18. Colin Murray Turbayne, *The Myth of Metaphor* (New Haven, Conn.: Yale University Press, 1962).

19. Cook and Fonow, "Knowledge and Women's Interests."

20. Donna Haraway, "Situated Knowledges: The Science Question in Feminism and the Privilege of Partial Perspective," in *Feminism & Science*, eds. Keller and Longino, 254.

21. Nancy C. M. Hartsock, "The Feminist Standpoint: Developing the Ground for a Specifically Feminist Historical Materialism," in *Feminism and Methodology: Social Science Issues*, ed. Sandra Harding (Bloomington: Indiana University Press, 1987), 157–80.

22. Harding, *Whose Science?*,105–137, 268–272.

23. Harding, *Whose Science?*, 268–312.

24. In a presentation at the University of Utah, academic year 1992–93, Henry Louis Gates argued that whites can and should teach in black studies programs.

25. Harding, *Whose Science?*, 277–95.

26. Sara Ruddick, *Maternal Thinking: Toward a Politics of Peace* (Boston: Beacon Press, 1989).

27. Patricia Hill Collins, *Black Feminist Thought: Knowledge, Consciousness, and the Politics of Empowerment* (New York: Routledge, 1991).

28. Harding, *Whose Science?*, 271–77.

29. "Politics and Feminist Standpoint Theories," special issue, ed. Sally J. Kenney, Helen Kinsella, *Women & Politics* 18, no. 3 (1997).

30. Ida B. Wells, *Crusade for Justice: The Autobiography of Ida B. Wells*, ed. Alfreda M Duster (Chicago: University of Chicago Press, 1970).

31. Alice Walker, *The Color Purple* (New York: Washington Square Press, 1982).

32. Nancy F. Cott, *The Grounding of Modern Feminism* (New Haven, Conn.: Yale University Press, 1987).

33. Sandra Harding, *The Science Question in Feminism* (Ithaca, N.Y.: Cornell University Press, 1986), 143, drawing from Hilary Rose, "Hand, Brain and Heart: A Feminist Epistemology for the Natural Sciences," *Signs* 9 (1983); and Hilary Rose, "Is a Feminist Science Possible," paper presented to MIT Women's Studies Program, April 1984.

34. Harding, *The Science Question in Feminism*, 68–69.

35. Harding, *The Science Question in Feminism*, 58–81.

36. Harding, *Whose Science?*, 45–46.

37. Emily Martin, *The Woman in the Body: A Cultural Analysis of Reproduction* (Boston: Beacon Press, 1987).

38. Harding, *The Science Question in Feminism*, 142, citing Hilary Rose, "Hand, Brain and Heart: A Feminist Epistemology for the Natural Sciences," *Signs* 9 (1983).

39. Sandra Harding, presentation at the University of Utah, 1992.

40. Others who are not feminists value acknowledging the connections between social life and science. For example, see Bruno Latour, *We Have Never Been Modern*, trans. Catherine Porter (Cambridge, Mass.: Harvard University Press, 1993), especially 135.

41. Harding, *Whose Science?*, 71.

42. Haraway, *Primate Visions*, 319.

43. Haraway, *Primate Visions*, 320–21.

44. Haraway is well aware of the playful ways in which she uses this word to show a nexus of meanings. See her work "Primatology Is Politics by Other Means," in Bleier, ed., *Feminist Approaches to Science*, 81.

45. Laurel Richardson, *Fields of Play: Constructing an Academic Life* (New Brunswick, N.J.: Rutgers University Press, 1997).

46. Claude Lévi-Strauss, *The Savage Mind* (Chicago: University of Chicago Press, 1966).

47. Paul Ricoeur, "The Function of Fiction in Shaping Reality," *Man and World* 12 (1979): 135.

48. Clifford Geertz, presentation at University of California at Santa Cruz as part of an NEH seminar, summer 1988.

49. For an argument to support this point, see Paul Ricoeur, *The Rule of Metaphor: Multi-Disciplinary Studies of the Creation of Meaning in Language*, trans. Robert Cyerny with Kathleen McLaughlin and John Costello (Toronto: University of Toronto Press, 1977), and the work of Harold Bloom, Northrop Frye, and C. Wright Mills.

50. Haraway, *Primate Visions*, 15.

51. For a discussion of a semiotic theory of language, see Eloise A. Buker, "Sex, Sign, and Symbol: Politics and Feminist Semiotics," in *Women & Politics* 16 (1996): 31–54.

Chapter 6

Rhetorical Moves:
Science As Storytelling

I have argued that feminist scientists show that scientific discourse does not simply offer facts, but organizes and composes phenomena into facts by means of statements. For a phenomenon to appear as a fact depends on some linguistic representation, some rhetoric. Meaningful statements happen when rhetoric works. Talking about scientific discourse as constructed information emphasizes that scientific work involves rhetoric—that is, putting information into meaningful formats. But even this statement deceives, for information is not had and then put into a format, but emerges within the context of its format. How facts are presented is part of the facts of a case; saying it is part of "it." Thus, understanding how scientific rhetoric constructs sex/gender imagery is part of scientific work. The point is not to expose scientific work as biased but to show how this rhetorical approach offers a new way of understanding scientific epistemology. My audience for this new approach includes scientists and consumers of scientific information. I have suggested that today, American citizens can understand science better by thinking about it as a collection of stories, rather than a set of propositions that describe the world. In this chapter I will show how this approach can liberate scientific discourse from the old model of objectivism that cut science off from public life.

Telling stories is important for discussing women's experiences because it enables speakers to introduce new and different ideas into a broad-based conversation. It is for this same reason important to science. Building on the metaphor of science as a story, I begin this chapter by talking about the ways in which feminist scientists have written folktales to critique scientific epistemologies. Turning to a discussion of the political implications of the story metaphor, I proceed by discussing how this metaphor can reconstruct scientific authority by desanctifying science and freeing it to embrace empirical rather than positivistic knowledge claims. This reconstruction aims to enable citizens to read science with greater respect, care, and clarity. I conclude this chapter by discussing how citizens can use the story metaphor to reconceptualize science in order to integrate scientific truth more fully into social life— that is, public life, politics.

Second-wave feminists called for women to tell their stories. Feminist scientists have used this process as a metaphor to explain how science works as a cosmology rather than simply as a collection of facts. Harding credits Ruth Hubbard with this insight: "Hubbard stresses science as a social construction, a historical enterprise that tells stories about us and the world around us."[1] Both Donna Haraway and Sandra Harding claim that scientific inquiry is more like *telling* a story than *discovering* an object. This position fits with the philosophy of second-wave feminist scholars, who encouraged women to find their voices. Carol Gilligan, while not offering a new epistemology, signals a clear paradigm shift in her book, *In a Different Voice*;[2] Marcia Millman and Rosebeth Moss Kanter in *Another Voice: Feminist Perspectives on Social Life and Social Science* employ a similar metaphor.[3] The voice metaphor fits with storytelling. But if feminists and/or women speak in a different voice, they do not correct science by drowning out the old masculine voices. Instead, women introduce a new song that requires a new way of listening. The two metaphors, voice and story, work together to suggest that women's voices need to be heard and that their voices will change science.

HOW CAN FOLKTALES DO SCIENTIFIC WORK?

The story metaphor began its work for feminists as early as the 1940s with Ruth Herschberger's *Adam's Rib* (1948). Ruth Bleier uses Herschberger's folktale to critique science in her work in the 1980s. By assuming the voice of the female chimpanzee, "Josie," Herschberger shows that Josie sees her situation quite differently from her distinguished researcher (biographer), Robert Yerkes. Josie argues that Jack, her male companion, gets a favored reading from the human male observer:

> When Jack takes over the food chute, the report calls it his "natural dominance." When I do, it's "privilege"—conferred by him. . . . While I'm up there lording it over the food chute, the investigator writes down "the male temporarily defers to her and allows her to act as if dominant over him."[4]

This rhetorical device not only shows patriarchal biases, but also points out an epistemological difficulty that confronts scientists studying subjects who cannot speak. Unlike social scientists, these scientists lack the corrective resource of verifying findings with their "subjects." Social scientists whose subjects can respond have some clear epistemological advantages that may have made it easier for them to avoid the error of claiming exhaustive descriptions. Herschberger's folklore enables her to "supply" the subject's response to show that one interpretation may not exhaust all plausible explanations.

Following this folklore tradition, Ruth Ginzberg shows what might happen if food preparation and eating were treated as an activity requiring the same level of scientific scrutiny presently devoted to childbirth. Her mock argument for the defense of food regulation goes as follows:

> Science had already well documented the large numbers of bacterial organisms found in virtually every home kitchen, and its increasing knowledge of the role of bacteria in disease made it obvious that untrained cooks, usually women, in bacteria-laden kitchens could no longer be trusted with the important responsibility of feeding the general population.[5]

Discussions about the medicalization of childbirth are important to feminists,[6] and Ginzberg's analysis extends that critique to reveal the authoritative power of scientific discourse. Her tale questions what sort of activity citizens should put in the hands of technical scientific experts and what sort of activity should be protected from such interventions.

Showing how the folktale adds a moral, ethical component to scientific discussions, Ruth Bleier creates a fable about a society in which females do all the weaving. In the context of this tale, she asks if citizens would assume that males, because of their physical inheritance, were inferior weavers.[7] This tale counters various tales that grant superior status to men, including the modern testosterone story, which argues that men are stronger and more aggressive because of higher levels of testosterone. Because such talk distracts speakers from paying attention to what might count as stronger or more aggressive, this story can unwittingly preempt investigations of women's status by simply assuming the biological inferiority of women. Thus, such assertions block efforts to investigate social and biological phenomena that reveal women's equality with men. In contrast, scientific tales dealing with "disease" draw on a complex combination of biological-medical approaches to address human problems. In the case of women, women's so-called "inferior" condition is regarded as untreatable— even natural, even good.

But "women" are neither a disease nor a problem. The problem exists in the way science treats sex as an unproblematic, independent variable. If sex is taken as a permanently fixed characteristic that shapes other phenomena, it becomes an uninvestigated assumption in scientific research. This makes it more possible to use sex to assert female shortcomings. Making sex a dependent variable encourages the exploration of the phenomena that shape sex distinctions. Problematizing the way science constitutes sex can open up new ways of thinking about females and males, and valuing women can reframe scientific assumptions. If science can investigate sex as a dependent variable shaped by other phenomena, sex is not so easily isolated from the social phenomena that define it. Bleier's folktale about weaving raises questions about how sex differences become rigidly attached to social practices.[8]

These folktales use humor to examine how scientific rhetoric articulates gendered social assumptions. While avoiding the usual methodological critiques that derail conversations by focusing on methodological quibbles about degrees of certainty, these feminist scientists show how folktales can expose gender biases and refocus attention on scientific truth. Since scientific certainty is difficult to obtain, the methodological merry-go-round is nearly always available to someone who wants merely to challenge evidence rather than to consider its merits. This playful folktale approach makes room for innovative rather than defensive responses to such challenges and offers feminists a strategy for opening up closed questions.

In addition, science fiction can raise important scientific issues. It provides science with a genre that avoids the reification and rigidity often attached to scientific articulations of THE truth. Folklore and science fiction invite readers and writers to play with scientific ideas rather than just to assert and test them. As such, they offer an epistemological strategy for generating questions, hypotheses, philosophical insights, critique, and reflection. If science fiction is both truthful (in the sense that it represents real issues) and imaginative, it can inspire and support good scientific work and help citizens appreciate science more fully. If it is based on false understandings that degrade science and/or politics, it can be harmful. I am not suggesting that harmful science fiction should be censored and the author silenced. But I am suggesting that those who tell stories need to consider the social implications of the arguments their narratives make. These examples of how folktales question scientific assumptions are a first step in the epistemological work that feminist science performs by treating science as a story.

CAN THE STORY METAPHOR DESANCTIFY
SCIENCE AND MAKE TRUTH CLAIMS?

Folktales work to make points about science. But to call science a story is a different and more radical move. It is radical in the context of the Western accounts of how science works. Since the Enlightenment, scientific propositions have been accorded the status of truth, and the metaphor of story has suggested imagination, embellishment, even lies. Calling science a series of lies is not helpful. So, how then can the metaphor of story help citizens use science more effectively and respect it more fully?

To answer this question, I want to begin with a brief sketch of how science has come to be linked with the authority of the state. In the pre-Enlightenment era state powers were just emerging from a feudal state. In the United States, the founders were so uncertain about a nation-state governance system that they created a federal system. The abuses of kings had made persons suspicious of all governance. With the Enlightenment, scientific authority and the modern state had displaced the church and the feudal system. Just as kings and religious authorities combined forces to rule subjects, so the state and scientific authorities began to work together to govern citizens. Like religion, science could offer guidance on how to live. Just as feudal lords had coordinated social life, the modern state stepped in to coordinate actions for collective living. Just as premodern individuals turned to religion to save them from eternal death, so modern citizens turn to science for salvation from premature death. The rise of science came, in part, because modern science promised a broader, more global, basis for coalition building and economic trade than did religion—especially Christianity. The emerging state systems and their capitalist allies needed strong central authority, systems that valued organization, reason, and political deference. Newly formed states could ill afford loyalties along cultural lines that were contrary to state divisions or loyalties to such entities as religious organizations that claimed higher powers. Wary of constituencies whose loyalties could be transnational— such as those encouraged by the major religions—state leaders praised abstract reason as a guiding authority. Reason promised to serve as a unifying, non-threatening force. Furthermore, the quality of absolute authority attributed to religion was ill-suited to democratic states. Certainly, if some participants could be seen as speaking for God, they would gain too much control and upset pluralities. In many respects, this antidemocratic characterization of religion misunderstands it; but, nevertheless, mistrust of religious authorities created a power vacuum now filled by natural law and its spokesperson, scientific authority. Science has emphasized skepticism and doubt and scientific values—reason, critique, and doubt—have seemed better suited for democratic discussions, because scientific discourse promised a rational moral order devoted to preserving life— at least most lives, at least important lives. Because skepticism not only problematizes knowledge but also problematizes relationships, undermines trust, and questions personal experience reports, some feminists have difficulty in embracing the types of social critique that have come from Enlightenment science.

By the early 1900s state authority was secure, and by the end of World War II, the United States had emerged as a powerful model for combining democracy, capitalism, and science. But by the 1960s these hard-won achievements were beginning to attract attention as hegemonic forces. Critics began to talk about the military-industrial complex, which had involved us in Vietnam and created huge defense contracts to fuel a war effort, and behind this military-industrial complex was the alliance between science and the state. Not only did the modern state rely on science for its weaponry, demographic data, and policy analyses, but it also used science to justify social controls, such as control over medical practices, food and drug distribution, and housing conditions. Citizens turned to science as well for guidance on how to live safely. White lab coats became the new priestly vestments automatically accorded public deference. A new laity had emerged as science appeared too complex for ordinary citizen review.

By the late twentieth century, with the new economic order, the end of the cold war, and the everyday application of cybernetics, science became an even more important partner in state authority. Medical government forces, the National Science Foundation, the National Institutes for Health, the Food and Drug Administration, and other bureaucratic components have successfully challenged corporate forces—the tobacco industry, the asbestos industry, and a variety of other corporate interests. Scientific discourse can address key public concerns— tobacco smoking, environmental contamination, abortion, health care delivery, air travel, suicides by medical means, sex, AIDS, and others. The wars on drugs, poverty, and disease have made the state even more dependent on scientific discourse to keep citizens safe. In turn, citizens believe in science as an equal-access, public guardian angel.

The separation of religion from public life helped science move into the power vacuum left by relegating religion to private life. Exploiting the tensions between science and religion, Sandra Harding uses a religious metaphor to show how science had come to stray from its critical roots: "The project that science's sacredness makes taboo is the examination of science in just the ways any other institution or set of social practices can be examined."[9] By employing a religious allusion, Harding shows how scientific authority has become like religious authority in the pre-Enlightenment era. Just as science undid religious hegemony, so scientific hegemony can itself be undone. The religious analogy gives Harding's readers hope that such hegemonic force can be challenged: "After all, the legitimacy of the theological justifications once presented for scientific (and mathematical) claims and practices was eventually undercut by the claims and practices of modern science."[10]

But second-wave feminist scholars, hesitant to take on scientific authority, often left it instead to its own devices. Women's studies scholars gravitated toward the humanities, and activists satisfied themselves with critical reviews of the effects of scientific activities like childbirth practices and birth control. Haraway says of these scholars that "we"—meaning we feminists—have "perversely worshiped science"[11] by rejecting the natural sciences as disciplines that should inform feminist theory and by treating "nature" as an enemy of feminism.[12] Rejecting science reiterates a mind/body split and leaves issues of the physical body to science, while limiting feminist concerns to matters of the mind and culture. Reversing the popular U.S. tale that has "woman" represent body, while "man" represents the mind, does not help. It is important that feminists address both sides of the mind/body dichotomy to interrogate it. Putting definitions of the body, sex, and sexuality—which are controlled by scientific discourse—outside of feminist reach depoliticizes feminist work.

For Harding, the problem with science is its insistence on "one true story." Haraway shows how careful attention to science reveals that science can and does tell a multiplicity of stories. Feminists have challenged the "man-the-hunter" story by providing evidence that in many tribes "women-gatherers" sup-plied the majority of the food. Haraway anticipates that scientific tales will con-tinue to change as new cultural situations foster new insights:

> The challenge facing those who generated the figure of woman the gatherer is to mutate her further to tell better heteroglossic stories of sexual difference and differ-ence within sex—while remaining responsible scientifically for constructing and reading the data of "Sex and Gender Two Million B.C."[13]

For some empiricists, the bold affirmation of the power of reading "data" may seem jolting, but for Haraway it is not a trick of the imagination. The natural world both shapes and is shaped by our discourse. While not a proponent of the language-does-it-all theory, Haraway makes use of language philosophy to show the role that language and story play in the continuous construction of science.[14] For Haraway, data are never raw but are always already socially processed by lan-guage practices. However, she is not proposing a social constructionist or rela-tivist viewpoint. Truth is not created by human belief. Nature and material condi-tions cannot be altered to become whatever a citizen desires. The social world shapes articulations *of* the material world, and the material world shapes scientific observations. Physical materiality is not separate from language just as meanings are not separate from natural phenomena. The organic connection between mean-ing and materiality has important implications for scientific method.

What Haraway reveals is that science cannot free itself from human persons or from politics—not even by developing better methods to get the real data. "Data" is a product of social practices, including an empirical research design, which itself comes out of a social context with particular linguistic habits. Sci-ence cannot extricate itself from the struggle over how humans can live together—with each other, with other organisms, and with the physical elements that compose life on earth. By recognizing this struggle, citizens can acknowl-edge value conflicts and make self-conscious political choices. Haraway makes this point in the title of her article: "Primatology Is Politics by Other Means."[15] In suggesting that science is involved in politics, Haraway does not diminish the social value of scientists. However, she values scientists who can acknowledge the connections between their work and social life. Inviting feminists to take empirical science and nature seriously, Haraway rejects the old positivist dogma that advocated scientific separatism.

By connecting literature, narrative, and primatology, Haraway does not diminish the power of science but shows how science is a series of narratives that create powerful effects:

> . . . by altering a "field" of stories or possible explanatory accounts, by raising the cost of defending some accounts, by destabilizing the plausibility of some strategies of explanation. Every story in a "field" alters the status of all others.[16]

Speaking about science as a narrative shows how scientific discourse connects concepts and propositions in a set of interlocking relationships that together make sense of the world. By making connections among phenomena, scientists tell stories. Not only does this web of connections tell a story at a variety of levels, but the narrative is shaped by a variety of social, cultural, historical, and spiritual values. So scientific discourse communicates the truth in ways that go beyond merely providing accurate descriptions and predictions. For example, scientific discourse shows how healthy female bodies work, determines what counts as a sick female body, and suggests what might be done to change a sick female body into a healthy one. Furthermore, scientific discourse on aging guides employment practices, health care, government medical support, and food consumption. Scientific truth is not limited to physical descriptions but includes social meanings because science is a story told by humans to humans. Thus, the key question is not "Do scientists offer accurate accounts?" The question is "What does scientific truth mean in the context of citizens' lives?"

WHAT POLITICAL WORK DOES THE
STORY METAPHOR PERFORM?

I will explain the political work the story metaphor performs by discussing three ways the story metaphor connects politics and science: First, it politicizes knowledge in such a way that citizens are able to consider science as one among many ways of knowing, thereby including science in public discussions. Second, it enables science to respond more directly to public policy issues by encouraging scientists to access a variety of epistemologies in their analyses. Third, it extends the evaluation of projects beyond descriptions to include reflections on social values and ethics.

In politicizing knowledge, the story metaphor encourages citizens to turn to science as only one among many sources for knowledge—one story among many that citizens need to hear before resolving factual disputes or making policy decisions. Placing scientific knowledge in such a context undercuts a hegemonic interpretation of scientific discourse as the one and only way to gain objectivity. Letting go of science as the *only* means to gain knowledge enables science to resign as THE savior of the state and to take its place as one method among many that enable humans to know. Adopting an interpretive view of science can free science from the burden of presenting THE final answer. While undoing the social autonomy of scientific discourse has some costs, characterizing science as the holder of the "keys" to all truth has costs both for citizens and scientists. Furthermore, the story metaphor does not argue that science presents only opinion and/or false images. Linking scientific knowledge to social practices does not contaminate the "purity" of a science as truth. What makes the story metaphor liberatory is not only its ability to undercut the "one-true-story" version of science, but also its ability to integrate a variety of ways of knowing. It is the *Rashomon* quality of narrative genre that offers science a new paradigm. Because citizens so often call on scientific discourse within a medical context, medicine offers a good example of how this story metaphor can work. Abandoning the salvation image can help protect physicians from the unrealistic expectation that they can save all lives. While medical malpractice certainly does in some cases focus on the inappropriate actions of physicians, the image of the physician as savior leads to condemnation and blame when he or she fails to save lives. Unrealistic views of scientists as saviors create expectations that are bound to be frustrated. Science cannot solve all problems; reason, logic, and scientific truth have as much to teach citizens about the limits of knowledge as about the solution to problems. Medical decisions require patients to integrate medical information with other sorts of information concerning social, religious, cultural, and economic concerns in order to make decisions about medical procedures. Treating science as one narrative among many can facilitate this integration. For politics the process works in a similar way. Regarding science as a story makes scientific fact comparable with other types of information—personal experiences, artistic insights, imaginative visions, economics, religion, and intuitive perceptions. Treating science as only one story among many makes it easier to mix various ways of knowing to reflect on public policy issues. This consideration can strengthen communities and science because it permits science to connect with public political conversations without dominating them. Furthermore, it encourages scientists and citizen alike to recognize that scientific truth depends on acknowledging the limits of knowledge. Politicizing scientific knowledge by connecting it to social practices enables citizens to use scientific knowledge to develop policies without the danger of unmindfully determining those policies.

Politicizing scientific discourse presents two difficulties. First, neoconservatives already argue that feminist science is PC—that is, politically correct, by which they mean that it is *politically coercive* in terms of a social agenda. Both neoconservatives and feminists worry that science can be used by ideologues to dominate society. It might appear that calling science a narrative will reduce all science to PC status and only make such domination more respectable. However, this PC charge only works if science is accorded a value-free, neutral status. Once citizens realize that the PC charge itself has a political agenda that attempts to shut down debate by hiding behind a false notion of scientific neutrality, it no longer works. Rather than being embarrassed by the charge, citizens need to recognize that political correctness is better than political incorrectness or political indifference. Politics is not an evil activity but the obligation of every citizen. Rather than seeking a value-free position above and beyond the politics of everyday life, citizens need to speak openly about their value conflicts. Scientific discourse can encourage citizens to talk about the values that shape understandings of the truth.

Harding identifies a second difficulty that the story metaphor presents. She is fearful that U.S. feminist scientists, who work in the context of one dominant

tale, "The Patriarchy Story," cannot afford to give up attempts to create a coun-
terforce with "'one, true, feminist story of reality'"[17] She worries that the story
metaphor could lead to relativism, leaving feminists with no basis from which to
judge one political action (or one tale) better (more reasonable, more truthful)
than another. To solve this problem, Harding combines the metaphors of story
and standpoint. Employing the materiality of the standpoint metaphor, she avoids
arguing for a proliferation of narratives, and instead, emphasizes how societies
construct interpretations that are held constant within a particular historical cultural context. Time and the material anchor the scientific narrative. Thus, Harding argues that science can make legitimate claims about its "access to a real
world,"[18] and so she claims for science a "strong objectivity." But this strong
objectivity does not mean that science will automatically correct itself, nor does
it mean that science has already freed itself from patriarchy. Strong objectivity
requires hard political work that demands critical discipline. The image of a story
depicts the contingent nature of this work and encourages citizens to understand
science as one way of knowing without making it the one and only way of knowing. Politicizing knowledge frees scientists from the temptation of making false
universal claims and frees citizens to take account of a variety of ways of knowing. For societies to make good decisions requires information from a variety of
ways of knowing. So, the story metaphor works politically to integrate science
narratives into public life by arguing that science offers one way of knowing but
not the one and only way of knowing.

The second way the story metaphor works politically is that it facilitates conversations about social goals and public policy that include scientists. These conversations can be difficult for feminist scientists because some policy issues are
designed to achieve patriarchal goals. Drawing on the work of Elizabeth Fee,
Harding argues that a feminist science cannot even be imagined until a feminist
society exists.[19] Because society is part of the grounding for science, until some
of that ground has the right nutrients for feminist principles, science cannot be
expected to be free from social bias. Once some areas of that ground have
become fertile for gender-inclusive social practices, science can focus energy on
this area. But the point here is not that science just has to wait for social change.
Waiting for a utopian society simply denies the possibility for any politics at all.
Harding is showing how feminist work in the sciences responds to areas where
there has been social change and then opens the way for wider examinations of
a variety of standpoints. It is a step-by-step process that needs to set aside utopian
style dreams. The story metaphor can make these conversations about truth easier because it does not require a rigid adherence to a fixed set of propositions to
exchange ideas. Story encourages a back-and-forth style conversation and so
encourages the exploration of truth claims rather than their assertion.

For Harding, this story image supports reflexivity. Harding's strong objectivity expects scientists to become aware of their own cultural contexts, the points
at which they stand. What is important about Harding's epistemological solution

is the emphasis on the scientist's responsibility to build moral social environments as well as accurate knowledge archives. Harding's analysis anticipates changes that go beyond methodology, accurate description, and a correspondence theory of truth. Her narrative evokes a moral tale that demonstrates how science does more than merely pass on "facts" or information. However, she is not suggesting that science is corrupted by politics but instead that science is a social practice that should be shaped by the values of a particular society and should critique that same society. Harding argues that feminist quests for strategies for acquiring knowledge are "transitional meditations"[20] that will serve to display contradictions until society offers an ungendered context in which to do science. Taking a position similar to Harding, Helen E. Longino also shows how science relies on social practices. Longino explains that feminist scientists make choices between correcting the masculinist bias in science by using established empirical methods, and constructing a "new" way of doing science by creating a "dialectical evolution" that preserves methodological continuities.[21] Explaining that correcting masculine bias in science is insufficient, she nevertheless does not argue that feminist science requires a "radical break with the science one has learned and practiced."[22] Longino is calling for intellectual courage, not deference to a particular political ideology. She argues for a feminist science composed of feminist, not feminine, values.[23] But certainly new cultural practices will call for new knowledge strategies, as well as old semi-abandoned ones, to respond to shifting needs and structures of meaning.

Longino embraces what she calls "contextual empiricism," which takes into account the ways in which texts shape scientific discourse.[24] Thus, she acknowledges linguistic limitations, while simultaneously affirming empirical methods. Her story of science does not evoke a paradigm shift but emphasizes continuity with previous models of science to develop gender-inclusive practices. Her tale is not about revolution but reformation. Nevertheless, she acknowledges that science involves political commitments.[25] She is less interested in a critique of androcentric science than she is in the development of political and social conditions that support a new, more comprehensive science. Her science narrative, like Harding's, relies on a utopian vision to anchor the dream of a better, gender-inclusive science. But, in the meantime, they both advocate the gradual elimination of sexism from scientific work. Both Haraway and Longino anticipate a time when science will be free of power struggles and so avoid explicit political questions about gender.

Aware of the multiplicity in the narrative genre, Haraway invokes the story metaphor with a postmodern turn. Not only does she reject a transcendental universal viewpoint, but she also manages to embrace a variety of truth claims from social constructionism to sociobiology. By reading scientific discourse as science fiction, she asks her reader to follow the work of biologists with keen and respectful interest. Rather than emphasizing how society and/or nature anchors narratives, Haraway pays attention to the author-scientist's imagination and how the text evokes the reader's response. Fiction has been better at explaining imagination than nonfiction. Combining the political use of utopias with Haraway's allusions to science fiction, Hilary Rose explains that feminist scientists use science fiction to make productive political proposals.[26] Suggesting a productive relationship between science fiction and science, Rose calls science fiction the "feminist laboratory of dreams."[27]

What I find important about talking about science as narrative is the way in which the story metaphor supports discussions that connect society, gender, ethnicity, and nature. Science is not a set of propositions to be measured against observations in natural settings, but a way of putting together "facts" so that they make sense, tell a story, and explain how things work. Haraway does not worry about relativism, but she does worry about how citizens can become reflective. Her position establishes a basis for citizens to judge an imperfect world and so she is not afraid of calling her work political and including it in public conversations about social change.

The third way in which the story metaphor connects science and society is that the story enables scientists and their readers to become more reflective. The story metaphor, developed by feminist philosophers of science, shows that scientific truth depends on social practices. The old model of science—science as mere description—articulated knowledge as a true/false dichotomy. Readers either agreed or disagreed with scientific conclusions. This true/false dichotomy encourages verification processes, intersubjective validity, and popular surveys. Although this old model offered some room for qualifying answers, its logic restricted truth to a singular articulation. Old science employed a methodological fundamentalism that treated certainty as desirable, prediction as the test of truth, and relativism as a threat. Old science lauded narrowness and turned ambiguity, flexibility, and imagination into vices. Old science judged truth on the basis of methodological purity and replicability. Feminist scientists introduce a new scientific empiricism that evokes the genre of narrative to emphasize both imagination and accuracy. Such feminists emphasize that the meaning of the story needs to be both accurate in detail and sufficiently general to allow the reader to make use of the information. For science to work it must be socially meaningful.

If science is understood as a set of meaningful stories that guide citizens, then scientific truth needs to be evaluated, in part, in terms of its ability to provide that guidance. Scientists already use such criteria in evaluating projects in terms of their fruitfulness—although some may limit that fruitfulness to scientific work. More general broad-based significance depends on scientists being able to speak with political leaders and citizens. In a democratic society, scientific fruitfulness needs to anticipate a broad audience. The story metaphor can encourage scientists to define their audiences more broadly and to refine their thoughts by speaking more clearly about how their projects draw from and contribute to social life. Thus, the story metaphor expects scientists to be reflective about their work.

This reflectivity depends on science addressing a broad audience that will enable scientists to take account of the way social life makes their work significant. The value of projects cannot be measured merely in terms of predictability, replicability, and accuracy. Without discarding these standards, scientific projects need to be evaluated in terms of how they contribute to social meanings and so make life better. Making the world a better place is not simply an abstraction, nor is it divorced from ethical matters. For example, Haraway rejects any natural or social science based on domination—domination among humans or between humans and nature.[28] Discussing the social values in a scientific project can encourage scientists to become reflective about the ethical dimensions of their work. While this ethical concern seems like dangerous territory, confronting such dangers can enable science to be more fully integrated into social discourse. Avoiding scientific separatism has benefits for scientists and citizens alike. The story metaphor helps science to make more complex epistemological connections between scientific and social practices.

I am proposing that this story metaphor can be used to generate new and more complex criteria for judging the merits of scientific work. I am arguing that scientific projects be judged on the basis of the type of relationships inherent in their structure, articulated by their format, and fostered by their outcomes. For example, if the political values that frame a project make domination the only or the best form of interaction, the project should be treated with some suspicion. If the project assumes that some persons must dominate others or that persons must "dominate" nature rather than work with natural phenomena, the project should be regarded as suspicious because it is projecting negative social actions onto scientific phenomena. Projects need to be evaluated not only in terms of their replicability but also in terms of the assumptions and projections that construct their narration. Projects that encourage and support good relationships need to be given priority over projects that foster bad relationships. This is one criterion for judging projects. Of course, employing these values does not dispense with the old standards; projects must also offer workable, accurate models. But projects are not to be rejected on the basis of epistemological commitments alone; they might also be rejected on the basis of the types of relationships embedded in the structure of their inquiry. The relationships between the variables and between independent and dependent variables are not merely descriptive, but tell a moral tale, and the moral import of that tale needs to be examined. Employing the metaphor of story to explain how science articulates descriptions about the world may make it easier to examine the ethics of scientific work. The story metaphor can invite scientists to articulate in an open and playful way the judgments and moral codes that inform their work so that they will not be hidden. Thus, such judgments become explicit, and unspoken values are given public voice.

Scientists already take some account of the ethical aspects of research by reviewing the use of humans and animals in experimentation. This new criterion evaluates how projects articulate and advocate relationships. This criterion extends the ethical dimension beyond the confines of issues about the treatment of the subjects in an experiment to include the way the project constructs relationships throughout its structure. It also encourages the evaluation of scientific projects on the basis of how they construct relationships in the world. Projects that open up possibilities for better relationships among persons, between persons and animals, and/or between persons and inanimate beings are to be evaluated higher than those that do not create good relationships. While there will be differences in assessing these relationships, it is the process of assessment that is important. Scientific narratives will be judged not only on the basis of their accuracy or their ability to predict actions, but also on the basis of their ability to articulate the possibility for *good* actions that nurture good relationships and sustain environmentally beneficial human social practices, respectful of all beings. While this criterion may seem very hard to use in an evaluation process, I will later argue that it can be achieved through conversations among citizens rather than through the enforcement of rules or some reward/punishment system. This new criterion depends on a variety of epistemological strategies—empirical, interpretive, postmodern, hermeneutical, phenomenological, and pragmatic. But more importantly, public and private discussions can enable individuals to evaluate actions in terms of their ethical significance. Laying aside the old viewpoint that the scientist is merely the disembodied voice of the all-powerful "nature," revealing "her" natural laws as "he" discovers them, citizens can use the story metaphor to understand science as a *human* activity that makes important contributions to moral/ethical values.

I am suggesting that the source for good science is to be found in a good society, and good societies need to look to science in order to move closer to goodness. This is not a vicious hermeneutical circle but an appraisal of the interactive quality of the relationship between scientific truth and social structures. Citizens can understand the good, the moral, and the ethical by bringing the discourse of scientific truth and the discourse of public life together. Separating them has not only separated science from society but has also given science a sacred space beyond social critique. This separation deprives science of critical reflection and prevents citizens from appreciating the rigors involved in scientific work.

An examination of how science constructs relationships can offer a new understanding of the connection between truth and politics. Because scientific truth has served as the model for truth in modern America, the story metaphor can be useful for reformulating other public conversations. Rather than insisting that truth calls for one and only one course of action, citizens can appreciate how truthful propositions depend on narratives that arise out of a cosmology of values and assumptions about human, social, and environmental relationships. The implications for scientific truth as a narrative can reach beyond science to suggest an epistemological strategy for talking about the truth in a number of different discourses without resorting to either relativism or hegemonic monism.

NOTES

1. Sandra Harding, *The Science Question in Feminism* (Ithaca, N.Y.: Cornell University Press, 1986), 125.

2. Carol Gilligan, *In a Different Voice: Psychological Theory and Women's Development* (Cambridge, Mass.: Harvard University Press, 1982).

3. Marcia Millman and Rosebeth Moss Kanter, *Another Voice: Feminist Perspectives on Social Life and Social Science* (Garden City, N.Y.: Anchor Books, 1975).

4. Ruth Bleier, *Science and Gender: A Critique of Biology and Its Theories on Women* (New York: Pergamon Press, 1984), 28, quoting from Ruth Herschberger, *Adam's Rib* (New York: Harper & Row, 1970), 10.

5. Ruth Ginzberg, "Uncovering Gynocentric Science," *Hypatia* 2 (1987): 96.

6. Emily Martin, *The Woman in the Body: A Cultural Analysis of Reproduction* (Boston: Beacon Press, 1987); and Valerie Lee, *Granny Midwives and Black Women Writers: Double Dutched Readings* (New York: Routledge, 1996).

7. Ruth Bleier, "Sex Differences Research," *Feminist Approaches to Science*, ed. Ruth Bleier (New York: Pergamon Press, 1986), 158–59.

8. Another example can be found in the folktale of Ruby, a "freeze-thawed, living Australopithecus female fossil," told by Adrienne Zihlman and Jerrold Lowenstein, which debunks the myth of the passive dependent female; Donna Haraway, "Primatology Is Politics by Other Means," in *Feminist Approaches to Science*, ed. Bleier, 112.

9. Harding, *The Science Question in Feminism*, 39.

10. Harding, *The Science Question in Feminism*, 141.

11. Donna Haraway, "Animal Sociology and a Natural Economy of the Body Politic, Part I: A Political Physiology of Dominance," in *Sex and Scientific Inquiry*, ed. Sandra Harding and Jean F. O'Barr (Chicago: University of Chicago Press, 1987), 219.

12. Haraway, "Animal Sociology, Part I," 219.

13. Donna Haraway, *Primate Visions: Gender, Race, and Nature in the World of Modern Science* (New York: Routledge, 1989), 348.

14. I know of no serious scholar who thinks that language is the prime cause of all social phenomena, although postmodern theorists do construct language as the basic social element.

15. Donna Haraway, "Primatology Is Politics by Other Means."

16. Haraway, "Primatology Is Politics by Other Means," 81.

17. Harding, *The Science Question in Feminism*, 28.

18. Harding, *The Science Question in Feminism*, 137.

19. Harding, *The Science Question in Feminism*, 139.

20. Harding, *The Science Question in Feminism*, 141.

21. Helen E. Longino, *Science As Social Knowledge: Values and Objectivity in Scientific Inquiry* (Princeton, N. J.: Princeton University Press, 1990), 187–94, especially 193.

22. Helen E. Longino, "Can There Be a Feminist Science?" in *Feminism & Science*, ed. Nancy Tuana (Bloomington: Indiana University Press, 1989), 54.

23. Longino, *Science As Social Knowledge*, 187–214, especially 188.

24. Longino, *Science As Social Knowledge*, 215–32.

25. Longino, *Science As Social Knowledge*, 194–213.

26. Hilary Rose, *Love, Power, and Knowledge: Towards a Feminist Transformation of the Sciences* (Bloomington: Indiana University Press, 1994), 208–29.

27. Hilary Rose, *Love, Power, and Knowledge*, 228–29.

28. Haraway, "Animal Sociology, Part I," 231–32.

Chapter 7

A Reflective Feminist Science:
Scientist-Citizens and Public Policies

In this chapter, I discuss six basic components of a citizen-friendly, reflective science that I have developed from a close reading of feminist scientific discourse. Without disparaging other ways of knowing, these six components affirm both quantitative and qualitative empirical research, privilege reflection as well as observation, and honor cultural and historical limits as vital components of scientific work. My goal is to facilitate public policy conversations between scientists and citizens. Democracy depends on citizens and scientists having these conversations and so this communication has important consequences for such political institutions as universities, hospitals, government agencies, and local communities. This reflective science avoids neutrality; equally important, this approach refuses to reduce knowledge to individual opinion and/or know-nothing relativism. Following my discussion of the six components, I will show how feminist science can be used to build a reflective science that connects truth and politics.

HOW IS FEMINIST SCIENCE CONNECTED TO PUBLIC POLICY?

One of the primary challenges for scientists who want to talk about the connection between truth and politics is figuring out how to do so without undercutting knowledge claims. For those who believe that truth requires a value-free science, any such connection is an unspeakable pollution. For others whose epistemological stance is empirical rather than positivistic, the inevitable link between the "context of discovery" and the "context of justification," the connection between science and society is unavoidable, but regrettable.[1] For those who go further to invoke reflexive epistemologies, the link between science and society makes science meaningful.

Rather than seeing the connection between science and society as a problem, I have argued that it solves problems.[2] It is a solution in that such connections make science meaningful and enable scientists to reflect on the social factors that can and do shape their work because science emerges not from a pure, empty interest in knowledge, but from a desire to know something that serves particular human-centered interests. Those interests might be utilitarian, in which case science solves social problems. Those interests might be ends in themselves, in which case science offers an appreciation of the beauty of natural phenomena that simply delights scientists and their readers. Nevertheless, all such scientific projects—those that serve utilitarian purposes and those that serve aesthetic ones—are framed in social terms. In both cases, science addresses human needs and speaks to a human audience who is located in a particular historical, cultural context. These social connections make scientific discourse meaningful and relevant.

But in order to extend the meaning of research projects, scientists embrace abstractions. Some of these abstractions have universal claims for application to all historical periods and social circumstances. But many generalized abstractions are so obvious as to have little significance. For example, the abstraction that all persons need food or the observation that all objects like baseball bats when dropped on earth outside a vacuum fall are too general and obvious to be of much significance. They demand particulars to explain their significance. For example, what counts as food in one culture may be considered unhealthy in another. Bats dropped in the water don't fall in the same way as bats dropped in the air. These particulars create significance and connect broad generalizations to particular social and physical circumstances. Science is most engaging at the intersection of points of universal generalization and variations. The tension between the generalization and the particulars is not only a key issue in summarizing observations; but it makes science vital and epistemologically challenging. Meaningfulness requires some level of specificity—some level of particularity that makes it possible to apply the findings to particular situations. Because situations differ, even what might be considered the exact same findings will become meaningful to specific groups of people in differing ways. Because all scientific projects are conducted within social settings, the interface between scientific findings and social meanings cannot be avoided, and attempts to avoid such connections generate dishonest claims and produce epistemological errors.

Some will argue that scientists should not be directly concerned with policy issues because they know nothing about this field and so should stick to the narrow business at hand. But such narrowness is based on a false compartmentalization. Scientific questions come out of social practices, and their explanations and answers reform social habits. At some general level, scientists admit that they deal within human contexts, but sometimes this admission is at such a high level of abstraction that its significance disappears. For scientists to say that their questions arise out of social contexts is correct but insufficient. The nod to such generalized connections to social life is insufficient to give science its necessary rigor and respect. For example, investigating the differences in nutritional needs in males and females produces information that can prevent false assumptions about similarities between male and female bodies, and testing heart medicine on women as well as men is important to protecting the health of women. Science and social practices are not separate. Obviously, such scientific observations have gender significance, but a careful exploration of research projects will reveal that scientific discourse is not so abstract as to be removed from everyday life but only appears to be so because such connections may often be unspoken. For example, nutrition and body image have ramifications for women's health and social status. If science emphasizes thinness as healthy, it can contribute in unwitting ways to popular discourses that denigrate heavy women because they take place in the context in which fat women are treated differently than fat men. So citizens may hear messages about thinness in ways that contribute to creating anorexia in women.[3] Because of the ways modern culture privileges scientific narratives, citizens can give scientific explanations too much unwarranted control and so use science to guide decisions that are best made by considerations of the interaction of social and natural factors. By including in their scientific work reflections on social factors, scientists can avoid subversive politics and articulate some of the social factors that impinge on their human research. The goal of such considerations is to make science reflective and so more rigorous and to make citizens more aware of the ways in which natural scientific factors shape and are shaped by sociocultural factors.

Science can and does work toward building a better society—not a better society in general, for all persons in all places and times, but a better society within the historical and cultural contexts in which it operates. While many scientists are well aware of this fact, it has been difficult to bring those values into public conversations about scientific projects. Of course, scientists cannot articulate all the public issues to which any particular project is connected because many will be unanticipated. But many *are* anticipated and can be discussed. By specifying these components, scientists can develop a heightened awareness of what they are doing at every level of the research process. Dialogues on a project's social significance can include a variety of experts—social scientists, artists, medical doctors, technicians, and other citizens whose work and interests intersect with the scientific project. Already, this dialogue begins silently in the head of the scientist as she or he works. While making the dialogue systematic, rigorous, and critical can strengthen scientific projects, scientists fear that it could also lead to control and censorship. However, control and censorship already exist in the philosophical social structures that shape scientific discourse and in the practical day-to-day operations used to allocate financial resources. Nevertheless, scientific public conversations can be conducted in a spirit of mutual support, and scientists along with others can shape these conversations. But the point here is that scientists should be encouraged, not forced, to reach beyond narrow definitions of their work to include policy discussions as a part of it, not as an addition to it.[4] Such encouragement constructs science differently. Developing reflectivity in the inquiry process can enable scholars to discuss their projects more fully with citizens. A reflective science can encourage scientists to abandon the personae of magical, mystical beings whose methods work wonders and instead to present themselves as everyday citizens who, like others, have contributions to make. Feminist philosophers of science like Sandra Harding, Donna Haraway, and Helen Longino offer insights on how this transformation can be accomplished. Taking account of the connection between science and society, feminist scientists can offer some leadership in moving toward more reflective scientific work.

This leadership takes two forms. First, it serves to correct errors in empirical science. Certainly, feminist scientists have helped reduce false universal claims caused by unreflective androcentric biases. Feminists using this approach emphasize the need for correcting "bad" science by using typical empirical methods; this approach works best in discussions with scientists who are unfamiliar with philosophical critiques of scientific activity.[5] These scholars believe that the scientific process is sufficiently robust that in time it will correct androcentric errors without altering scientific methods. The correction is made by additional observations, which continue to use methods developed in ways that are believed to be independent of social cultural factors. This viewpoint argues that scientists may not be neutral but the scientific method is. As Sue Rosser suggests, this good/bad science approach evokes liberal feminist values. This approach brings women into scientific view without changing the way things are viewed or the methods used to substantiate observations. In contrast, a feminist scientific approach argues that the methods themselves are shaped by androcentric values and so to view women requires some adaptations in scientific method. This approach argues for a paradigm shift and is more closely an ally of radical feminist scholarship.[6] Rosser has found that methodological, epistemological conversations that involve questions about objectivity and scientific method are a primary barrier in discussions between feminist scientists and scientists who focus on other matters.[7] Feminist scientists who seek deeper understandings of scientific practices may well find the reflective approach more useful. It has greater radical potential in that it works to transform scientific method itself. It does offer an adjustment not only in the content or focus of scientific observation but also in the methods and procedures for observations.

For those engaged in scientific research, it may be helpful to consider how science might continue to evolve, not only in terms of facts and hypotheses but also in terms of its methods. There is no reason to believe that the scientific method, articulated in the early part of the Enlightenment, represents the last word on scientific epistemology. Reflectivity can be included in scientific inquiry without discarding empirical methods. But even without such reflectivity, feminist scientists make important corrections to "bad" unselfconscious, androcentric science. Science can be corrected by extending research to include females, by scrutinizing gendered metaphors, and/or by limiting claims to the masculine database represented in the research. Because practicing scientists still build their work on value-free scientific belief systems, both correcting "bad" androcentric science and reframing scientific epistemology are necessary. However, my focus is on the latter because it offers more opportunities for articulating the connection between politics and science.

To form the basis for reflective scientific work, I respond to six questions by proposing six key practices for reframing scientific epistemology. These practices are designed to support citizen-scientist dialogues as well as to encourage dialogues among scientists, feminists, feminist scholars, and other types of citizens.

CAN THE TELOS OF SCIENCE BE CONNECTED TO THE WORLD?

First, it is important that scientists understand that their goal involves the production of knowledge. Knowledge production depends on a language, which itself depends on a set of social meanings. In this sense, all knowledge enhances social life because it adds to its social meaning. Even science performed out of wonder and curiosity—for no end other than delight in the wonders of the natural environment—makes life better.[8] For example, a scientist who wants to understand the marvels of the ant world connects with citizens by conveying the marvel of the ant world to a socially situated human audience through a specific language. The magic of making that ant world meaningful to a particular group of humans makes science work, and it is this connection that I want made explicit. So, scientific work need not make the world better by reducing cancer, prolonging human life, feeding more people—even though these are all fine goals. What I mean by improving life is creating a deeper level of understanding. For example, the case of ant research illuminates how ants work together to sustain life. These structures have social meaning because humans also participate in an organized work life. The ant world is explained in terms that make sense in the context of human existence. Of course, the argument is not that humans are just like ants. Articulating similarities and differences enables scientists to give those who have not studied ants a sensible understandable view of this world, but it also can encourage self-aware reflections on the ways in which ants and humans are both similar and different.

All meanings set forward a set of ethical values. But science is not addressed to the lone scientist who sets down comments for his or her own purposes, it is addressed to others (humans) who read the work. Thus, scientific reporting is an act of communication. Even if the message is simply to appreciate the natural world, this appreciation can make a better world and so contribute to social practices, which, in turn, shape social policies. This understanding of science constructs the scientist as a communicator whose mission involves conveying information to others.

In some respects, this goal to make life better is a universal one. But within current scientific discourse, this purpose places less emphasis on the "pure/applied" distinction and more emphasis on the ways that even pure science enhances human existence. Furthermore, science does not become pure by separating it from life situations, nor do scientists gain "purity" by separating themselves from society. In the eighteenth and nineteenth centuries, the pure/applied distinction created some room for scientists to pursue projects that were not directly connected to mundane instrumental goals. However, in these times this distinction works to shield scientists from productive conversations and access to interdisciplinary knowledge. Modern and postmodern citizens now know that even the value of understanding the natural world is a human goal with political significance. If citizens take pleasure in the natural world that sustains them, they may be less likely to destroy it. Just as citizens treasure man-made art and even woman-made art, aesthetic beauty composed by natural beings may be also treasured—the art of a rock or an ant's life, or a growing tree. While scientists may not be able to specify exactly how society will be improved by a project, they do seek to add to social meaning through their projects.

The distinction between pure knowledge and applied knowledge did protect scientific work from social control. While such protection may have been important during the founding days of scientific practice in the Enlightenment era when science challenged the hegemony of church authority, this distinction no longer serves the same purposes. In fact, this separation produces a sacred space for science that is increasingly inappropriate because of the way in which it grants hegemony to scientific discourse. Dropping the image of "purity" could enable science to relinquish its old struggle with religion and get on with its modern critical goals. Letting go of the ideological commitment to a "pure" science frees science from its "holy, pure, separatist" pretense. More reflective scientific projects could more easily avoid such ills as were created in the alliance between science and the Nazis in World War II. Science does not become "pure" by staying away from government. By denying connections to society (and the government purposes which society has) makes scientists defensive, secretive, and unreflective about the ways in which their work can harm and benefit society. Scientific projects like all other human projects have their benefits and risks. It is only in a society that requires a radical separation between good and evil that science must pretend to do only good. That society, if it ever existed, exists no more.

Feminist scientific discussions recognize that science is a political practice and analyze how science allocates power, shapes public practices, and offers delight to readers. But science is not a political practice only in the sense that it is corrupted by persons abusing science to get their wants satisfied: it is political in that science adds to human life. While it might be the case that scientists abuse their power, my point is different from this. I am suggesting that science entails social political values. While some scientists see social value as a secondary factor goal, I am suggesting that it needs to be a primary consideration. That primary goal may be expressed as a quest for knowledge for knowledge's sake or as a curiosity inspired by topics or questions, scientific practice creates meaning. That meaning not only delights humans within social settings, but it also delights them in particular ways that have political-social significance. Acknowledging these political connections avoids the corruption that can be bred by denying them. For example, in controversies over AIDS research and breast cancer, both citizens and scientists can reflect on how science allocates resources in pursuing these issues. Such controversies can enable scientists to be more reflective about how they make decisions and how their work is used in the decisions made by others. This sort of politics need not be a problem, but can serve epistemological ends. Recognizing social-political connections enables scientists to consider ethical issues along with methodological ones and can facilitate reflection in all aspects of a project, from the formulation of a research design to the written report.

I am arguing that the examination of the ethical issues that emerge throughout the execution of a project is a vital part of the work. It is not an aside. Bringing ethics into scientific conversations reduces the absolute authority of scientists in social-political matters. By emphasizing how citizens and scientists can share in the examination of the ethical issues embedded in scientific research, I am emphasizing the responsibility that each citizen has to articulate the ethical values that inform their judgments. In the old hegemonic scientific tale, Nature and *her* spokespersons, scientists, fought off the evil dragon death and rescued humans. Giving up their image as the knight in shining armor and their image as the lone savior in the white coat, scientists can gain a place in the world rather than a pedestal above and separate from it. Scientists, then, can become partners with others in making the world and the humans, who inhabit it, better.

CAN A NEW RHETORIC GIVE SCIENTISTS A PUBLIC VOICE?

To achieve this partnership, scientists need ways to speak about the value judgments that shape their work. By speaking in the third person, as a distant other who reports observations, scientists discredit themselves by suggesting that they do nothing. This depersonalized rhetoric makes scientific practice a message with no messenger. While useful at one point in Western history, this rhetoric no longer serves, because it radically separates nature from culture and thereby reduces nature to a "thing," a tool to be used rather than a phenomenon to encounter. For example, using their own voice releases scientists from the pretexts exemplified by such statements as "the data say that. . . ." Scientists construct and interpret data; scientists speak; data do not speak. Rejecting the image of "speaking data" permits scientists to speak more precisely.[9] The taboo on the use of the first person singular, "I," in the scientific genre encourages scientists to eliminate themselves from their reports and thereby stifles aspects of scientific inquiry. By self-consciously making their human circumstances (including their historical and cultural contexts) part of the scientific enterprise, scientists avoid the prideful temptation to see their "fields" as places in which to grow supermen who fly above all others to save the world.[10] But more importantly, by rejecting the superman, third-person voice, scientists invite their readers to appreciate science as a part of the human experience rather than an activity separate from it, and the scientist takes responsibility for his or her part in this process. Such appreciation might lead to better environmental practices because it might enable scientists to speak about their own delight in a tree, a fly, or a rocky cliff.

By asking scientists to make explicit connections to political-ethical values, I am not suggesting that feminist scientists should abandon empirical methods. By seeing their own judgments as part of the scientific enterprise in all of its stages, scientists can more fully acknowledge their real talents and rid themselves of the burden of presenting themselves as manifestations of super secretaries who merely record observations. For even to record all the observations for a single moment in a single room is itself an impossibility. Scientists make selections in the process of their inquiry. Such selections compose the story. They do not tell all, and their criteria for selection develop out of social-political commitments; in failing to take account of this connection they miss a central aspect of every scientific project. Including the voice of the scientist in the project can enhance the rigor and accuracy of scientific reporting. Finding a public voice for scientists can increase the public's awareness of the value not only of science but of natural phenomena. This rhetoric might reduce instrumentalist orientations toward nature.

CAN REFLECTION ENABLE SCIENTISTS TO BROADEN THEIR GAZE WITHOUT LOSING FOCUS?

Acknowledging the connection science has to society not only enhances the reflective capabilities of scientists; it also opens up a new set of practices for scientists. Scientists can look in two directions. They can look at the world out there and the cultural values within them. They can examine not only the objects to be observed but also their own responses to them. For example, a scientist examining disease in the body can speak about the social activities that produce that disease and how the developing treatments will transform social life for the patient, as well as about the models of the healthy body that constitute those phenomena as a "disease." A scientist who examines the structure of a molecule in the context of her or his research will not be barred from asking what social issues bring this structure into view and what possible new social practices will be produced by the research.[11] While these issues might seem to expand scientific discourse, they may not. This broadened gaze involves reflections, and scientists are already involved in such reflections. Of course, they still will need to select what becomes important in the context of such questions and what does not. The point here is to cast the conversation more broadly so as to make the work more explicit. Recognizing social factors can enable scientists to take larger views of their activity and invite a more systematic and explicit examination of their projects. By bringing rigorous, systematic, social-scientific analyses into science, scientists can examine the social and political components of their projects.

These reflections can make scientists more able to talk about what they know and what they do not know—the boundary between knowledge and ignorance. I do not mean that science should create a black hole, a pit of ignorance, which will someday be enlightened by fancy new flashlights. The black hole image of science anticipates a time when ignorance will disappear. I am suggesting that when some ways of knowing come forward, others disappear because knowledge is shaped by social practices.[12] I mean that science should discuss the limits of scientific discourse itself. Such reflection can, in turn, make citizens more comfortable with characterizing themselves as knowing some things and not knowing others. So scientists can teach citizens about the limits of knowledge and assert into public discourse a habit of expressing such limitations. To do this requires abandoning the all-knowing voice of the third-person objectivist viewpoint and taking up the first-person voice of an individual who sees the world from a viewpoint—not from all viewpoints. It means replacing the quest for complete knowledge with the quest for clearer articulations of the boundary between knowledge and ignorance.

For this kind of reflectivity, scientists need empirical skills that can enable them to speak more accurately about their work. Greater accuracy could avoid situations in which scientists either make rash and unrealistic claims about the effects of the research or make no claims at all. In the absence of such claims, others (nonscientists) sometimes make rash and unrealistic claims about the research. While speculation and rash claims would still be with us, systematic examination of the complex social factors that compose scientific projects could enable scientists to give fuller accounts of their work and not only reduce the incidence of such claims but also their impact. Many grants already require discussion of such social factors. Making this aspect of research more systematic would encourage all scientists to develop fuller understandings of their own work. I am arguing that such discussions are vital for a good public life, which is the goal of politics. Care in articulating what is both known and unknown can lead to better conversations and to better decisions. Such discussions can facilitate better scientific work by making scientists more aware of the multiplicity of facets in their work and can make scientists less vulnerable to social fads, political pressures, and historical prejudices. Enabling scientists to take account of the notions of the *good* embedded in scientific projects authorizes talking about scientific values. Since every scientific project assumes, normalizes, and even advocates a value system that embodies models of the good human community and its relationships with other beings, it is important that scientists make these values explicit.

HOW IS SCIENTIFIC AUTHORITY
EXERCISED WITHIN COMMUNITIES?

I also want to propose changes in the type of authority claims scientific discourse makes. By acknowledging the ways in which scientific practices are a part of social structures, scientists will no longer be required to maintain the impossible pose that science is untouched by human hands. Maintaining the distinction between "pure" and "applied" science has encouraged scientists to separate themselves from public life. Scientists who realize that even so-called "pure" science is not separate from social practice but is itself a social practice can find freedom in that insight. Becoming reflective about cultural values can enable scientists to take fuller account of their own work. Being open to a greater array of social factors, scientists can produce deeper conversations with citizens and avoid situations in which a bevy of experts use specialized discourse to talk past one another. Rather than competing to become top dog, scientists can use such conversations to speak about the value conflicts that divide them. The point is not to avoid conflict but to engage in it productively.

This reflective approach does require scientists to give up the image of the sacred researcher, who is untouched by worldly things (as well as untouched by mundane concerns). Rejecting their magical mystical powers, scientists can more easily explore a wider range of aspects of their work. However, reflective science does not require that scientists articulate all the connections between projects and policies. There will be surprises in scientific discovery, and room needs to be made for them. There will also be surprises at the epistemological level, and scientists can respond at this level, for there is no reason to expect that scientific methodology has arrested its development with the empirical approach that is so popular today.

Abandoning its quest for the "one true story," science can acknowledge that its projects depend on particular cultural contexts and historical settings. The moment a scientist chooses a language—for example, English, Chinese, German—to articulate her or his project, that project is limited by the cultural meanings within that language. Even mathematics as a communication system mixes everyday language with its codes. Such linguistic necessities preclude universal articulations because no *universal* language exists, even though attempts have been made to create one. While the patterns analyzed by science may well hold true in "foreign" cultural contexts, their social meaning will vary.[13] Empirical methods cannot rescue scientists from their cultural roots, even though within that cultural context they produce reliable, objective knowledge. But this limitation is not to be regretted, even though it makes scientific projects more meaningful to some communities than to others. Thus, translating a scientific project from one culture to another is like translating a poem. The meaning will change, and its social reception will differ. To the degree that science conveys meaningful information, it depends for communication on a complex of social cultural meanings for communication that shapes the messages scientists send. Recognizing this cultural element enables scientists to take account not only of the outcome of their projects but also of the ways in which those outcomes are understood by readers.

Scientific authority need not depend on finding the one true meaning for all times in all places. Science can instead provide citizens with an articulation of an objective truth that yields meaning in the context of particular historical cultural contexts, interests, and needs. Although this pragmatic or contextualized understanding of truth requires science to make more modest claims, it does not leave science without authority. Its authority rests with the community of scholars who are the practitioners of science and the community of citizens whom science serves. Claiming some independent, separate authority base that transcends social life is not only inappropriate, but it is also counterproductive. Scientific authority, like the authority of other knowledge systems, is not above and beyond that of the arts, humanities, or social scientists. Science is knowledge made by humans for humans. The distant god's-eye view is no longer credible; scientists need to see their lab coats as one uniform among many uniforms rather than as a priestly garb that gives them privileged access to THE truth. Citizens need no longer place scientific discourse above and beyond all political and social realities. In the international, intercultural postmodern world, scientists do not transcend social worlds to serve as gods, or even as the primary guardians of reason.

HOW CAN SCIENTIFIC JUDGMENTS ASSESS RELATIONSHIPS?

Science offers more than verifiable descriptions; it traces interactions—actions and reactions. Because these actions develop out of the assumptions and beliefs of a particular community, science can help citizens live better lives within the context of that community. Science not only offers an accurate interpretation of reality, but offers it in terms that make sense to citizens in the course of their interactions with the world.

Thus, I am arguing that scientific truth be evaluated not only in terms of the accuracy of its descriptions but also in terms of the ethics of its prescriptions. Asking questions about how science constitutes relationships moves in this direction. For example, a scientific investigation of aging assumes some notion of what counts as a healthy body, which itself assumes a healthy body at a particular age. Scientists who reflect on how a project on aging constructs the relationships between age and social life add a vital dimension to their projects. Investigations of pregnancy assume what counts as health in both the mother and the fetus/baby as well as what counts as either a fetus and/or a baby. Questions need to be asked about how scientific projects articulate these relationships. All scientific projects constitute relationships—relationships between citizens and nature, between citizens and the universe, and among citizens. Because constructing these relationships is unavoidable, it often goes unnoticed. My point is not that such constructions are unscientific or inappropriate. My point is that the way in which science constitutes such relationships merits examination and evaluation.

Constructing poor relationships—even if they are composed of accurate accounts—can harm citizens. I do not mean to suggest that scientists should lie to produce good relationships; rather, I am suggesting that science needs to take account of both the truth of its propositions and their social significance. For example, earlier periods in American science emphasized "man's" control and domination over nature. Scientific truth was used to promote strip mining, deforestation, air and water pollution, and the depopulation of some animal species. While science cannot be held solely responsible for these negative consequences, scientific claims to absolute objectivity and the separatist model of science have made misuse easier. Scientific discourse created conditions in which some scientists and some citizens could use science to smuggle in assumptions about the necessity of "man's" dominating and controlling nature. Making these assumptions more explicit by linking science and social ethics will make such smuggling operations more difficult. While even explicit links do not guarantee that abuses will not occur, they make abuses less likely. Unacknowledged values have secret, subversive powers. A more reflective science enables the examination of these relationships not only by scientists but by citizens as well, and serves as a check on abuse as well as a means for encouraging the appreciation of the contributions scientific discourse makes to the art of living.

Reflective scientific discourse is explicit about the types of relationships and values that are a part of every research project. If the work exposes the wonder of natural phenomena, that too can be made an explicit part of the project's values. Because the truth of science relies on a social viewpoint and a particular language practice that expresses that truth, the values embedded in communication need to be made explicit. Citizens and scientists increasingly expect that cultural and linguistic viewpoints—that is, values—will be a part of scientific investigation as well as a criterion for awarding public support for such investigation. Science is not only about procedures; it is interwoven with a communication system that brings along with it the commitments to a particular historical, cultural community. Some commitments can support wrongful actions; others can be merely irrelevant. I am not arguing that care should be exercised because data can be misused. Unfortunately, human creativity makes misuse and abuse a potential in all projects. I am arguing that scientists need to be mindful of how their narratives authorize certain types of relationships and obscure others.

Obviously, research that accepts the assumption that females are inferior to males can foster poor relationships. Such research is not value-free and so cannot hide under the cover of absolute objectivity. This sort of research merits critical review to see how ideological forces may have shaped the project and how such judgments of inferiority have been articulated. Terms like "strong," "aggressive," "tender," "nurturant" need scrutiny, and scientists need to be suspicious when their research appears to serve unethical goals and/or ideological purposes.[14] Scientists can make explicit the value tradeoffs that are involved in the formulation of their projects. My point is not that the key issue is that scientists will be tempted to give in to pressure groups. My point is that cultural stereotypes can and do shape projects. Thus, research reports and the evaluation of those reports need to make extra effort to take account of how projects support the development of good relationships between men and women, between nature and humans, between humans and other animals, or between humans and machines. As citizens develop more elaborate understandings of the criteria that can be used in judging the truth, the public will become more adept at talking about these criteria. But such considerations should not abandon methods, scientific rigor, or unpopular positions. Contextualized truth expands the criteria by which projects are judged; it does not make truth meaningless.

I am drawing on feminist science to open up conversations about how science constitutes relationships and thereby contributes to social conventions, habits, and ethical values. I hope to bring a new question to the foreground that includes but goes beyond methodological accuracy, and I hope to raise questions about the constitutive nature of a research project by asking, "How does a scientific project construct relationships?" In this regard, I draw from feminist science to make greater demands on science for epistemological rigor.

WHY DOES SCIENCE NEED TO TAKE ACCOUNT OF GENDER?

A key step in reflective scientific discourse is an explicit examination of how scientific projects articulate the relationship between men and women. This means that scientists and citizens need to review how projects characterize females. At this historical point, failure to ask explicit gender questions threatens to leave patriarchal biases intact and often unnoticed. Gendered images and masculine-feminine metaphors appear not only in the context of discovery (in the questions and in the ways in which research projects are framed), but also in the operationalization of variables, the deployment of descriptions, and the use of metaphors to describe relationships among variables. The gendered representation of objectivity and subjectivity adds to this problem. I am not arguing that gender is the most fundamental category for all times and all places. However, at this time, it is important that gender-specific interrogations occur. Without such interrogations, even the most liberated scientists and/or citizen is likely to overlook androcentric biases.

Thus, citizens and scientists alike need to ask what tales a scientific project tells about females and males, as well as what tales those projects tell about science itself. Scientists who are unaware of gendered imagery can unwittingly employ old feminine-masculine images in their projects. When these old models of gender are pointed out, scientists who unwittingly use them are surprised,

sometimes embarrassed, and more often than not, grateful. The old science supported male domination because it was so much a part of the unexamined fabric
of everyday life. But such male privilege no longer passes without note. If science does not keep up with new social understandings, it can lose its credibility.
To avoid error, scientists need to ask specifically how gender images, metaphors,
and rhetoric appear in their discourse. Both scientists and citizens can work at
bringing scientific discourse up to the level of gender sophistication found in current public conversations about women and men.

Asking gender questions can connect science more fully with social life and
liberate science from an old separatist, puritanical conception of it. In many
ways, this transformation has already occurred because scientific discourse has
problematized the use of "race" as a category of analysis. By reflecting on the
way social ideologies used race, scientists have opened up new possibilities for
understanding ethnic differences and have made it harder for citizens to use scientific discourse for racist purposes. But it is also important to extend such
reflection to other categories of identity and the relationships that they put forward—whether they be constructed around gender, race/ethnicity, humanity, or
age. This critical review is essential for scientific inquiry to become more truthful and less ideological. The interrogation of gender can enable scientists to
review research in terms of the ways in which it constructs relationships between
males and females. Equally important, this interrogation can eliminate masculine
bias in scientific representations.

But attempts to interrogate all social categories present serious political dangers. Neither citizens nor scientists can take on all issues at once. If the argument
is made that science must interrogate all social identities—able-bodiedness, ethnicity, sexuality, class, region, religion, age, gender, body shape, etc.—before it
can proceed, analysis can become impossible, and many may be tempted to alleviate this problem by returning to the old value-neutral talk. At this time, I am
suggesting that scientists and citizens begin such interrogations by asking questions about gender, a move facilitated by the interrogation of "race." But interrogations concerning gender are not the end-all of interrogation. Gender interrogation offers one place from which to begin critical work that can move on to
include other social categories—but not all of them, all the time. The end goal is
an understanding of science as a social-political practice; such an understanding
will then support the integration of scientific discourse into public discussions as
one of the many voices that should shape public life.

CAN FEMINIST SCIENCE SERVE TRUTH AND JUSTICE?

I have discussed how important it is that truth be understood in the context of
social conventions and practices. It is equally important that justice be socially
contextualized. Within the United States, the late twentieth century has empha-

sized two theories of justice—distributive justice and procedural justice.[15] Procedural justice fits with the old science that emphasized scientific methods as procedures for gaining the truth. Methods and procedures produce fairness by following rules. But if the rules are formed by special interests, such as patriarchal or racist practices, justice is harder to achieve for women and ethnic minorities than it is for men and Anglo majorities. In contrast, distributive justice requires that justice occur in the distribution of resources as well as in the procedures followed for such distributions. I am suggesting that employing procedural and distributive justice can inform scientific discourse by encouraging scientists to pay attention to the methods that guide the way in which their projects articulate and thereby normalize relationships. By combining scientific empirical method with reflection at each step in the research process, scientific truth can be responsive both to social meaning and natural phenomena. To achieve this sort of justice requires scientists and citizens to understand themselves as making judgments. Taking responsibility for such judgments authorizes citizens to act on behalf of their values in a reflective, collective way. Before such action occurs, it is important that citizens and scientists discuss the value tradeoffs that compose various projects and the value differences that inform their lives. Such public discussions are vital parts of the process for achieving reflectivity as well as for arriving at collective decisions. In some respects, this focus on reflection is a premodern concept of justice that emphasizes how integrity and wisdom make good judgments possible. This contrasts with modern emphases on rules and their application.

Justice requires paying attention to the articulation of research—how the researcher constitutes things/concepts/ideas/relationships in words and symbols. Rhetoric matters; each linguistic formulation articulates values and so distributes resources. Justice requires becoming aware of the ethics involved in these rhetorical moves, which form scientific projects and readers' apprehensions of them. Metaphors cannot be avoided, but they need to be handled carefully.

The notion of justice I articulated in the first section on law shows that citizens need to take responsibility for making judgments. I am making a similar argument for scientific discourse. It is important for scientists to speak in their own voice to make explicit the value judgments that compose their research projects. Justice requires ongoing commitments to reflections on the truth. However, there is more to my understanding of justice than this simple model of reflection. I am arguing that for public life to work, it needs to support public political conversations about moral issues. Cornell West, bell hooks, Jean Bethke Elshtain, Hannah Arendt, and others have lamented the lack of opportunity for serious public conversations about ethical matters. Iris Young has called for a deliberative democracy that seeks justice by making such opportunities available.[16] Scholars are debating how left socialist democratic theories can incorporate gender, ethnicity, class, and sexuality to compose a new radical democracy.[17]

I have argued that justice requires such conversations, because not only do citizens need to take responsibility for their duties to judge, but they also need to discuss those judgments in order to make them fairly. Such conversations—that is, deliberations that provide a give-and-take base—are necessary for procedures to work and for distributions to be evaluated. But justice is not a matter settled once and for all by the right public policies. Both procedural justice and distributive justice depend on public conversations about values and their application to particular cases. These discussions cannot be abstract but must include deliberations about particular actions in concrete cases because it is only by the scrutiny of both value abstractions and particular actions that citizens can develop an ongoing conversation about justice. Justice depends on scientists and citizens who are willing and able to make judgments to engage in public deliberations about conflicting values, to scrutinize the rhetoric in scientific discourse, and to engage in the process of reforming justice through its applications to particular situations.

Feminist scientists challenge the earlier epistemological positions that claimed objectivity required methodological distance from a subject subordinate to the researcher. My approach argues for a more egalitarian relationship. Furthermore, I argue that the *truth* does not depend on a posture of neutrality and proceduralism. Feminist scientists show that this so-called objective pure posture depends upon a false separation of scientific practices from society. Social neutrality rests on a lie because ungendered persons do not exist and so cannot be found to do gender-neutral science. Citizens are all in some way connected to matters under review, and it is this connection that makes all judgments—including good judgments—possible. Cultural practices, values, and experiences make truth meaningful; they are not merely dirty burdens to be set aside to discover the truth. In fact, great distance from a cultural value system might well render a judgment meaningless. Absolute distance is not only unattainable, but undesirable. So-called neutral positions often distort the truth. Rigorous epistemologies require citizens and scientists to become more aware of their own viewpoints in order to judge more accurately and fairly.

Feminist scientists show citizens how social power works to support scientific discourse. Because modern science has been a powerful discourse within the U.S., science touches many aspects of public life. The distinction between males and females has been articulated as a biological one, allowing science to shape the ways in which citizens think about sex/gender differences. To understand how science itself is shaped by social practices is to understand how patriarchal bias gains entry into scientific discourse and then comes back to us as scientific "knowledge." Reevaluating the relationships between science and society enables citizens to begin the work of eliminating patriarchal bias from scientific research. To support more just relationships among humans, animals, and inanimate beings, feminists are reformulating the representation of Western dichotomies, including nature/culture, objectivity/subjectivity, male/female, human/animal, and masculine/feminine. This work requires linking politics (which is the quest for a good and just society) with science (which is the quest for a clear understanding of social life) and feminism (which is the quest for just gender relationships).

Feminist scientists offer a new understanding of the connection between science and society and so reveal a more complex connection between truth and the politics of everyday life. This connection has become especially important because of the opposition that modernity has created between culture and nature. Enlightenment science relied on distance as a path to objective truth, but at the same time it relied on nature for a moral code to replace the pre-Enlightenment religious code. With the critique of positive science, citizens realize that nature and "her" spokesperson, science, cannot provide such a code. Science is not an innocent activity. Not only paradise is lost but also scientific purity is lost, but this "fall" does not mean that society can construct the world in any way it pleases. Scientific materialism and cultural practices limit such constructions. To keep their commitments to truth, scientists need to be open to critique and reflections that include the development of new methods of inquiry. While scientific studies cannot provide definitive answers to policy questions, they can offer assistance in the struggle for truth. Such truth is necessary for making political decisions better. Certainly, the understanding of truth offered by empirical science needs to be included in policy analyses.

I have argued that feminist scholars need to examine scientific discourse because sex has functioned as a dichotomous variable that constructs male and female difference. While such difference is real, its construction has been based on biased social projections that in turn limit the lives of women and men as well as limit the usefulness of science. Sex distinctions and their accompanying metaphors might be productively considered as a continuum rather than a dichotomy. Sex or gender as an independent variable for predicting behavior falls short of the truth, and its limited use as an independent variable has contributed to the stereotyping of women. Examining even physical differences between males and females often reveals more variation within each sex than between the sexes. Science can correct social misunderstandings so that citizens treat maleness and femaleness as flexible, continuous categories rather than rigid, dichotomous ones. This knowledge can enable citizens to rethink "woman" and "man," restructuring social and political institutions so that they will not use unwarranted stereotypes to confine males or females. Thus, citizens can develop a set of practices that move away from phallocentric human biologies in which "woman" is weak, dependent, and emotional, while "man" is strong, independent, and rational. In connecting truth and justice, I am asking citizens to pay attention to how science constructs relationships between humans and natural "things" and between men and women.[18] I am suggesting that a key part of political work is the conceptualization and articulation of situations. Part of the scientific message is in its discourse—its talk, its rhetoric—which takes place not just in the methods employed, but in every aspect of the process of inquiry. Scientific truth depends on reflections about its social messages as well as its empirical methods.

Feminist science makes way for an understanding of truth that incorporates a variety of paradigms and voices to describe and interact with the world. This understanding of truth emphasizes that scientists seek the truth as citizens who live in a community. In this sense, all scientists are political scientists whose work is creating a better, more just world. Truth depends on reflective, just judgments.

NOTES

1. The terms "context of discovery" and "context of justification" are used by philosophers of science to examine the values that frame scientific projects.

2. For a discussion of this subject, see Eloise A. Buker, "Feminist Social Theory and Hermeneutics: An Empowering Dialectic?" *Social Epistemology* 4 (1990): 23–39.

3. For an analysis of this discourse, see Susan Bordo, *Unbearable Weight: Feminism, Western Culture, and the Body* (Berkeley: University of California Press, 1993).

4. Eric Voegelin offers a broad value-based definition of science that he develops from pre-Enlightenment and post-Enlightenment reflections in *The New Science of Politics: An Introduction* (Chicago: University of Chicago Press, 1952).

5. For a discussion of good/bad science, see Anne Fausto-Sterling, *Myths of Gender: Biological Theories about Women and Men* (New York: Basic Books, 1985) 208–22.

6. Sue V. Rosser, *Re-Engineering Female Friendly Science* (New York: Teachers College Press, 1997), 81–101.

7. Sue Rosser, National Women's Studies Conference, St. Louis, Mo., summer 1997, in response to the question "What counts as the greatest barrier to scientists taking feminist scholarship seriously?" indicated that the primary barrier was discussions of objectivity.

8. I wish to thank Lee Swedberg for helping me think about science as "wonder" and avoid an instrumental view of science.

9. For this insight into science, I thank Michael J. Shapiro, University of Hawaii, lecture, 1978.

10. The medical version of this detachment appears when physicians say, for example, "Tests indicate this medication," rather than, "My interpretation of the test is that you should have this medication." Abandoning the superman image of medical practitioners could have the very positive result of relieving them of the responsibility of *saving* all their patients and reducing expectations that doctors can win over all odds. This false expectation may be a factor in the rise of malpractice suits.

11. For an analysis of the imagery of the cell, which is constructed from a masculine viewpoint, see Bonnie B. Spanier, "Gender and Ideology in Science," *National Women's Studies Association Journal* 3 (1991): 167–98.

12. For example, in Truk, modern harbor authorities insisted that ships use scientific navigation tools, which displaced earlier Polynesian navigation technologies, many of which have now been lost.

13. In a talk given at Denison University, in the spring of 1995, Sandra Harding argued that all sciences are ethnosciences because they arise out of cultural interests, but that they retain universal significance and hence are properly called sciences in cases in which their results hold true across cultural contexts.

14. For an overview of scientific bias in research about gender see Susan A. Basow, *Gender Stereotypes and Roles* (Pacific Grove, Calif.: Brooks/Cole Publishing Co., 1992).

15. For a discussion of procedural justice and distributive justice in terms of feminist theory, see Mary Hawkesworth, *Beyond Oppression: Feminist Theory and Political Strategy* (New York: Continuum, 1990).

16. Iris Marion Young, *Intersecting Voices: Dilemmas of Gender, Political Philosophy, and Policy* (Princeton, N.J. : Princeton University Press, 1997).

17. David Trend, ed. *Radical Democracy: Identity, Citizenship, and the State* (New York: Routledge, 1996).

18. The connection between humans and nature is an important aspect of ecofeminism and cultural critiques of Western science that develop out of cultures, such as the Native Hawaiian culture, which do not construct an opposition between the categories of "human" and "nature" in which humans are expected to dominate nature.

Part III

❖ ❖ ❖

Postmodern Feminism: Ethics and Citizenship

My first encounter with postmodernism was in graduate school in Hawaii, where I engaged in a year-long field study in a community that was working class, multi-ethnic, and rural. This field experience came after my coursework in political science, which had emphasized postmodern analyses. I suspect that the Hawaii Political Science Department was engaged in critical reflections on postmodern theorists before many on the United States mainland because of the ways in which postmodern theory opens up analyses of multicultural aspects of public life by emphasizing the power of symbols in shaping relationships. It is clear in Hawaii that symbols play a key part in shaping political life in the islands. So, I began my fieldwork in rural Hawaii with an interest in symbols and storytelling, which had been nurtured by my teachers, who believed that symbols were important for understanding politics. The area where I lived and studied for over a year included Native Hawaiian homestead land and so was especially influenced by Hawaiian cultural practices. My fieldwork in Hawaii came at the time of the Hawaiian renascence, and so I was able to see how symbols could transform a social-political environment. The influence of Hawaiian cultural values is immediately apparent to anyone who lives in Hawaii.

This is illustrated most clearly in the ways in which Hawaii has preserved Native Hawaiian words in everyday speech practices and in geographic names. While Native Hawaiians compose less than 20 percent of the population, the influence of Hawaiian cultural values is a key part of the culture of Hawaii. This influence has not come about as a result of their majority status, and it does not come about because Hawaiians occupy key roles in large corporations or government.[1] The influence of Hawaiian culture over the lives of those who live in Hawaii today comes about for a complex of reasons, but one feature that stands out is the emphasis on storytelling and symbol. Even tourists are made aware of the importance of storytelling in Hawaii, because a part of that storytelling is communicated through dance, music, and the visual arts. But the political value of storytelling is clear to those who live in Hawaii. Hawaiian cultural values, which are preserved and communicated through stories, offer important ways of building ethical responses to social life. This works especially well in a multiethnic setting because stories enable the exploration of value differences, as different figures in a story can represent different points of view.

Hawaii's multiethnic political culture fits well with postmodern analyses because postmoderns emphasize the importance of symbols, stories, and cosmologies in shaping politics and so explain the power in symbolic representations. Often there is as much power exercised by symbols as there is by large corporations, by landowners, by the military, and by government systems. Hawaii shows that the power of symbols and narratives can work to transform political practices, institutions, and public policy. The influence that the Native Hawaiian culture exercises in Hawaii has increased in power and momentum because Native Hawaiian imagery and narratives shape life in Hawaii. For example, with the Hawaiian renascence, more and more people not only have seen sacred versions of the hula danced but are becoming aware of the dance's cosmological significance. If it ever was, it is no longer the case that the Waikiki hula is taken seriously by people who live in the islands. It serves only as an embarrassing reminder of the ways the islands depend on tourism for economic wealth.

In this situation, postmodernism helped me in three ways. First, it helped me to reframe my understanding of social positions and political identities. In particular, it helped me to abandon an essentialist understanding of ethnicity, culture, and race and to embrace contextual understandings of identities and cultural practices. In this community, as in many in Hawaii, people draw upon a blend of cultural heritages. They may have a Chinese grandmother, a Hawaiian grandfather, an Irish-American mother, and a Japanese father. In different contexts, they bring forward different aspects of their cultural identity so that in one context they may present themselves as Chinese-American and in another, as Hawaiian. Seeing ethnic identities as cultural performances, rather than as essential characteristics, supports political coalitions in a way that essentialized identities often frustrate. Performing multiple ethnic identities does not mean that ethnic tensions disappear, but it does mean that there are a number of persons who bridge such tensions because their own heritage offers a blend of practices, cultural habits, and ethnicities. This postmodern de-essentialized identity has been advocated by some activists in the Hawaiian renascence. In the 1970s a group was formed called the Kaho'oalawe O'hana. The word "o'hana" means family in Hawaiian but it is important to realize that family does not necessarily assume blood ties. Families may be created by rituals that bond persons into familial relationships that operate like Western blood kin. Kaho'oalawe is a small island in the Hawaiian chain that has played an important part in Hawaiian religious practices. The island had several sacred ritual sites; it is an important navigational point for early travel by the Native Hawaiians from Polynesia. So the island was seen as having both sacred and practical significance, even though it had not been recently inhabited by humans. The United States Navy had been using this island as a target for air raid bombing practice, which was resulting in the destruction of the land, the sacred sites, and the archaeological artifacts on the island. This bombing was an affront to Hawaii culture. The Kaho'oalawe O'hana was focused on ending the bombing. At a meeting of the O'hana, a Hawaiian wise elder Emma DeFries (a kahuna) gave all present permission to call her Auntie Emma. She explained that all who practice love, aloha, are Hawaiian in their hearts. In this way, she authorized the participation of a variety of ethnic groups to participate in a political movement, de-essentialized ethic identities, and created a workable coalition.[2] In this community, I could become an Irish-American whose identity included Hawaiian cultural values. This helped me to think about my own identity in ways that did not fix me once and forever within one single ethnicity, but which invited me into a multiethnic community in which I had a part to play. While my Irish-American foreparents offered me a position from which to enter this social world, others did not use my ethnicity to interpret my behavior because this multiethnic context made ethnicity itself a complex and unstable category of analysis. Taking up such a position that includes my Irish-American heritage enabled me in part to drop the privilege of a Euro-American who pretends to be *no one* so as to represent *everyone*. Such a pretense permits Euro-Americans to gain ascendancy over other ethnic groups by referring to their own culture as a neutral position.[3] Postmodern explanations about the multiplicity of identity offered a way of talking about the politics of this experience. It also has helped me to acquire an ethnic identity for myself without being trapped either by the riches of my heritage or by its shortcomings. While I inherit white skin privileges I also inherit white skin ugliness, which has included such events as the enslavement of blacks. This has encouraged me to take some responsibility for addressing previous wrongs by getting involved in politics. Postmodernism can help, then, avoid the celebration of victim status and encourage the contextualization of experiences in historical, cultural traditions that are examined for flaws and virtues. Postmoderns argue that individual citizens change by acting with others politically. Thus, I came to understand that social change in part brought about personal change in the very process of a political act.

Just as practical hands-on experience teaches skills, practical hands-on political work teaches citizens how to re-form themselves as they reform others. Ethnic practices, heritages, and family values serve as beginning points from which to engage in this work but they are not end points.

Secondly, the postmodern understanding helped me develop an epistemology that was both open and closed, which moved me from scientific positivism with its rigid notions of objectivity to interpretive empiricism. Realizing that value-free social science, positivism, is both impossible and undesirable was an important aspect of my ability to do fieldwork effectively, because in the community where I worked and lived people believe that each person has a set of political values. If I had attempted to claim to be a value-free neutral investigator, I would not have been able to work effectively. But this was not merely a pose on my part. I understood my own work as framed by values. This fit between my own self-understanding and the community's shared understandings made my project work better. Community members do not understand themselves as neutral but representing a mix of cultural values and political positions. Neutrality is seen as a pose that dishonestly attempts to gain advantage. But more than this, neutrality is a dangerous pose that encourages persons to see themselves as passionless, unattached, and uncaring. To interact with people in this community I needed a value position that recognized emotions as a part of intellectual life. Postmodern epistemology offered such an understanding.

Third, postmodern thought helped me to focus on symbols and local narratives rather than on larger global narratives like capitalism and marxism, which have constructed social relationships on the basis of economics. In the community where I worked and studied, both marxism and capitalism fail to present convincing narratives because both emphasize global activity and materialism. And that very globalism has created serious problems for this community. Captain Cook and his thirst for global passage brought disease and destruction. Multinational corporations—especially in sugar and pineapple—have sucked the fertility out of the land and raised the salt levels in the ground water. Tourism, with its eye on the global traveler, has pushed many Native Hawaiians and the poor who grew up in Hawaii to the mainland for economic survival even though this means living far away from friends and family.

The rejection of both marxist and capitalist metanarratives, and the recognition of local authority with its complexity of relationships and loyalties were articulated in a comment by Native Hawaiian kahuna Auntie Emma DeFries. She said to a large group of political activists, "If your kahuna tells you that there are seven spirits, there are seven spirits; if your kahuna tells you that there are five spirits, there are five spirits." What that statement meant to me was that everyone did not have to have the same cosmology to work together. An absolute final truth was not a precondition for politics. Ambiguities do not necessarily create social disorder. Differences could be a part of a comm(unity).[4]

The emphasis on the transformative power of symbols and local narratives—not grand universal narratives—as guides for public life is a central feature of postmodernism. The term "talk story" has special significance in Hawaii because it describes the process by which strangers and/or friends listen to each other tell stories that explain life cosmologies, cultural values, personal tensions, and political contradictions.[5] Postmodern thought encourages telling and listening to local stories. What has taken me some time to understand is the way in which this storytelling offers a public genre for discussing moral issues that avoids polarizing issues and thereby reifying partisan positions. But more importantly, postmodern feminism offers a way of seeing our moral codes as articulations of what we take to be the good in our cultural heritage. Stories in this context are not didactic lessons but ways of talking about ethical matters. Rather than offering laws and rules that guide behavior by preventing certain types of actions, stories offer examples for thinking about what might emerge as good choices in particularized concrete social situations. The fact that the story is an example encourages the story listener to apply the narrative situation rather than to obey the moral of the tale. Rules and laws offer carrots and sticks to "discipline and punish" citizens.[6] Narratives offer a moral code that gives a story listener a very different sort of moral inspiration. The freedom of application that stories create encourages citizens to use the story as a guide toward good actions. Arising out of a need to explore the complexities involved in moral decisions rather than a need to control citizens, talk story and telling stories enable citizens to share different understandings of social justice. Stories can give complex views of good and ill that encourage a back and forth dialogue rather than the simple application of good and ill labels. But I am not arguing for an open system in which citizens need no controls. They do. I am suggesting that telling stories offers a way of discussing the ethical values in social practices and serves some important functions not accomplished by conversations that focus on laws and the formation of social regulatory policy. This may be why feminists have been so interested in telling stories. In this part, I will explore postmodern feminist discourse to examine how it illuminates ethics in the practices of everyday social life. To begin with work, I will examine how postmodern feminists construct the connection between ethics and politics.

NOTES

1. Noel Kent, *Hawai'i: Islands under the Influence* (New York: Monthly Review Press, 1983).
2. Observation in Honolulu, 1976, at a Kaho'olawe O'hana meeting. "O'hana" means family and refers to an extended family, including "adopted" children who are designated by such terms as uncles, aunties, sisters, and brothers. The term was used to form a "politi-

cal coalition" in the Hawaiian renascence movement to stop the bombing of Kaho'olawe and preserve the island as a sacred site for Native Hawaiian study and worship. The O'hana was run by traditional Hawaiian values and included a leader and a special advisor to the leader, a wise elder, a Kahuna. Auntie Emma DeFries served in this capacity.

3. For more details on the nature of this field research and what I learned from studying in this community, see Eloise A. Buker, *Politics through a Looking-Glass: Understanding Political Cultures through a Structuralist Interpretation of Narratives* (New York: Greenwood Press, 1987).

4. For a discussion of the problem of unity, see William Corlett, *Community without Unity: A Politics of Derridian Extravagance* (Durham, N.C.: Duke University Press, 1989).

5. Eloise A. Buker, *Politics through a Looking-Glass*, and Introduction to *A Time for Sharing: Women's Stories from the Waianae Coast,* ed. Women's Support Group of the Waianae Coast (Honolulu: University of Hawaii Press, 1982).

6. Michel Foucault, *Discipline and Punish: The Birth of the Prison*, trans. Alan Sheridan (New York: Vintage Books, 1977).

Chapter 8

Critical Feminism: Putting-Off and Putting-On the Postmodern

This part focuses on the intersection between politics and ethics.[1] In Western thought, ethical concerns are often constructed as moral principles accompanied by rules that offer transcendent guides for human behavior. Western understandings of reason assume citizens will be able to recognize and apply moral principles by using their rationality. Thus, rationality and rules can be used to articulate and enforce a moral order.[2] Whether the transcendent base for those rules is dictated by nature, God, or other forces, humans can lead *good* lives by finding and following the universal principles. Although I am not ready to deny the existence of some universal principles, I am less sure that they can be articulated by the particular language and cultural contexts that all citizens inhabit. While I honor quests for the universal good, my project is more modest. I want to examine the moral demands that public life makes on U.S. citizens. While moral demands appear in the laws that regulate and maintain order, the moral demands that take the form of cultural practices are broader. These moral demands compose daily life practices and make life itself meaningful. Sometimes moral codes are ambiguous; sometimes cultural codes offer immoral guides. A careful examination of cultural codes can enable citizens to reflect on the politics of their lives together. In fact, a democratic society relies on its citizens to distinguish the moral from the immoral, the good from the ill.

Because postmodern analysis is useful for examining the power of symbols and because postmodern feminists focus on gender issues, I turn to postmodern feminism to explore how feminists can speak about the politics of symbols in cultural practices. I argue that these cultural practices offer a constitution that guides citizens toward the culturally constructed common good. By making these patterns the focus of my analysis, I want to encourage citizens to reflect on how cultural practices shape gender relationships to see if those received cultural codes create just relationships between men and women. Although postmodern

143

feminists, like other postmodern writers, avoid searching for universal guidelines, they can help citizens critique what is currently set forth as the good. Rejecting the assumption that moral codes will progress, postmodern feminists expect politics and struggle to continue as societies attempt to realize the good and just. Abandoning utopias, they invite citizens to make self-reflective ethical commitments. While many feminists find postmodern feminism intellectually engaging, others fear that it might be politically damaging and thereby set feminist politics back because it eschews universal codes and the moral agency that such codes imply.[3]

I begin by giving an overview of postmodern feminism. Then I discuss four political difficulties that postmodernism presents for feminist politics: (1) its apparent support for a conservative political agenda that protects male privilege; (2) the elitism of its discourse that fails to serve women in their everyday lives; (3) the problem of relativism, which encourages depoliticizing citizens by supporting cynicism; and (4) the problem of agency, which decenters individual citizens as the source of social change. While considering these difficulties, I suggest some of the feminist political practices and policies that postmodernism can support. In the next chapter, I offer a reformulation of the term "politics" by analyzing four sets of metaphors within postmodern feminist conversations—hybrid selves, the body, geography, and language—to show how postmodernism can be used to articulate new understandings of the self, the cosmology of beings, the state, and power. Next, I offer a critique of our two-gendered system by developing a twelve-gender system that challenges the taboo of the two-gendered system and produces a new set of political possibilities. This twelve-gender system demonstrates the deconstructive and reconstructive possibilities for a playful postmodern feminist turn. I close with a discussion of the political gains and losses that are created through such postmodern redefinitions. In chapter 9, I develop a feminist ethic that blends postmodern theory, critical theory, and liberalism. I argue that postmodern feminism supports moral agency by encouraging citizens to see themselves not only as inheritors of a tradition but as its crafters as well. Cultural tradition, so much a part of everyday life, is nearly invisible. Making cultural analysis visible, postmodern feminism supports reflection—reflection that serves as the basis for evaluating cultural practices. I close with reflections on my own struggle to use postmodernism to develop a moral discourse that can realize the goals of feminist politics and gender justice.

HOW DOES POSTMODERN FEMINISM PERFORM POLITICAL WORK?

The term "postmodernism" is used to refer to a philosophical orientation as well as to designate a current historical era. I am using the term as a philosophical orientation that refers to a way of talking about and apprehending a worldview, even though these two definitions share some common points.[4] I will begin with a short discussion of my interpretation of postmodernism, which I develop in order to use postmodern understandings to do political work.

One of the most serious consequences of modern thought has been the separation of ethics from politics—a practice that reduces politics to debating games and consigns ethics to private matters. Ironically, it is the neoconservatives who have brought ethics back into political discourse.[5] Ancient classical Greek definitions of politics describe it as an activity designed to move a community closer to the good and that good was anchored by the belief that humans could discover a universal harmony that would enable them to come out of the cave to transcend their mundane existence. The Hebraic, Christian, and Moslem cultures anchored the universal good in God who enables humans to transcend the illness that composes their worldly lives. However, the Enlightenment brought forth a narrative that problematized these old anchors. Positivism and secular humanism avoided religious commitments and sought transcendent truth with the aid of a transcendent Being. While retaining some of the characteristics of Greek epistemologies that found truth in the harmony of the universe, post-Enlightenment citizens found themselves in a multicultural context so unlike the early Greeks that even a generalized view of a harmonious world was difficult. Even the notion of a common good seemed not so possible, and if collective political action depends on finding a common good, collective action itself becomes difficult. Communities cannot decide what actions they will take by simply following the will of the stronger or even the majority. The question remains how can good decisions be anchored so that the community can find sufficient agreement to act collectively. I will use these four feminist concerns to interrogate postmodernism to see if it can support a productive feminist politics that values women as well as men and that makes collective commitments to action workable. Within my interrogation of postmodern feminism, I will intersperse suggestions about how feminists can use postmodernism to develop new policies for American political life that are designed to realize these goals in everyday practices.

While postmodern feminism places language at the center of its understanding of public life, it would be a mistake to think that postmoderns reduce material life to words, or the world to a text.[6] Although postmoderns do not argue that "language is all there is," they do say that humans use language and speech to organize and share a world and to make relationships among persons and between persons and things intelligible. Language thus composes all analyses because it is a basic ingredient in knowing the world. Language does not change things, but it can change our understandings of them. For example, for most purposes, citizens define my watch as a "decorative instrument used to tell time," but it can become a "bookmark" if I use it as one. Shifting contexts changes relationships and so the definitions of things. In this example, the watch does not change, but understandings of it do. This is not simply a functional definition of a situation but also an illustration of the ways in which use patterns, practices, and situations work together to shape understandings.

Despite postmodernism's aversion to definitions, I will briefly sketch my use of three key terms: poststructuralism, deconstruction, and hermeneutics. Postmodernism is an umbrella term that I use to refer to a philosophical orientation that subscribes to a post-positivist epistemology that rejects universalism in favor of historical cultural contexts, celebrates local narratives in place of such grand narratives as capitalism and marxism, asserts a semiotic theory of language that makes communication a central feature of human understanding, and considers cultural practices primary factors that shape individual choices and public performances. Poststructuralism, which began with social linguistics and semiotics, represents one method or strategy of interpretation within postmodern thought.[7] Poststructuralism grew out of structuralism—an empirical analysis, rooted in a semiotic language theory that examines the structure of symbol, language, and speech.[8] It differs from structuralism by refraining from making an objective empirical claim to discover a deep structure beneath the surface. Poststructuralists argue that interpretations take place at the surface level as witnesses view actors (that is, others in their social environment) perform. Meaning takes place as such witnesses interpret actions or decode them according to a cultural code. Critiquing scientific objectivity, poststructuralists use such methods as genealogies to trace the shifting surface understandings of social phenomena such as mental illness, crime, and sexuality.[9] For example, Foucault shows how those who "acted out in society" were treated in earlier times as persons possessed by the devil and in need of a priest and exorcism, whereas modernity has considered such persons "mentally ill" and in need of medical doctors with their apparatus of surgical operations, drugs, control, and isolation. This creates a set of social medical practices designed to respond to the metaphor of "medical illness," which differs from the earlier metaphor that suggested such persons were possessed by demons, which required a religious set of social practices to correct the problem. Such analyses of social behavior arise out of connecting the naming of actions (for example, calling something mental illness) with the social practices that accompany them (treating the "ill" with medical strategies as opposed to religious ones). Poststructural analyses rely on binary oppositions and their mediations to decode such meanings within symbol systems.

Another example can be found in the work of Claude Lévi-Strauss, who analyzes cultures by using the binary opposition between the raw (natural foods) and the cooked (culturally processed foods); this opposition is mediated by the rotten (a blend of natural processes and culturally designed treatments).[10] His claim is that an objective meaning is not obtained by "discovering" what is there but instead is obtained by "making" an interpretation. In this sense, his anthropological approach avoids the claim that he can discover some deep meaning within another culture but instead constructs a meaning of a performance (such as serving raw and cooked food) by considering the intersection between his or her own cultural practices and those of the society that he observes. Lévi-Strauss's approach suggests that other interpretations remain possible as contexts and concerns shift. Because he is examining genealogies, the male-female binary plays a central role in his analyses. While feminists use this gender binary differently, this binary property of poststructural analysis leads easily to analyses of the opposition between male and female and such in-between characters as the hermaphrodite or the male in drag.[11] For some feminists, this opposition involves a power reversal that displaces masculinity with femininity. Such an analysis leans more toward structuralism than toward poststructuralism, since it depends on a binary power relationship that is asserted as an end point rather than as a series of cultural possibilities. Poststructuralism invites a continuous play between binaries that deconstructs or softens the effects of the binary's operation. In other words, male/female distinctions are held more lightly by poststructuralists than by moderns.

Deconstruction, represented by the work of Jacques Derrida and Gayatri Chakravorty Spivak, contrasts with the genealogical approach developed by Michel Foucault and used by such feminists as Kathy Ferguson, Nancy Fraser, and Shane Phelan. Deconstruction represents a second method of analysis that relies on postmodern thought. Deconstructionists analyze the construction of texts (both written and oral) and argue that part of what is said is contained in how it is said. The term "text" here is used metaphorically and literally to refer to both written documents and other symbol systems like dance, gestures, music, and fine art, all of which communicate through representations that involve writing, speech, and/or other forms of performance. Deconstructing texts does not entail their rejection or destruction. Unfortunately, the popularization of the term "deconstruction" has led some academics to use it interchangeably with the term "destruction." Donna Haraway makes an important point when she argues that one should only deconstruct that which one loves.[12] Deconstruction requires a commitment to that which is deconstructed in order to perform this analysis from the inside. Outsider interpretations that ignore the meaning system under scrutiny are no more useful than are comments by those who can't read a language or text. Non-Spanish speakers are not asked to interpret Spanish texts. Outsiders to a meaning system cannot interpret it effectively because interpretation depends on at least a partial insider position that requires "standing under" some premises, which then makes under-standing possible.

Although hermeneutics has not been given much attention in postmodern discussions, I include it in my discussion of postmodern thought. My focus is on philosophical hermeneutics, represented by such philosophers as Hans-Georg Gadamer, Paul Ricoeur, Zygmunt Bauman, and Stanley Fish, as well as such feminist philosophers as Georgia Warmke and Susan Hekman.[13] Hermeneutics is important to feminist considerations of postmodernism because it advocates variety in the interpretations of texts and thus opens the way for feminist readings of documents, even documents that exclude women. Hermeneutics can also assist feminists in constructing "readings" of situations that compose the text of a life.[14] While poststructuralism and deconstruction offer critical readings of cultural phenomena, hermeneutics stresses that readings take place within tradition.[15] In this sense, hermeneutics can be useful in preserving, honoring, and extending women's traditions. Giving tradition over to patriarchy, or even to male histories, leads to a rejection of women's art, narratives, wisdom, and analyses, even though such works have always been a part of history. Women's contributions to society have been undervalued. More importantly, hermeneutics suggests that textual readings are directed toward attempts to act better in life situations. This activist element is important for feminist politics. Emphasizing hermeneutics and conversation as a transformative political activity can help citizens pay attention to women's contributions.[16]

All three approaches, poststructuralism, deconstruction, and hermeneutics, share a critique of positivist epistemology. All three demonstrate the impossibility of gaining a dis-interested, value-free view of the world, and they claim that all knowledge comes about through a situated position in the world composed by cultural practices. Second-wave feminist scholars share this value-laden understanding of social epistemology as do many social scientists who replace positivist claims with empirical ones.[17] Empiricism offers methods for observations about the world, while postmodern approaches encourage analysts to examine how those observations generate meaningful symbolic relationships. By examining meaning systems, analysts seek to understand the self/other distinction as a mutually constitutive act. Empiricism emphasizes bracketing values in analyses, while postmodernism examines values as part of scientific investigation. Poststructuralism emphasizes using binary oppositions to expose the structure of cultural practices. Genealogies trace the history of those structures. Deconstruction examines the way in which texts, both written and oral, construct values. Hermeneutics emphasizes a reflective process that includes looking back and forth between the external world inhabited by others and the self (whether that be an individual or collective self). This means that the analyst focuses on the construction of meaning while arguing that interpretations never exhaust all possible meanings. All three approaches—poststructuralism, deconstruction, and hermeneutics—are part of an emerging postmodern body of thought.

Because postmodernism and feminism share many concerns and because postmodernism emerges as a central philosophical orientation in the latter part of the twentieth century when feminism has also become prominent in social analysis, it is surprising that feminist analyses are so absent from postmodern texts.[18] In contrast, feminists have read the postmoderns and rely on them to develop a feminist postmodernism even though this effort has proceeded with some difficulties. I will now turn to four problems that threaten to put feminists off of postmodern thought.[19] The first problem is the charge that postmodernism supports a conservative agenda.

IS POSTMODERNISM A FORCE FOR CONSERVATIVES?

First, postmodernism, in general, has been criticized for its politics; both Jacques Derrida and Michel Foucault have been accused of conservatism, and this charge has been extended to postmodern feminists.[20] A conservative political ideology in the United States has often produced antifeminist politics. But the problem in using the terms liberal, left, conservative, goes beyond this difficulty. In developing these three ideological categories—conservative, liberal, left—political scientists were attempting to explain patterns in male political behavior. Furthermore, these explanations focused on cold-war relationships. Current politics, which now includes women, and a post-cold war era makes these categories less useful. In particular, they fail to explain many of the alliances that feminists make. For example, left feminists like Catharine MacKinnon and Andrea Dworkin work with political conservatives on pornography, while radical feminists oppose legal controls on pornography and take up what appears to be a liberal agenda.[21] Feminists like Jean Bethke Elshtain exemplify a conservative viewpoint and yet differ from such conservatives as Camille Paglia or Christina Hoff Sommers.[22] Third-world women, women of color, and other women have criticized the ways in which second-wave feminism repudiates the "traditional."[23] Although the use of these categories always encountered exceptions, the problem that now exists is that they simply no longer work as general explanations. While a suspicious orientation toward tradition is a tenet of modern liberalism, radical feminists and even liberal feminists like Carol Gilligan reclaim feminist traditions. Feminists seeking an ERA, abortion rights, and employment opportunities turn to government for protection and Zillah Eisenstein explains that even liberal feminism has an unavoidable radical side to it.[24] Perhaps the term "conservative" needs to be reformulated in the light of women's politics. If "conservative" includes recognition and respect for women's historical traditions and practices, it might better explain feminist politics. Perhaps these terms are categories that no longer work for the twentieth-century political world.

Another way in which postmodern feminists support a conservative agenda is through their denial of the possibility of revolutionary change. In extreme cases, liberals recognize the need for political revolution, even though they argue that structural changes can come about through constitutional reforms as well as revolution. Marxists believe that revolutions are inevitable. So both marxists and liberals believe that revolution is possible. Because postmoderns argue that real change comes about through changes in the language, a revolutionary would require a totally new language. They are suspicious about claims to total political revolution and they are more likely to explain changes as evolutionary. This political position can lead citizens to believe that they can do very little, and thus it can encourage citizens to retreat from politics and embrace what may pass for sophistication but in reality is merely cynicism.[25] A deconstructive philosophy whose only purpose is a critical view of what is—that is, a deconstruction of the Big Is[26]—can leave citizens with no hope for or vision of anything other than the unsatisfying present. While the Big Is (including a Big Feminist Is) needs to be deconstructed, citizens also need to gain understandings of how they can use such an analysis to work toward political change. The loss of political hope in a democratic society disenfranchises citizens.[27] That loss can actively promote the status quo, because political change depends on active citizens who believe in the possibility of reform.

As a part of their critique of revolutions, postmodern feminists advocate resisting patriarchy rather than dismantling it. But resistance may be a subversive strategy that fails to take advantage of situations in which greater change is possible. If, as Hester Eisenstein argues, feminists have become "femocrats" who now occupy a variety of powerful positions,[28] then greater change may be possible now than ever before. While it may be that total revolution is a mere utopian ideal, at some historical points more rapid change may be possible. If the goal is mere resistance, moments for dramatic change may be missed.

In their critique of revolution the postmoderns also reject the story of human progress. According to the postmoderns, citizens do not move progressively away from a paradise or toward a utopia. Things are just different from before and will be different in the future; life mixes the good and bad.[29] Naming utopian talk dangerous, postmodern feminists argue that such imagery is used merely to manipulate people by using future promises in order to extract present dues. Nevertheless, Drucilla Cornell argues that deconstruction depends on an "unerasable trace of utopianism." This trace of the utopian offers plans for change but does not hold citizens hostage to an idealized future that must be realized. Cornell permits a trace of a utopianism, anticipating a changed value system in which women receive justice, but she stops short of supporting social blueprints designed to produce a new order. Such a blueprint might well produce a nightmare of rigid controls designed to realize THE one true vision. While postmodern feminists avoid utopias, they are willing to offer political goals designed to realize more immediate values. Sidestepping the ends/means debate, postmodern feminists emphasize that politics is an evolving process. It does not necessarily involve reframing, realigning, or shifting paradigms. Thus, formulating goals within a particular context makes sense, while movement toward some utopian vision that leaves such a context behind does not.

While postmodern feminists disparage revolution and so delegitimate radical feminists, the difficulty of revolution is not news to feminists. Because feminists are aware of how stubbornly patriarchal culture holds onto its misogynist practices, they may find comfort in the postmodern view that argues revolutionary change is a counterproductive utopian dream. Consolation can be taken from the fact that no one else has accomplished a revolution either. However, feminists have dreamed of a new society where gender equity exists and so the delegitimation of utopian imagery can also be disturbing. While such imagery has inspired feminist activists to make sacrifices for the future, this imagery can also be used to generate feminist puritanisms that reduce all political negotiations to sell-outs. In 1990s American politics, the religious right has labeled this sort of puritanism "political correctness" because the right can use this term to distract from its own political agenda while discrediting those who oppose them.

This postmodern feminist critique of revolution can make feminists less vulnerable to such puritanisms. A combination of utopian imagery and American puritanism can produce strong antipolitical sentiments in citizens who think that the really "good" and "pure" stay out of politics until the revolution miraculously arrives. Postmodern feminists offer an alternative viewpoint. These feminists encourage citizens to engage in incremental changes that develop out of concrete political goals rather than seeking to change the "entire system" at one time. Postmodern feminism insists that political struggles cannot be settled by the recovery of or the realization of a perfect social order that embodies a universal value system. In a postmodern feminist understanding, there is no natural harmony, even though there are contingent orders established through language, cultural practices, and other governance mechanisms.

From the perspective of postmodern feminists, objects are linguistically constituted, and language is arbitrary. Their emphasis on language as an ordering force fits with the rejection of a natural order of things. Thus, they are suspicious both of ecofeminists, who rely either on goddess imagery or on nature's patterns and laws, and of radical feminists, who rely on feminine goodness to provide "the" good social order. Even support for abortion as a feminist litmus test does not fit well with postmodern feminism. No universal positions can be put forth because all moral codes depend on sociopolitical contexts. Postmodern feminists have been so influential in their critical evaluation of essentialist stances that almost all feminist scholars are wary of essentialism and consider such a charge a serious allegation.

Gayatri Chakravorty Spivak argues that postmodernism makes it difficult for "fundamentalisms and totalitarianisms of various kinds" to function.[30] For feminists, this essentialist critique helps combat even "feminist fundamentalisms,"[31] which threaten to silence critical reflection. Antiessentialism rhetoric avoids the difficulties presented to feminists from a variety of philosophical positions: platonic fundamentalism, which reifies the form of things in Western thought; Christian fundamentalism, which utilizes biblical literalism to defend such practices as slavery, misogyny, and other forms of objectification; biological fundamentalisms, including the current version, sociobiology, which locates all laws in nature, interpreted by a priestly class of physical and natural scientists; marxist fundamentalism, which reduces human activity to material production and reproduction; and cultural fundamentalism, which reduces human activity to cultural relativism by suggesting that humans can and should make the world any way they choose. All threaten to reduce an understanding of human life to a single unitary force.

For postmodern feminists, antiessentialism means that there is no perfect feminist and no perfect feminist victim. Antiessentialism thwarts attempts to establish some women as the most oppressed, by virtue of their race, ethnicity, sexual orientation, class, ablebodiedness, or some combination of these. All persons and groups represent a mix of power/powerlessness and oppressor/oppressed. In a patriarchy, struggles over the one true feminism make it far too easy to defeat feminist agendas. Postmodern feminists discourage puritanical politics and rigid community boundaries, advocating instead, flexible coalitions, formed by the expectation that the differences will make the focused action effective rather than weaken the group's resolve.[32]

While postmodern feminists may appear to support cultural determinism, they do not, but instead, invite readers to deconstruct cultural formulations to show how changes in the symbol system can reorder social understandings. For example, middle-class, white women can reformulate their social positions by changing the way motherhood is symbolized. Or Hawaiian women can emphasize their female identifications in some contexts, while in others they can foreground their connections with indigenous people. Leaky boundaries can open up a new politics. With postmodernism such flexibility makes sense, while within social constructionist or natural-law viewpoints, such moves can be dismissed as merely anomalies. Postmodernism takes citizens beyond the insider/outsider dichotomy to illuminate how all citizens are within some context, which can be understood broadly as the universe or narrowly as a couple.

While postmodern feminism does not inspire politics through the promise of a revolution, it also does not endorse the totalitarianisms that often evolve from the fundamentalist visions that such revolutions offer. Postmodern feminism occupies a critical middle ground. However, it is more consistent with liberalism than with communism, because of its stance on utopias, revolution, and cultural phenomena, even though postmodernism remains ambivalent about capitalism and its ally, modern empiricism.

IS POSTMODERN FEMINISM AN ELITE JARGON-FILLED DISCOURSE?

A second political difficulty with postmodern feminism is the complexity of its discourse, which has discouraged many, even academics, from participating in its conversations. Plain talk is in short supply. This complex discourse does not sit well with feminist commitments to democratic practices that depend on inclusiveness. Part of the problem is that postmodern feminists think that speech and language are the medium through which all other changes can be effected. Thus, political changes require changing speech and language practices. Such changes occur by analyzing language and changing it. This requires not only a change in vocabulary but also a change in the way American citizens understand language. Rather than employing a referential theory of language, which argues that language is a neutral tool that points to things, postmoderns use a semiotic theory of language, which explains how words constitute the world and thereby name and order it. Words and sentences order things.[33] But even without the advantage of postmodern thought, second-wave feminists were aware of this aspect of the politics of language. Obvious examples come easily to mind. Second-wavers pointed out that the term "girl" has political import when it is used to refer to adult females. The second-wave transformed the use of masculine pronouns to represent all persons as well as the so-called generic use of the term "man." But postmodern feminists take this argument even further by explaining that all words involve political action. Words constitute persons and phenomena, and this constitution gives such persons and things meaning by incorporating them into a cultural-political value system.

To create a new politics, therefore, requires a new set of words. However, the more new words deviate from the established order, the more difficult it is for citizens to understand what is being said. At some point, the most radical new politics would be unintelligible to almost everyone and so totally ineffective. Thus, postmodern feminism creates tension between its desire to engender a new order by building a new discourse and the necessity of communicating to a wide number of people. Such communication depends on the use of present discourse, a discourse that often devalues women. So postmodern feminists use new and fresh discourse to articulate new ideas. But it is also the case that postmodern academic feminists create power for themselves by generating a new and complex set of terms. Frequently, being the newer younger folks on the block, they gain status from excluding more established scholars, and they benefit from the modern ideology that assumes that newer and harder is better. In this sense from a modern viewpoint, postmodernism can be seen as better on two accounts. First, it cherishes more complex, difficult articulations and so is harder to understand. Second, it mimics the so-called "hard" sciences by using a third person, distant voice, even though scholars like Foucault and Derrida claim that such "scientific" objectivity is a political move rather than an epistemological choice.

Nevertheless, it is clear that the degree to which postmodern feminists adopt the already-in-place common discourse is the degree to which they abandon change. Postmodern feminists explain how the terms of the conversation are political and show that to give way to another's discourse, whether it be legal, medical, religious, empirical, marxist, or whatever, is already to have conceded much of the argument. Hence, postmodern feminists want to contend over definitions[34] and to contest verbal characterizations—even their own. Definitions are not prepolitical struggles. Terms and their definitions compose a discourse, and discourses establish political authorities, grammars, rules, behavioral norms, and practices. Those practices rule citizens, and gender plays an important role in those practices. Citizens learn how to be men and women by paying attention to speech patterns, voice pitch, and other behaviors that are prescribed to distinguish men from women. Discourses inscribe gender and are inscribed by gender. One small example can illuminate how these such everyday practices are gendered. Medical discourse often takes for granted a masculinized authority figure who doctors and a feminized caretaker who nurses. Thus, women, as well as men, are defined, confined, empowered, and normalized. Women are not only discouraged from pursuing degrees as physicians, but all women are encouraged to see themselves as persons who "nurse" others. To fail to contest such characterizations is to leave patriarchal language in place.

While language and speech are important areas in which politics takes place, language is not all there is; language is only one area of politics. So, postmodern feminists need not deny the importance of other types of analyses, including those that examine the distribution of material resources and the exploitation of women and people of color through the manipulations possible by large-scale capitalism. The postmodern argument is that all speech *is* political action and that language is both a vehicle for communication and a medium for establishing political gains. Their argument is not that language is all there is to social power. Postmoderns believe that if some symbolic political gains are realized, others will be lost, obliterated, forgotten, forced underground, silenced, or killed. A contest over words is a political contest with consequences.[35] Once this premise is understood, its struggles become clear. Postmodern feminists endeavor to be aware of their own desire to communicate, while being clear about their own will to power, which includes the violence that their speech will do as it silences other discourses—other ways of talking, other ways of being. Such clarity is not always pleasant.

DOES POSTMODERN FEMINISM DEFER ACTION AND SUPPORT RELATIVISM?

The third difficulty that puts feminists off of postmodernism is their fear that postmodernism inhibits political action. Unlike the marxists, who seek change in the transformation of work conditions; and unlike Freudians, who find change in altered attitudes; and unlike empiricists, who find change in external behavior; postmodern feminists seek change through alterations in symbol systems. Rejecting notions of a common, universal good, they anticipate that change will produce only contingent, temporary goods that do not reach beyond their cultural historical contexts. By problematizing absolute knowledge claims, postmodern feminists remove the Enlightenment hope that reason will lead all citizens to act on behalf of the good. They explain that both reason and empirical certainties—facts—are products of a particular culture's ideology and do not come about by "discovering" a compelling universal truth. Feminists are concerned that citizens may be unwilling to act without such certainty. Thus, tenuous knowledge claims may paralyze the citizenry.

But postmodern feminists do act decisively. What Haraway's *Primate Visions* demonstrates to her readers is that she can write 383 pages of very convincing prose while holding to her position as a so-called relativist.[36] Postmodernism has not paralyzed her. Nor has it depoliticized her by preventing her from making choices or being reflective about those choices. The world is so arranged that cit-

izens can and must act because they are intricately woven into the social political fabric of life. Citizens cannot choose to withdraw from politics; they can only
choose to become inactive in it. But even inaction constitutes a political decision
with consequences. It is only when citizens require that universal reason rule
over them and that certainty serve as the foundation for politics that contextualized truth becomes paralyzing. Those who charge postmodernism with relativism
may be hoping that *Reason* can rescue them from uncertainty and provide them
with clear, unambiguous paths toward the good and just society. Such certainty
would avoid politics, technicalize problems, and remove citizens from social
struggles and negotiations. However, it would provide citizens with one aspect
of the liberal dream—a world that maximizes private life and relieves citizens
from public responsibility. But such relief would be the end of public life, of
community, and of societies. By contextualizing truth, citizens can remind themselves that communities and coalitions must continually figure out what to do by
struggling to understand situations; citizens cannot simply turn themselves over
to *Reason*. Putting off politics is not possible. Politics is in what citizens do here
and now, and in what citizens do *not* do here and now. In this sense, absolute relativism is impossible, for deferring action articulates a position on the truth of a
political situation.

Jane Flax takes a somewhat different approach toward the problem of relativism by explaining that it represents a shift from a search for the truth to a
search for the "art of conversation or persuasive speech."[37] Some might think
that the art of conversation is then based on an epistemological relativism in
which the best debater wins. But this is not what Flax means by persuasion. If
conversation is actually conversing back and forth, then persuasion is not a
process by which one person convinces another to their already formed point of
view. Persuasion is the process by which all parties to a conversation reformulate
their positions through dialogue. This means that arriving at the truth requires
constructing meanings with others. Meanings are created through negotiation.
Hence, truth is a negotiated concept; it comes into being through a process of
communication and it is linguistically dependent. It is made—not owned and not
discovered. If truth is understood as a negotiated concept, it depends on free and
ongoing conversations among citizens who together produce meaningful truths.
This view of truth emphasizes how citizens depend on each other to come to the
truth and is more consistent with a democratic political process than with an aris-
tocratic one. While this notion of a negotiated truth fits traditional liberal views
of truth as well as postmodern ones, the postmodern understanding of agency is
more problematic for liberal politics.

Postmoderns argue that individuals act out of cultural patterns and belief systems as much as they do out of some individually determined behavior. This
means that cultural practices shape decisions that individuals make within that
culture. Citizens do not so much act on their own as they act out of patterns articulated by their received culture. Cultures rather than individuals guide actions.

The problem with this formulation is that it locates everyday decisions with an unspecified group, the culture, rather than with particular individuals involved in the actions, and it makes the connection between particular types of individuals and actions more contingent. If the concept of "woman" is a cultural construct shaped by group actions, it can be reshaped by group actions. On the one hand, this has liberatory promise because women are not stuck with a contemporary derogatory view of women. On the other, it problematizes the connections between "woman" and a set of actions or social obligations. For postmodern feminists this creates two difficulties. If groups rather than individuals shape everyday politics, then it is harder to show how individual feminists can act in ways that make a difference. This can create the belief that feminists cannot really do much, and so they might as well not try. Second, if "woman" is a cultural construct that depends on cultural performances rather than on fixed categories, the category "woman" is destabilized. The question of who is a woman is much more difficult to answer. The question is, "Can feminism continue to flourish without a stable, even essentialist, definition of 'woman'?" By problematizing such categories, postmodern feminists decenter subjects and reframe identities as performances rather than as states of being. Moving from understanding "woman" as a cultural construct to understanding "woman" as a performance opens up new possibilities for postmoderns by emphasizing that being a "woman" involves choices about actions rather than having a fixed set of bodily configurations. "Woman" involves a set of actions, performances, that cannot be reduced to some social, biological features of persons. Being a "woman" depends on a regular commitment to a type of performance.

DOES POSTMODERN FEMINISM DECENTER SUBJECTS AND MAKE WOMEN DISAPPEAR?

Decentering the subject raises two key political questions: Are cultural forces so strong that individual motivations, intentions,[38] and responsibilities are immaterial? Who is a woman? While many may be tempted to use postmodern feminism to hide behind the culture and to say, "The culture made me do it," postmodern feminists hold citizens responsible for their actions, even though their culture scripts those actions. Responsible citizenship requires the scrutiny of cultural patterns and the rejection of harmful cultural patterns. In this sense, a postmodern feminist's understanding of responsibility focuses not only on individual actions but on cultural patterns as well. In this regard postmodernism emphasizes how citizens perform or enact ethical values. So a postmodern understanding of who counts as a "woman" focuses on the quality of womanhood as a performance. The issue of who counts as a woman is bound up with the issue of how cultures shape identities and how individuals choose to play our/their identities. Cultures give citizens a laundry list of types of identities or "subject positions" that they can inhabit—things they can "be." The act of citizenship is choosing how to perform these subject scripts.

Beginning with the de-emphasis of the author as author(ity) over the text, postmoderns emphasize how cultural norms shape action. By explaining that actions begin outside individuals, postmodern feminists decenter actors, or subjects. Such decentering shows how modernity constructed a story about an inner, secret self that commanded the actions of a citizen. Deconstructing this tale of an inner, secret self reveals how cultural forces shape citizen action and, moreover, delegitimates the old tale of how personality traits make persons act in particular ways. Even though postmodern feminists accept that some aspects of individuals are unique, they argue that such uniqueness is overrated in an individualized Grand Narrative that fails to note how social forces form identities, intentions, desires, motivations, and actions. In another time, another place, a person would "be" something else. Politically, this has a mutliplicity of implications. One example is that it suggests that social change may not result from removing so-called bad persons from office and replacing them with so-called good persons. Change is achieved by restructuring an office and the cultural norms that shape it. This position lies somewhere between the socialist desire to restructure government institutions and the liberal hope that finding the right person will do the job. The postmodern approach avoids demonizing or sanctifying individuals and undercuts a simplistic politics that seeks change by "throwing the bums out." Furthermore, the emphasis on culture and symbol can be useful in promoting democratic practices, since almost all citizens have some access to symbols. While some have greater skills in poetry, news reporting, medical discourse, or legal discourse, all citizens have some access to symbol use. Although some have greater access than others, it is less costly to use a symbol than it is to run for office or hire an attorney. Thus, political change can begin with any part of the system—the bottom, top, or sides.[39] All citizens can employ symbols to begin changes within the contexts of their own social groups and spheres of influence. In a rapid-paced communication system, that sphere of influence can spread quickly and so create a broad-based change.

On the other hand, Chris Weedon argues that although the time for the deconstruction of the male subject may be at hand, the time for decentering the female subject may not be. Weedon argues that feminists need to emphasize a different aspect of postmodernism from that emphasized by men to use postmodernism for feminist political projects.[40] What Weedon does not say is that it may not be possible to decenter the female subject because she has not yet been fully centered.[41] Gayatri Chakravorty Spivak makes a similar point:

> You cannot *decide* to *be* decentered and inaugurate a politically correct deconstructive politics. What deconstruction looks at is the limits of this centering, and points at the fact that these boundaries of the centering of the subject are indeterminate and that the subject (being always centered) is obliged to describe them as determinate.

Politically, all this does is not allow for fundamentalisms and totalitarianisms of various kinds, however seemingly benevolent.[42]

She goes on to say that if deconstruction were used as a foundation for politics, it would be either "wishy-washy pluralism" or hedonism.[43] From her viewpoint, citizens cannot turn to postmodernism to gain a viable politics.

Nevertheless, deconstruction has offered an important strategy for American feminists engaged in undoing racism, heterosexism, and sexism, because it shows that an important site for that struggle is linguistic practices—stories, films, philosophies, news accounts, social theories, research reports, and conversations. Deconstruction enables feminist academics to understand themselves simultaneously as activists engaged in politics, scholars engaged in analysis, and the subjects of their own self-critical reflections. To the degree that feminist academics are able to engage in all three of these activities, they find themselves able to go beyond wishy-washy pluralism and self-centered hedonism. More importantly, postmodern feminism encourages academics to give up on the devious politics produced by the pose of epistemological neutrality.

Susan Hekman and Judith Butler give a different turn to the problem of the decentered self.[44] Butler argues, "The deconstruction of identity is not the deconstruction of politics; rather, it establishes as political the very terms through which identity is articulated."[45] Butler wants her reader to understand that identities can be constructed in and through coalition politics. In her analysis, *fixed* identities inhibit politics. She believes that citizens acquire identities through actions: "My argument is that there need not be a 'doer behind the deed,' but that the 'doer' is variably constructed in and through the deed."[46] Postmodernism does not eliminate subjects and agency, but rather makes way for citizens to evolve into a variety of subjects. But it is important to note that this evolution is not a return to the old, liberal romantic view that citizens are "self-made men," or even "self-made women." The subject is not solely the product of her or his own doing but is a part of the collective action of a community—identity, subjecthood, and being emerge through action. A different sort of action constitutes a different sort of subject.

What is politically important about such evolving subjects, such multiple selves, is the way in which they free persons from cultural definitions that turn them into mere representations of categories. White feminist Nancy Hartsock is not merely a white feminist; Patricia Hill Collins is not merely a black feminist. Both represent class, sexual, and regional viewpoints among other things not yet identified—things yet unsaid by anyone. In Butler's analysis, *fixed* identities—that is those established as *essential* characteristics of persons—unnecessarily limit political processes. bell hooks argues that this emphasis on the cultural production of identities helps African-Americans to avoid essentialism in their construction of black identity and to "affirm multiple black identities, varied black experience."[47] Adrienne Rich's definition of lesbianism as a continuum evokes a similar politics and encourages coalitions between heterosexual women and lesbians. Are both heterosexual and lesbian identities changed when citizens do politics together? Is such change a fear or a hope? The decentered subject offers new opportunities for a more diverse community because it can resist various dominations, including the domination of Western individualism.[48]

Hence, postmodern feminists emphasize the contingent dimensions of the self. Such categories as male, female, black, middle class, marxist, Irish, teacher, and attorney are social constructs of a particular historical culture. They are not things that citizens are by nature. Citizens can be labeled with such categories because they are among the things that one can choose to be within a particular context. Labeling cannot be avoided, for speaking itself requires the use of some "name," some label. But the understanding of how such names and labels function can be changed in ways that create more flexibility. However, such flexibility does not mean that all citizens can put-on any category. White citizens have a hard time choosing to present themselves as black, even though white and black are products of a culture that could reconstruct itself in other terms as Anglos and African-Americans. Even this moderate reconstruction changes the categories. While I may fit into the white category, my Irish-American heritage excludes me from the Anglo one. While some blacks from India might fit into the black category, referring to them as African-American would be inappropriate. Some identities have historically disappeared, and it is likely that those very identities that citizens have chosen to put-on today will someday be gone. Even in the present, different locations reform identities. For example, as I moved from the United States to China, my identity shifted from a middle-class white person to a white foreigner. When I moved to Hawaii, I became a "haole wahine" (white woman), even as I reconstructed my own heritage as an Irish-American woman. But I also became a political scientist, who often saw herself as some gender hybrid—composed by a masculinized discipline and a feminized life history.

A new story of the self emerges as postmodern feminists emphasize cultural practices. But this new story is not a retelling of the old liberal narrative that "you can be anything you want to be." In times of despair, this dream of an open system in which anyone can be anything they want can be appealing. But this super-culture dream of the "made man" or "made woman" regularly falls prey to two problems. First, it lends credence to the story of blaming the victim—if you don't succeed, it is "your" fault.[49] Second, it encourages citizens to think that they can just make themselves and others over so they will fit in. If citizens can make themselves into "anything," they can also make over others? There is political efficacy in believing that citizens can make the culture anew; there is frustration in acknowledging that citizens share in the blame for its present inadequacies. Postmodern feminists offer contingent subject positions, but this does not mean that citizens can be anything they want. Their positions are fixed not only by their own choices and self-understandings but also by cultural practices that locate individuals in particular ways. A woman exists not only because "she" chooses to act like a woman but also because there is a history in which others have chosen to treat "her" as a woman. For the category "woman" the social ritual that characterizes an individual as a woman often begins at birth. For other categories it may begin at another point.

For postmodern feminist politics "woman" is a contingent category. "Woman" will continue to evolve, shift, and change as political life changes. Because so much of American feminist politics has been built on coming together as women, problematizing the term "woman" creates difficulties. Without the central organizing symbol "woman," the women's movement can no longer rely on a common identity to recruit loyal supporters. Traffic between the categories "male" and "female" emerges. But this traffic can play into the hands of liberals who want citizens to be happy just being persons, de facto "men." Destabilizing "woman" challenges the privileged status of women in the women's movement, for if men can be women, they can also be feminist leaders. Women's space may no longer make sense because woman is a cultural performance. Can "men" enter women's space if they are willing to perform as women for the day, for an hour, for a week, for a few years? Furthermore, if women can be men, they can avoid oppression by simply crossing over. Can American feminism work without a biological definition of "woman?" Many are not sure that it can; even Spivak argues for strategic essentialism when politically necessary.

By problematizing "woman," postmodern feminists appear to move citizens toward what might be called a postfeminist era at the very moment when feminism has begun to challenge patriarchy. Certainly, affirmative action looks quite different if the categories of ethnicity and sex are so problematized. The neoconservative agenda to replace women's issues with so-called family values may be aided by the deconstruction of "woman." On the other hand, deconstructing "woman" can free feminist politics from reducing woman to a pure victim, to a pedestaled queen-mother, or to an incomplete man.

HOW DOES POSTMODERNISM PUT-OFF FEMINISTS?

While each of these dimensions of postmodernism presents barriers to feminist politics, each also promises to liberate feminism from some of the limitations created by Western patriarchy. First, while postmodernism can be used to support a conservative agenda, that agenda is not necessarily antifeminist in that it can be used to affirm women's traditions. Although postmodernism gives up the language of revolutionary change, it also gives up the domination that often accompanies such revolutionary talk. Second, although postmodern feminists use a difficult discourse, they also introduce new ways of thinking and talking about American politics that encourage citizens to analyze symbols, language, and popular culture. Thus, postmodern feminism can enable citizens to examine the constitution of their daily lives, which regulates and rules citizens in ways that have gone unnoticed under empirical, liberal, or even marxist frameworks. Postmodernism supports a broad-based feminist politics that encourages work at the level of daily life.[50] Third, postmodern feminists emphasize how cultures shape individual actions and limit understandings of the truth to cultural and historical situations. However, such limits do not mean that actions are forever deferred until cultures change. Politics involves deciding both when to act and when to refrain from action. Similarly, the lack of certainty and/or access to universal truth cannot keep citizens from political action, for even their failure to act shapes political life. Fourth, the decentering of the subject opens up space to rethink the categories of male/female as well as gender and so encourages the creation of a new politics that takes better account of the ways in which cultural patterns shape identities and choices. These four dimensions of postmodernism promise to offer feminism a new politics. The next chapter utilizes the images and metaphors from postmodern feminism to articulate dimensions of that new politics.

NOTES

1. For comments on an earlier draft, I wish to thank Robert Cahill, Henry S. Kariel, Laurel Richardson, Jane A. Rinehart, Tom Rukavina, and the Postmodern Faculty Feminist Seminar at Ohio State University, 1987–88.

2. For discussion of morality as rule-guided activity in Western thought, see Zygmunt Bauman, *Life in Fragments: Essays in Postmodern Morality* (Cambridge, Mass.: Blackwell, 1995), 257–65.

3. Diane Bell and Renate Klein, eds. *Radically Speaking: Feminism Reclaimed* (North Melbourne, Australia: Spinifex, 1996); and Linda J. Nicholson, ed., *Feminism/Postmodernism* (New York: Routledge, 1990).

4. For discussion of postmodernism, see Fredric Jameson, *Postmodernism, or, The Cultural Logic of Late Capitalism* (Durham, N.C.: Duke University Press, 1991).

5. George Lakoff, *Moral Politics: What Conservatives Know That Liberals Don't* (Chicago: University of Chicago Press, 1996).

6. For a review of the benefits of poststructuralism for feminist analyses, especially in regard to the role of language, discourse, agency, and deconstruction, see Joan W. Scott, "Deconstructing Equality-versus-Difference: Or, the Uses of Poststructuralist Theory for Feminism," *Feminist Studies* 14 (1988): 33–50; and Judith Butler, Joan W. Scott, eds. *Feminists Theorize the Political* (New York: Routledge, 1992).

7. I refer to poststructuralism as a more narrowly focused field within postmodernism. Poststructuralism emphasizes semiotics and develops from structuralist linguistics, as is manifest, for example, in the work of Roland Barthes. For a feminist analysis of poststructuralism, see Chris Weedon, *Feminist Practice and Poststructuralist Theory* (New York: Blackwell, 1987).

8. For a more detailed description, see Robert E. Scholes, *Semiotics and Interpretation* (New Haven, Conn.: Yale University Press, 1982).

9. Michel Foucault demonstrates this analysis in *Madness and Civilization: A History of Insanity in the Age of Reason*, trans. Richard Howard (New York: Pantheon Books,

1965); *The History of Sexuality*, Vol. I, trans. Robert Hurley (New York: Vintage Books, 1985); *The Use of Pleasure*, Vol. II, trans. Robert Hurley (New York: Pantheon Books, 1985); *The Care of the Self*, Vol. III, trans. Robert Hurley (New York: Vintage Books, 1986); and *The Order of Things: An Archaeology of the Human Sciences*, trans. A. M. Sheridan Smith (New York: Pantheon Books, 1970). Kathy E. Ferguson uses a genealogical feminist analysis in *The Man Question: Visions of Subjectivity in Feminist Theory* (Berkeley: University of California Press, 1993).

10. Claude Lévi-Strauss, *The Raw and the Cooked*, trans. John and Doreen Weightman (New York: Harper & Row, 1969).

11. The male in drag is employed by Judith Butler in *Gender Trouble: Feminism and the Subversion of Identity* (New York: Routledge, 1990).

12. Donna Haraway's presentation at Cultural Studies Conference at the University of Illinois, 1990.

13. Georg Wilhelm Friedrich Hegel's emphasis on the subject, Edmund Husserl's interest in phenomenology, and Martin Heidegger's focus on language all play roles in constructing philosophical hermeneutics. For a discussion of the connection between hermeneutics and postmodernity, see Gary Brendt Madison, *The Hermeneutics of Postmodernity: Figures and Themes* (Bloomington: Indiana University Press, 1988), and John D. Caputo, *Radical Hermeneutics: Repetition, Deconstruction, and the Hermeneutic Project* (Bloomington: Indiana University Press, 1987).

14. For a more direct discussion of the uses of hermeneutics, see Eloise A. Buker, "Feminist Social Theory and Hermeneutics: An Empowering Dialectic?" *Social Epistemology* 4 (1990): 23–39, and *Politics through a Looking-Glass: Understanding Political Cultures through a Structuralist Interpretation of Narratives* (New York: Greenwood Press, 1987).

15. For an analysis of the connection between hermeneutics and politics, see Richard J. Bernstein, *The New Constellation: The Ethical-Political Horizons of Modernity/Postmodernity* (Cambridge, Mass.: MIT Press, 1991).

16. For an argument to support this point, see Jane A. Rinehart, "Feminist Theorizing as a Conversation: The Connections between Thinking, Teaching, and Political Action," *Women & Politics* 19 (1998): 59–89.

17. For summaries of this approach in the social sciences, see Richard J. Bernstein, *Beyond Objectivism and Relativism: Science, Hermeneutics, and Praxis* (Philadelphia: University of Pennsylvania Press, 1983); and for feminism, see Sandra Harding, *The Science Question in Feminism* (Ithaca, N.Y.: Cornell University Press, 1986), and *Whose Science? Whose Knowledge?: Thinking from Women's Lives* (Ithaca, N.Y.: Cornell University Press, 1991). In addition, the work of Jürgen Habermas and Richard Rorty articulate the distinction between empiricism and positivism.

18. For examples, see the work of Michel Foucault, Jacques Derrida, Richard Rorty, Fredric Jameson, Hans-Georg Gadamer. While a few occasionally mention women, the mention of women and feminist theory is rare. With the recognition of the work of Judith Butler in the mid-1990s, feminism has begun to appear with greater regularity in collections of postmodern thought.

19. For an earlier version of this analysis, see Eloise Buker, "Rhetoric in Postmodern Feminism: Put-Offs, Put-Ons and Political Plays," in *The Interpretive Turn: Philosophy, Science, Culture*, eds. David Hiley, James Bohman, Richard Schusterman (Ithaca, N.Y.: Cornell University Press, 1991), 218–44.

20. Jürgen Habermas, "Modernity—An Incomplete Project," originally delivered as a lecture in Frankfurt, September 1980, when Habermas was awarded the Theodor W. Adorno prize, trans. Seyla Ben-Habib, reprinted in *Interpretive Social Science: A Second Look*, ed. Paul Rabinow and William M. Sullivan (Berkeley: University of California Press, 1987), 141–56, especially, 156. For feminist critical commentary on postmodernism, see Nicholson, ed., *Feminism/Postmodernism* and Bell and Klein, eds. *Radically Speaking*.

21. Clinton Rossiter makes the argument that the left/right ideologies are better understood in reference to a circle rather than a line because the left and the right are often together as they position themselves in opposition to a middle liberal position. Thus, left and right are not polar opposites, *Conservatism in America* (Cambridge, Mass.: Harvard University Press, 1982).

22. Jean Bethke Elshtain, *Public Man, Private Woman: Women in Social and Political Thought* (Princeton, N.J.: Princeton University Press, 1981); Camille Paglia, *Sex, Art, and American Culture: Essays* (New York: Vintage Books, 1992); and Christina Hoff Sommers, *Who Stole Feminism? How Women Have Betrayed Women* (New York: Simon & Schuster, 1994).

23. Penny A. Weiss and Marilyn Friedman, eds., *Feminism and Community* (Philadelphia: Temple University Press, 1995), see section 1 "Women in Traditional Communities," with articles by Lila Abu-Lughod, Del Martin, Patricia J. Williams, Emily Honig, and Kate Rushin, 21–81.

24. Zillah R. Eisenstein, *The Radical Future of Liberal Feminism* (New York: Longman, 1981).

25. For an analysis of this, see Henry S. Kariel, *The Desperate Politics of Postmodernism* (Amherst: University of Massachusetts Press, 1989).

26. The phrase the "Big Is" is from Robert S. Cahill, who uses it to point out the political significance of taking our present ways of doing things and our present situations as the only way things could ever be. Lectures in Honolulu, Hawaii, University of Hawaii, 1977–80, and discussions in Spokane, Washington, 1984–90.

27. Cornell West, *Race Matters* (Boston: Beacon Press, 1993).

28. Hester Eisenstein, *Gender Shock: Practicing Feminism on Two Continents* (Boston: Beacon Press, 1991).

29. Drucilla Cornell, *Beyond Accommodation: Ethical Feminism, Deconstruction, and the Law* (New York: Routledge, 1991), 107.

30. Gayatri Chakravorty Spivak, *The Post-Colonial Critic: Interviews, Strategies, Dialogues*, ed. Sarah Harasym (New York: Routledge, 1990), 104.

31. I want to thank Reba Keele for this phrase, conversation at The University of Utah, 1993.

32. For a discussion of the issue of community and difference, see William Corlett, *Community without Unity: A Politics of Derridian Extravagance* (Durham, N.C.: Duke University Press, 1989).

33. For an argument about the way in which language and culture shape social order, see Foucault, *The Order of Things*.

34. For an argument about the importance of contesting definitions as a central political issue, see William E. Connolly, "The Politics of Discourse," in *Language and Politics*, ed. Michael J. Shapiro (New York: New York University Press, 1984), 139–67.

35. For commentaries on the violence of language, see Jacques Derrida, "Violence and Metaphysics: An Essay on the Thought of Emmanuel Levinas," and "The Theater of Cru-

elty and the Closure of Representation," *Writing and Difference*, trans. Alan Bass (Chicago: The University of Chicago Press, 1978), 79–153, 232–50. For a feminist examination of the violence of language, see Dale Spender, *Man Made Language*, 2nd ed. (Boston: Routledge & Kegan Paul, 1985).

36. Donna Haraway, *Primate Visions: Gender, Race, and Nature in the World of Modern Science* (New York: Routledge, 1989).

37. Jane Flax, *Thinking Fragments: Psychoanalysis, Feminism, and Postmodernism in the Contemporary West* (Berkeley: University of California Press, 1990), 32.

38. Bernstein in *The New Constellation*, 230–58, gives a brief explanation of how postmodernists like Richard Rorty avoid explaining behavior in terms of an actor's intentions.

39. Foucault argues that change comes from the bottom because cultural practices create change, *The History of Sexuality*, 92–102.

40. Weedon, *Feminist Practice and Poststructuralist Theory*, 173.

41. For this critical comment, I thank Mary Jo Bona, Gonzaga University, 1992.

42. Spivak, *The Post-Colonial Critic*, 104.

43. Spivak, *The Post-Colonial Critic*, 104.

44. Susan Hekman, in "Reconstituting the Subject: Feminism, Modernism and Postmodernism," paper delivered at the American Political Science Association Meeting, Atlanta, 1989, 7, moves feminists toward the postmodern position by arguing that postmoderns do not simply replace the subject with the culturally determined "dupe." She explains that the postmodern position challenges "the subject-centeredness of modernist epistemology." Butler argues in *Gender Trouble* that identity is formed by political action.

45. Butler, *Gender Trouble*, 148.

46. Butler, *Gender Trouble*, 142.

47. bell hooks, *Yearning: Race, Gender, and Cultural Politics* (Boston: South End Press, 1990), 28.

48. hooks, *Yearning*, 31.

49. William Ryan, *Blaming the Victim* (New York: Vintage Books, 1976).

50. While Bettina Aptheker is not a postmodern feminist, her work illustrates the key connection between feminism and daily life, *Tapestries of Life: Women's Work, Women's Consciousness, and the Meaning of Daily Experience* (Amherst: University of Massachusetts Press, 1989); and the work of Anndee Hochman provides a further illustration, *Everyday Acts & Small Subversions: Women Reinventing Family, Community, and Home* (Portland, Oreg.: Eighth Mountain Press, 1994).

Chapter 9

Gender-Sex Plays: A Metaphorical Reformation of Public Policies

Because postmodernism works by focusing on how language constitutes relationships, postmodern feminists often turn to rhetoric to reframe social relationships. While the most problematic move for feminist politics has been the deconstruction of "woman," postmodern feminists have also problematized other key terms in feminist discourse including sex, gender, masculinity, femininity, race, subject, experience, politics, materialism, body, and others. Postmodern feminists use rhetoric to encourage readers to pay attention to the political constructions of words such as (m)other, author(ity), in-between, racialized, con-fusion, and body matters. Thus, it makes sense to examine how postmodern feminists use metaphors to articulate their politics. I will begin this chapter by examining four sets of metaphors that play a prominent role in the postmodern feminist rhetoric: (1) hybrid selves, (2) the body, (3) geography, and (4) language. The first set of metaphors articulates the importance of mixed identities, hybrid selves, which reframe the way citizens understand the connections among themselves, their communities, and their cosmologies. For example, Donna Haraway's metaphor of the *cyborg* displaces the Western emphasis on transcendence, which highlights the connection between humans and God. Both the Hebraic Christian God images and feminist Goddess images suggest divinity involves transcendence of humanity. In contrast, the cyborg emphasizes immanence by connecting humans to machines. Because turning humans into machines is so strange in Western thought, this move reshuffles transcendence and immanence so that they are no longer polar opposites. This suggests that human life and things are intertwined. Furthermore, bodies and minds are not all that separate. The second set of metaphors that I examine uses the female body to create new political images. For example, Luce Irigaray's image of women's two sets of lips—the mouth and the vagina—explains how feminine imagery represents the similarities between material reproduction in the vagina and symbolic articulation—that is, between the body and the word.[1] An implication of this feminine metaphor is that politics needs to address human reproduction, the materiality that sustains life, and the symbolic cultural practices that give life meaning. A third set of metaphors calls on geographic and spatial images to invite readers to rethink the connection between citizens and public life. In some sense, language is itself a metaphor for representing nonlinguistic *material* things. Words are used to speak about concepts and material objects, but the words themselves appear in a form very different from the concept or object. Decoding a speech requires translating the rhetorical term into its representative word. Speaking a language performs metaphorical magic by using the materiality of the spoken word, or voice, and the materiality of the written word, or print images, to re-present ideas and experiences. For example, the word "chair" and the word "sitting" are made with letters that metaphorically re-present a reality of a lived experience of chairs and sitting—which are phenomena quite unlike the word "chair," which looks nothing like a chair. So, language works as a web of metaphors to re-present a lived world of things and ideas.

As I examine each metaphor, I will suggest ways in which each set of metaphors opens up new possibilities for public policy initiatives. As a conclusion to this analysis of metaphors, I will present a twelve-gender schema that shows how new images can reframe gender politics, which will, in turn, invite new sets of metaphors.

HOW DO HYBRID SELVES WORK POLITICALLY?

The image of a hybrid self challenges the notion that a citizen *is* one thing. Encouraging citizens to see themselves as representative of a multiplicity of identities undercuts notions of pure breeds. No one person can actually represent blacks, southerners, women, whites, Euro-Americans, and/or African-Americans. Citizens are not incarnations of their ancestors or of any other type of identity group. Instead, individual citizens can be thought of as hybrids who even embody polarities. This is especially attractive to feminists because of the ways in which Western cultures have restricted women by limiting them to a singular identity—as a "mother" or "wife" or "employed workers." This multifaceted identity offers one way for women to reconceptualize themselves without choosing a primary identity. In some situations, women may be encouraged to give up female attributes in order to present themselves as "true" professionals. Hybrid identities ease the harsh choices involved in these conflicting choices.

Donna Haraway demonstrates the political value of hybrid selves by using the cyborg image to critically review the transcendence-immanence polarity and the male-female polarity.[2] She hopes that the cyborg myth supports a progressive politics of "transgressed boundaries, potent fusions, and dangerous possibilities":[3]

Cyborg imagery can suggest a way out of the maze of dualisms in which we have explained our bodies and our tools to ourselves. This is a dream not of a common language, but of a powerful infidel heteroglossia. It is an imagination of a feminist speaking in tongues to strike fear into the circuits of the super savers of the New Right. It means both building and destroying machines, identities, categories, relationships, spaces, stories. Although both are bound in the spiral dance, I would rather be a cyborg than a goddess.[4]

Haraway's mythic cyborg figure replaces the goddess image that captured the attention of many second-wave feminists. Crossing the human/machine boundary at a time when technology is highly suspect by feminists, Haraway challenges feminist antiscience ideologies. Encouraging feminists to appreciate technology, machinery, and other representations of immanence, Haraway suggests that machinery and technology are not only merely patriarchal tools because these tools also can acquire mythic significance. This cyborg metaphor simultaneously reframes the sacred/secular distinction by denying god-goddess ambitions that have produced human arrogance. While affirming a self that connects with the inanimate, Haraway objectifies herself as machine while mystifying herself by the human-machine mix. She takes this image further in her discussion of technoscience and the twin icons, FemaleMan and Oncomouse.[5] Through technoscience, she recognizes an elaborate hypertext that models reality by displacing the materiality of the "real" with the semireality of an electronic image that occupies space differently—so differently that policing such cyberspaces by military, governmental, and corporate powers has become difficult. At the same time, Haraway avoids the mechanized metaphor of the Enlightenment, which reduces God or Power to a machine, politics to a system of flow charts, the human body to a road map, and the brain to a wired computer. Haraway's cyborg image, like Pirsig's motorcycle story, hints at an intimate relationship between two seemingly opposite beings—humans and machines.[6] If such an image is taken seriously, this new metaphor might even transform feminist notions of relationships themselves, as well as feminist relationships with machines—computers, cars, appliances, factory equipment, etc.

But Haraway is not interested in transforming some "original-authentic" person into a new *being*. She problematizes the notion of an "original" person because persons contain a multiplicity of beings that live in the intersection between change and continuity. Her image for this multiplicity of being is "diffraction."[7] Haraway's tale of life is that beings are not born so much as they emerge through life's unfolding processes. This makes quests for "original birth" information less important. Everyday is a birth-day. Rebirth is the everyday fare of living. Politically, this means that Haraway invites citizens to give more attention to caring for the immediate details of their lives than to planning for future lives or finding past origins. In mundane terms, it may be that planning for the future sometimes leaves little time for daily acts of kindness. Finding origins can turn "Americans" into Anglo-Saxons when they could just as easily be mideast-erners or Asians. But can Americans be all three and more? The old oft-told origin story says "no" because "the founders" came from Europe.[8] But is this true? Who were "the" founders? Or is the founding still in process? A quest that emphasizes the unfolding processes of making today's America offers a different response.

But Haraway is not satisfied with merely including diverse cultures in "our" American political community:

> I insist that social relationships include nonhumans as well as humans *as socially* (or, what is the same thing for this odd congeries, sociotechnically) active partners. All that is unhuman is not un-kind, outside kinship, outside the orders of significa-tion, excluded from trading in signs and wonders.[9]

In an earlier context, she calls upon the birth image to create a different sort of hybrid:

> Indeed, I have always preferred the prospect of pregnancy with the embryo of another species; and I read this "gender"-transgressing desire in primatology's text, from the Teddy Bear Patriarchs' labor to be the father of the game, through *Primate Societies'* developmental-evolutionary narrative fragment about a heterogeneous sibling group of "almost minds."[10]

Violating the animal/human boundary through the image of the pregnant woman gives the "mother nature" story a shocking turn. A different bond between the animal and human world could foster policies that enable persons to respond more fully to animal research, dietary decisions, and pets. This is not necessarily an argument for animal "rights" but instead suggests that "rights" talk itself is a problem because it depends on unrealistic notions of individual autonomy that seek to protect the so-called privacy of citizens from so-called government intervention. Such liberal rights talk does not build relationships but protects citizens from some of the negative consequences of relationships. Human animal relationships require an empathy that includes new ways of understanding the animal in ourselves.

Obviously, to read this text as an argument for vegetarianism interprets the policy too narrowly because vegetables can also be understood as beings to be respected. But treating animals or carrots with respect does not require us to treat them as humans. Respect requires recognizing differences and the different sorts of relationships among beings. Such an ethic may not forbid eating carrots but it does forbid wasting them, and eating them needs to be executed in a spirit that appreciates the gift other beings make to one's own life. The goal is to learn from the gift and pass it along in the appropriate way as is suggested by Maxine Hong Kingston's tale of the rabbit in the *Woman Warrior.* She tells of a rabbit who jumps into the fire to turn him or herself into meat to feed the starving woman warrior.[11] Haraway's and Kingston's narratives remake the relationship between humans and animals by transforming it from the modern one characterized by domination into a new one characterized by cohabitation. They suggest that care and sacrifice are honorable characteristics of animals, including human animals. Haraway's work continues to call upon these images of cohabitation in reviewing the racism, which serves as a subtext in Euro-American texts, as well as the assertion of her own desire for social relationships with animals.[12]

This shift to cohabitation offers humans a different politics. The well-fed and financially comfortable, who are asked to feed hungry poor citizens through taxes or other mechanisms, might be grateful for the sacrifices that many "beings" have made to sustain them as well-fed and financially comfortable. In this light, some sacrifices for other humans might not seem so unfair and/or difficult. Reading human life as a cautionary tale built on the sacrifice of other animals may produce a different calculus in evaluating such issues as diet, wetlands, exercise (for all types of animals including humans), zoning regulations, forestry, and clean water. Undoing the human mind/body dichotomy, Haraway uses animal-human hybrids to suggest a way of understanding human life as an interdependent political process.

Judith Butler offers a third hybrid in her explanation of how parody and irony can undercut domination. The man in drag and the cross-dresser dramatize gender power. Butler explains, "I would suggest as well that drag fully subverts the distinction between inner and outer psychic space and effectively mocks both the expressive model of gender and the notion of a true gender identity."[13] Haraway in *Modest_Witness@Second_Millennium.FemaleMan©_Meets_OncoMouse^{TM}* offers a technoscientific drag, the FemaleMan. In referring to her own "modest witness," Haraway uses the written image "s/he" to suggest that she is a person who is both male and female.[14] By suggesting that somehow a man in drag is really a woman but also really a man, the image transforms a rigid category into a fluid one. Checking the male/female box on the form is no longer so easy. Moreover, the drag figure mimics the liberal myth that "we" are all "just persons"—devoid of gender. Butler shows readers what it means to become a "person" who represents both sides of the male/female dichotomy. The male in drag is not a synthesis, but a productive confusion.

The drag image illuminates the simultaneous presence of both the masculine and the feminine in a single unsynthesized person; she/he is *both/and*, not an undulating *either/or*. The performance works because auditors are aware of the simultaneous presence of male and female. For an auditor who is fooled into thinking that the performer was only female, the act fails. Being too convincing spoils the show, because it depends on the simultaneous presence of both genders. Clearly, this drag figure differs from the liberal androgynous figure who blends the masculine and feminine until the two merge and gender disappears. But is the woman in drag also comic? Or is she merely the everyday banker dressed in her business suit to mask her feminine parts? Or is she a pitifully poor copy of a man? Does the comedy depend on the fact that men dress "down" when they costume themselves as women and so the humor is produced by the fact that a high person falls below his station? What would it mean if our gay pride marches had equal numbers of drag kings—women in tuxedos and military regalia, perched upon Cadillac convertibles, with names like Mr. Bull Dock and Daddy Dandee? What new political possibilities await feminists who can present a drag king in both comic-gay-lesbian and serious-hetero-straight roles? What powers can be found in such images?

These hybrid selves go beyond reminding citizens that identities are social constructions. Bringing a new interpretation to Simone de Beauvoir's insightful phrase, "One is not born, but rather becomes, a woman,"[15] postmodern feminists explain how a citizen's identity depends on contexts. In the context of America, the problem women encounter is that the category "woman" overrides all others. If feminists reify the category "woman," they contribute to, rather than, alleviate this problem. American men had the "luxury" of escaping their gender, but the women's movement has made it difficult for "men" to set aside their gendered identity. In exploring the intersection between cultural codes and individual choices, Butler examines the politics of this sex/gender story,[16] which has made sexed bodies foundational. Postmodern feminism revitalizes the sex/gender tale by using the "body" as metaphor that plays out a number of different contexts. The body represents an individual person who is encased in a body, the body represents women who are often "reduced" to their bodies, and the body represents the incarnation of the political state, which exists in the form of the bodies of its citizens and the territories they occupy.

HOW CAN THE BODY SERVE AS A METAPHOR?

Feminists were not the first to use the body metaphor to speak about the state. Rousseau uses the metaphor of the body to explain how politics requires organic connections among persons and institutional practices. Rousseau explains that the chief administrator represents the "head" of state, and the legislative branch represents the body's trunk.[17] Rousseau's organic view of politics contrasts with a different sort of body, the Leviathan, whom Hobbes uses to frighten citizens into obedience.[18] Both stories show that bodies matter.[19] Furthermore, body parts—skin, breasts, noses, hair, vaginas, penises—can be made to serve symbolic political purposes. Such body parts can be made to limit citizen access to public life by racializing and gendering certain types of bodies to mark them as "different" and so "outside" the normal body politic. Haraway refers to these racial-sexual markings as "stigmata,"[20] which alludes both to the politics of denigration and the political possibility of martyred status. But can body signs serve feminist values, or must all body metaphors be abandoned? Can a woman's body move beyond present Western representations to represent courage, friendship, and reason? Or can men's bodies become representations of fragility, sexuality, and emotion? Would not such mixed images encourage citizens to imagine women as part of public life and men as part of private life? Can the all-American citizen appear with dark skin, with long, straight, dark hair, with almond-shaped eyes, with a flat broad nose, with a small inconspicuous nose, or with a large high-ridged nose? How many different sorts of body types can "represent" the all-American citizen?

In Western cultural practices, women's bodies have symbolized sex and so have represented the private realm, the family. Susan Rubin Suleiman discusses the links among the female body, sexuality, and political symbols in "(Re)Writing the Body: The Politics and Poetics of Female Eroticism."[21] Feminist semiotic analyses examine the body both as an object of the gaze and as a medium of communication.[22] Many women report that their bodily presence makes a difference in conversations, changing the postures of other bodies in the room, the ways in which hostility and friendship are expressed, the pronouns in use, and so forth. Bodies represent both the presence of individual concrete persons and a range of metaphors that suggest connections that go beyond the present. Normalizing the female body, Luce Irigaray talks of women's two sets of lips to suggest the polyvocal features of communication and she emphasizes the connection between speech (the mouth) and reproduction (the vagina), while speech and reproduction articulate the intersection of the symbolic and the material.[23]

On the other hand, Susan Bordo demonstrates the costs of symbolic representations in *Unbearable Weight: Feminism, Western Culture, and the Body*. Utilizing Foucault's genealogical analysis, she explains how nineteenth-century women corseted themselves to display an exaggerated form of the fainting lady, while contemporary women starve themselves to manifest the sleek malelike body of the professional woman.[24] Recognizing the destructive elements in these actions, Bordo shows how political contexts entice women to reshape their bodies to gain some sense of control in their lives even as these behaviors get out of control. Bodily conditions reshape what may be an unconscious political protest into a health risk, created by women's pushing their bodies into shapes that threaten their very lives. Showing the dangers of using women's bodies as mere symbolic representations, Bordo's analysis asks readers to think about contexts that might evoke a different set of political messages—messages that are healthy for women.[25] Can feminists and others mix and match body parts to recompose everyday presentations of the self in ways that are healthy for women?

Butler, calling for examinations of how sex and heterosexuality work "in the crafting of matters sexual and political,"[26] shifts from the metaphor of the body as the "site" for politics to a metaphor of the body as a "performance medium." She explains that matter becomes meaningful through a *"process of materialization that stabilizes over time to produce the effect of boundary, fixity, and surface we call matter."*[27] This is no minor point. By critiquing the image of site or construction, she avoids the language of the "social construction of reality." Her solution to the culture/nature debate is not to accept that truth lies with both; rather, she suggests examining how discourse about "sex" regulates a boundary between cultural constructs and fixed, natural characteristics. She reformulates the radical feminist position—that is, the personal is political—by showing how the personal depends on public discourse, the political. Even sex cannot be private. At the same time, Butler welcomes crises in symbolic representations, which create conflict over what makes sense, "*over what constitutes the limits of intelligibility.*"[28] Tying sexual identity and politics together spotlights the fictive nature of symbols and thereby loosens their political hold so that citizens can be more open to change. In the chapter "The Lesbian Phallus," Butler urges phallocentric discourse to displace the phallus with such body parts as an arm, a tongue, or a knee.[29] The use of the body to reframe political imagery builds the polity from the "body" up. In her image system, body matters in new ways. Reproduction images that focus on the phallus, its absence, or even the vagina give way to sexual images that no longer link sex to reproduction.

Butler's gender-sex bending anticipates a new body politic, which moves away from nineteenth-century values that made the state the protector of families and men the protector of individuals within the family. Because the nineteenth-century citizen expected the state to create good conditions for commerce, the state focused on production, including the production of workers. As economics has extended its regulatory focus beyond population control, states have become less interested in controlling heterosexuality. As families have become less central in the manufacture and production of the goods and services, legal responsibilities have moved from families to individuals. Even in the case of married heterosexuals who jointly fill tax returns, the state has individuated responsibilities for errors in them. As citizens recompose themselves in a variety of family units, what counts as reproduction is less concentrated on the reproduction of human bodies and more focused on cultural practices and symbols. Abandoning reproduction as the central metaphor for family makes the gay-lesbian family intelligible, even sensible. If citizens define "family" as persons whose connections are forged by affection rather than for child rearing, gay-lesbian relationships are families. Nevertheless, this family image retains sex and pairing as a central feature of the bond that makes individuals into families. The body plays a key role in the bonding process through sexuality, but the body also signifies social bonding.

Bodies serve to represent social bonds. Citizens use their bodies as billboards that make identity announcements. Such messages come from a cultural grab bag of possibilities and mark a citizen's membership in a variety of groups—class, gender, ethnicity, political orientation, age, and sexuality among others. It is not only male street gangs who use color schemes and clothing codes. If such messages are not critical, citizens may fail to notice how they adorn themselves with signs that *sell* particular cultural values—business suits, ties, oxfords, dress scarfs, plain gold earrings. These too signal group/gang membership. As in all groups, the potential exists for group violence—physical, economic, or psychological. But citizens can avoid compulsive gang-type loyalties by becoming aware of how dress codes silently attempt to grab power. Aware citizens can more easily work with opposing "gang" members who come from other classes, ethnic groups, regions, genders, and sexual orientations. But body signs cannot be eliminated, for even nudity signals values. Postmodern feminists emphasize decoding the politics of body signals to invite citizens to self-consciously use the body as a performative tool for displaying a variety of political signs that display solidarities, boundaries, and coalitions.

Taking note of how citizens act with their bodies, feminists can move beyond such decoding to invent new performances for individual bodies, groups, and even the body politic. Butler's analysis suggests how everyday actions construct political life. A focus on the everyday makes politics immediate in the here and now rather than distant in the vote, court decision, or legislative outcome, and each citizen plays a part in crafting public life. National policies begin at the local level. So Washington, D.C. is just one among many sites for articulating and crafting cultural values that *constitute* the United States. This feminist version of embodied politics emphasizes not just face-to-face interactions but body-to-body politics, which makes communities dependent on interactions that include the body. Written communications, cyberspace interactions, and phone messages are insufficient to a full em-bodied politic communication.

But the process also goes the other way in that cultural symbols shape the way citizens see each other, even when they do so in person. But in person politics and body images have had long-range political implications for women. For example, the struggles of the pro-life, pro-choice movements are not simply about moral commitments. The struggle is also over how female bodies will be symbolized. In this sense, neither side has a winning position, for one casts women as persons whose freedom lies in the ability to reject motherhood, while the other casts women as natural, national breeders, whose lives are defined by their motherhood. Reducing women's images to pregnant bodies or potentially pregnant bodies has turned all women into dangerous breeders who may at any moment get into "trouble" and thereby trouble the social order. Providing women with the choice of what to do with their "own" bodies, abortion does little to escape the image of woman as "breeder," even though, to some degree, it makes the breeding at least dependent upon her decision. In this sense, the abortion debate, even its most liberal elements, reifies women as "potential" mothers and so limits women's options. Various symbolic representations shape women's experiences. Because welfare "mothers" are cast as irresponsible breeders, real-life working-class women encounter problems created by this stereotype and then must go to extensive lengths to prove themselves reproductively responsible. Such proof is not limited to government; welfare mothers must contend with their image as excessive breeders in a variety of relationships—with the men they date, the doctors who treat them, the employers who hire or refuse to hire them, and the landlords who consider renting to them. The terms of the abortion debate detract from women's full participation in the polity, because both sides define women in terms of reproduction. Postmodern feminist analyses suggest that women's bodies need to represent a range of activities that stretch beyond sex and human reproduction.

HOW DOES SPACE REPRESENT GEOGRAPHY, THE STATE AND "TURF" POLITICS?

Space metaphors represent a third set of political metaphors in postmodern feminist conversations. Postmodern feminists talk about conceptual mapping, bodies as sites of activity, computer networks as cyberspace, and linguistic distinctions as borders. Reminding citizens that anthropologists have recently extended their local cultural focus to include urban areas of the United States, postmodern feminists point out that humans are always already in a field.[30] This spatial wordplay underscores the way knowledge is shaped by a particular discipline and its surrounding locale—its geographic and cultural environment.[31] Reflecting on the space metaphor reveals the degree to which definitions of citizenship are tied to particular geographic locations. In the United States, the place of birth determines citizenship status. But if space is connected to birthright, as the U.S. Constitution suggests, then Native American indigenous people have prior claims on U.S. territory. Immigration regulation is a more complex issue than who comes into the United States; it articulates what types of persons can represent themselves as citizens. Not only do persons try to get in, but persons also try to get out, as the Native Hawaiian sovereignty movement and native American sovereignty issues continue to raise questions about how the geography of the "united states" constitutes citizenship.

Trinh T. Minh-ha demonstrates some of the difficulties in the term "native" by showing how it shifts with discourses and locales. In *Woman, Native, Other*[32] and in the film *Surname Viet Given Name Nam*, she shows how Vietnamese women can be natives in both Vietnam and San Francisco,[33] because cultures reach beyond nation-state boundaries. She shows how the term "native" is not a property or characteristic of a person but instead represents a situation in which some culture is momentarily fixed to a geographic location. The term "native" is a political designation determined by a historical story told from a particular political viewpoint. Her point has implications not only for so-called immigrants like the Vietnamese but also for all citizens. For example, I am a "native" of the United States and yet calling myself a "native American" will not work. While I am somehow attached to Ireland as an Irish-American, I am a "foreigner" in Ireland. If all citizens went back to their "native" land—that is, where their ancestors were born—where would "we" all go, and would it be crowded there?[34] Immigration is thus not simply about who can come into the United States but is also about what types of persons represent the all-American.[35]

By problematizing native status, Trinh T. Minh-ha shows that anchoring citizenship to geography illuminates how much the nation-state depends on geographic metaphors for its liveliness. In this sense, politics is tied up with geography. But geographic boundaries are at best suggestive. Postmodernism recognizes the contradiction involved in our commitments to pluralism and unity—a nationalism built upon a single unitary area, a space, which many endeavor to call a single culture, in spite of its multicultural dimensions. The name *United* States attempts to resolve such a tension.[36] Patrolling the boundaries of a culture that attempts to stabilize itself is even more difficult than patrolling the boundaries of a state.[37] "Alien" cultural practices seep through even the most vigilant border patrols.

So the state is not constituted only by geography. Cultural ties create state commitments. For example, the dismantling of the Berlin Wall shows the power of culture in overriding ideological divisions. Similarly, North and South Korea could unify. Movements in Ireland may echo another wall that cultural links could dissolve, even as religious rivalries divide them. State powers do not reside only in geographic boundaries. But rival forces threaten cultural boundaries as well. Such groups as feminists, religious persons, international workers, environmentalists, and multinational corporations have connections and loyalties that counter state powers. Like corporations, women's studies exists not in a particular geographic place but in an international verbal network supported by the Internet, the United Nations, conferences, universities, and circulating narratives. The geographic story of nationalism may be losing its readership or reforming with boundaries that are not linked to lands. Internationalism is an irresistible temptation.

Rethinking the connections between citizenship and geographic territory might invigorate nation-state politics. Postmodern feminists are unsurprised by proposals for representation based on communities whose constituents are non-territorial. For example, Mary Hawkesworth's proposal that Congress should have a minimum percent of female representation borrows from other nation-state practices, for whom territorial representations are only one model.[38] Rather than emphasizing congressional representations by territories (that is, states), the present model of representation in both the House and Senate, the representation could be based on nongeographic identities, such as ethnicity, gender, sexual preference, professional expertise, and/or a combination of all of these, including geography. While interest group politics offers opportunities for such groups to shape public life, perhaps the old geographic representation is no longer relevant. Does Hawkesworth's proposal signal a waning interest in state loyalties, especially on the part of women who have had difficulty gaining congressional representation under the U.S. territorial model?

Displacing the old mythic explorer and frontiersman, who conquered so-called wild *regions* (regions that actually already had inhabitants), the new citizen might try to care for "others" rather than conquer them.[39] Today's citizens look to the state not only for protection from so-called "outside" enemies but also for care and services. New images of the state might employ a so-called maternal figure, who loves the diversity of her children and encourages their interdependence. Maybe the Chicana lesbian who blends the spirit of politics with family life might help citizens rethink their relationships to each other as each citizen serves as an auntie, an uncle, a sister, or a brother to others. Maybe the femo-politico who teaches citizens active involvement in community life would be helpful. Maybe the black female teacher, like Sojourner Truth or Ida B. Wells, might enable citizens to see the state as a part of ourselves. This might even encourage citizens to see themselves as committed to all who are alive in the world. Such new metaphors could shock citizens into rethinking their commitments and that could recompose public life.

HOW DOES LANGUAGE WORK AS A POLITICAL METAPHOR?

Language itself serves as a metaphor that teaches citizens the interdependence of community and *communi-cation*. Not only does language serve as a rich source for metaphors, but semiotics explains how language itself works as an elaborate metaphor. Words are used to compare unlike things: three-dimensional life experiences (composed of the physical world, time, space, bodies, spiritual events, and emotions) are compared in a system of representations that translates them into two-dimensional figures, or *words* on a page. Americans pretend that the complexities of a relationship can be conveyed by the words "partner, husband, wife, lover, parent, child," or that the complexities of a life can be revealed in a biography, but semiotics reminds citizens that language systems translate experiences into speech acts that fall short of actually presenting what happened. Words and symbols re-present other life experiences. Semiotics does not, as some claim, argue that nothing exists but words and texts. However, semiotics does argue that the way citizens share experiences is by translating them into language systems, including dances, gestures, paintings, and other symbolic systems. Using the metaphor of grammar, semiotics shows how rules shape discourse, and how discourses shape social relationships. "Text" is a metaphor that represents not only a book but also a coherent social narrative. Using "text" in this way does not mean that the only real form of existence is a "text." This, too, is a metaphor that performs some tasks well because it preforms others badly.[40]

For example, Stanley Fish explores how a university classroom produces its own life narrative in his book *Is There a Text in This Class?*[41] Social analysts extend such images to speak about "reading" society. Even those less engaged by postmodern talk speak about "reading the ball" in racquetball.[42] Semiotics and postmodern insights emphasize that language systems support interpretations of everyday life situations. But social life is more than language, and taking these language metaphors too seriously is to misunderstand it. The value of the metaphor "it is raining cats and dogs" is lost if the auditor thinks cats and dogs are really falling from the sky. Similarly, language mediates social life, but it is not all there is to social life.

Postmodernism shows that social order depends on language and, in turn, communication depends on social interactions. Poststructuralists, calling upon the work of Ferdinand de Saussure, explain that meaning takes place in the circuit of communication between a listener and a speaker.[43] Meaning does not come about as a speaker defines terms but emerges as a speaker and a listener come to share some definitions of terms within a speech community.[44] A speech community includes not only languages, such as English and Chinese, but also discourses that create bodies of specialized meanings—legal discourse, medical discourse, academic discourse, etc. Meaningfulness is stabilized and institutionalized by a community of speakers,[45] but meanings continue to change as speakers introduce innovations. In this regard, poststructuralism emphasizes both the static and dynamic qualities of communication. Static elements are anchored in a language community. The dynamic elements come about as members speak and so introduce new phrases, terms, and grammars that reform language systems. "Lively" communication depends on both static fixed elements and dynamic new elements.

Philosophically, the static quality of communication means that understanding a different perspective might require switching to a different network of meanings. Such switches sometimes occur when a citizen travels to a new culture; it can also happen when academics cross over to a new discipline. A new mix of images inspires new understandings. Hermeneutics explains that citizens may need to change themselves to understand another person or culture. However, such changes are often accomplished only through struggle.[46] Just as anthropologists find that they must change themselves to comprehend the cultures they study—to understand new points of view—readers must be ready to change themselves to understand a new cultural insight, a novel, music, theory, or painting.

Politically, hermeneutics encourages citizens to see themselves as beings capable of change who can, in turn, change their culture. Some of this change is produced by symbolic, linguistic innovations. Because societies are not fixed, each citizen has some ability to alter cultural practices. However, politics via language change is slow and holds little hope for revolutionary transformations. It is not then surprising that postmodern feminists do not seek a feminist revolution because they assert that a pure feminism, devoid of patriarchy, may be a feminist dream that can only be achieved through totalitarianism.[47] Postmodern feminism offers a cautionary tale about political positions that claim to be pure, and it tells a story about the inescapable nature of patriarchal language that can comfort activists because it anticipates difficulties in changing women's status. Thus, postmodern semiotics can save feminists from feminist fundamentalisms that threaten to stamp out politics and public life.

Postmodern feminists emphasize language and so offer a critique of the material base of U.S. culture. In this political culture, words have been contrasted with the "real" world of "things"—captured by such slogans as "that is just talk," or "put your money where your mouth is," or "sticks and stones may break my bones, but words will never hurt me." Cutting through the thing/word dichotomy, postmodern feminists show how words constitute the world of things by naming them. Semiotics refocuses Western thought, turning it from a metaphysical preoccupation with nature and the physical-material dimensions of life to a more intense interest in language and symbolic representations of life. Because women fared so badly under the nature-physical American story, the new emphasis on language and symbols offers some promise for a liberatory feminism. For public conversations about gender differences, language metaphors may offer some advantages over material-body metaphors. Symbols are, after all, not all that hard to lift.

HOW CAN CITIZENS BREAK THE
TABOO OF "TWO GENDERS ONLY"?

Deconstructing the sex/gender boundary challenges positions taken by empirical scientists and second-wave feminists who constructed a distinction between sex—a biological characteristic based upon natural, physical male-female differences—and gender—a socially constructed male/female distinction. Postmodern feminists suggest that such distinctions, including the male/female distinction, is itself a cultural construct and so is, to some degree, arbitrary and contingent, even as it is occasionally also silly, tenuous, fragile, permeable, harmful, and helpful. Rejecting the salience of physical distinctions between sexes and/or genders, postmodern feminists avoid subscribing to the old liberal "we-are-all-just-humans," which reduces humans to make them all the same. Instead, they invite the reader to play with the male/female, masculine/feminine boundaries. Postmodernism offers a series of hybrid selves that suggest positions from which strong and playful citizens can emerge.

WHAT HAPPENS WHEN CITIZENS
PLAY WITH TWELVE GENDERS?

Postmodern feminists argue that one way to change political values is to make symbolic changes. For example, they challenge the way feminist scholars make an unproblematic distinction between sex and gender by suggesting that creating this boundary is itself a political act that may not serve feminism. Performing another political act, postmodern feminists problematize the boundary to argue that gender shapes what counts as sex in biological discourse and that sex, that is, biological features, shape how cultures develop notions of gender. Rejecting sex as a foundational category, postmodern feminists argue that a "sex-gender" system creates meaningful relationships between nature and culture. The same is true for the categories of male and female. Of course, postmodern feminists are not suggesting that cultures can reshape biological phenomena in any way that citizens choose. They are suggesting that the material limits of biology and the cultural limits of the human imagination work together to structure meanings. Postmodern feminist political analyses interrogate the boundary between such categories as sex/gender, male/female, and masculine/feminine to show how they constitute, nurture, and constrain relationships. Social practices maintain these categorical distinctions. So citizens, both female and male, who dress as females act to maintain the male/female distinction. When female citizens break into male-only spaces, including restrooms, they act to challenge it. Because the male/female distinction has become so sacred, the challenge does not dissolve the boundary. Just as the war to which no one came would end, so categories could be killed if no one used them. While postmodern feminists are interested in crossing linguistic boundaries and playing with distinctions, they are not interested in eliminating them, for to do so would be to silence everyone. Language is itself built on categories. Postmodern feminists invite citizens to play with distinctions in order to explore new political possibilities without necessarily giving up the old ones. In the spirit of this invitation to play with language, I will propose replacing our two sex-gender system with a twelve sex-gender system.

My new gender-sex system is developed from four dimensions. The first dimension works with the modern male/female distinction that divides persons on the basis of potential roles in human reproduction—that is according to "sex" organs—male/female. The second dimension develops a three-part division on the basis of how citizens perform Americanized versions of masculine and feminine characteristics. On this dimension, females can perform three distinct types of persons: feminized females, androgynous females, masculinized females. This dimension comes out of second-wave feminist interpretations of femininity. Doing the same for males produces three parallel categories: masculinized males, androgynous males, and feminized males. Dividing these six types of genders in terms of their sexuality produces six more categories of persons for a total of twelve types of genders. If the category of sexual partner were divided into three parts to include gays/lesbians, bisexuals, and heterosexuals, an eighteen sex-gender system would be produced.[48]

Twelve-Based Sex-Gender System

masculine hetero men	androgynous hetero men	feminized hetero men	masculine hetero women	androgynous hetero women	feminine hetero women
masculine gay men	androgynous gay men	feminized gay men	masculine lesbians	androgynous lesbians	feminine lesbians

There is no reason to believe that scientific inquiry would be unable to specify some biological as well as sociological differences among all twelve of these genders. How significant those patterns might be and what weight they would carry would depend on the ways in which a culture appropriated the differences into its practices. In other words, to make sense out of this twelve-point system would require a system of practices that would give them significance. Because there are presently few practices that support these categories, they don't seem important or reasonable. At this point in time, the twelve-point sex system is largely absent from practices and so is undertheorized by both everyday citizens and academics.

The political question that I want to raise is not, "Are there really twelve genders or really two?" My question is, "What political possibilities does the two-gendered system create and what different political possibilities would a twelve-point system create?" Certainly, the gay-lesbian movement has already expanded our understanding of gender differences. The second-wave women's movement altered notions of "woman," and thereby changed understandings of "men." But can this playful reconstruction of genders liberate citizens from a worshipful orientation toward sex-gender identities, so that citizens might inhabit such categories more contingently?[49] Can it generate a cultural understanding that appreciates gender violations—that is, men who act as women and women who act as men—as variation rather than as horrors?[50] Would such categories so devalue human reproduction that population growth would decline?

It is important to note that I am not arguing that nature has written onto the human body twelve or even eighteen genders for all times and all places or that biological differences determine there are twelve genders in the Homo sapiens species. It is also obvious that even a twelve-based gender system can still be understood in terms of a dichotomy. What multiplying our genders suggests is more ways to talk about gender-sex differences, which might enable citizens to appreciate more variety in the ways persons can be humans. But more importantly, such considerations can encourage citizens to consider gender categories less seriously, more tentatively, perhaps more creatively.

For example, the pejorative term "tomboy" might disappear as this term would refer to a "normal" masculinized heterosexual female, an MHF. Heterosexual men might find themselves able to express interest in fashion without confusing this interest with their sexual orientation; they would be feminized heterosexual males, FHMs. It might take quite a bit of social practice to undo the pejorative nature of this category but with practice and sufficient media support a new meaning could emerge that could leave the pejorative behind. Lesbian women could be seen in ways that include more than butch/femme images and some would be easily referred to as feminine lesbians, FLs. Middle-class white women might find it easier to move between styles that are both feminine and masculine without feeling that they had to give up being female to do so. While such movement might expand what counts as normal, the more important goal is to nurture appreciation of a wider range of differences. Such appreciation might displace the fear of difference that is presently such a feature of American society. But, of course, the new categories would in time produce their own disciplining codes.

The twelve-point system suggests that a sex-gender system can be thought of as a continuum. Might citizens replace this continuum image with that of a layer cake in which they simultaneously represent two genders within each person? It is important to note that this twelve-gender system does not eliminate sex as a category of understanding but instead invites citizens to ask how they choose to present themselves in gendered ways.[51] The system suggests that citizens perform some aspects of a male-female mix of possibilities. It encourages queries about how males have learned to be "professional" men, and how females have learned to be "professional" women. It invites crossing over to the other side to escape the constraints of one end of the male-female continuum. Such questions can expand choices and offer insights about the politics involved in those choices.

WHAT IS POLITICALLY GAINED
AND LOST THROUGH AMBIGUITIES?

Such playful reconstructions can be dangerous. bell hooks worries about how postmodernism conflates race and culture.[52] And hooks and other feminists worry about the ways in which postmoderns conflate sex and gender as well as male/female differences. Politically, such conflation can support a cultural relativism that accepts racism as merely another sort of cultural difference. For feminists, the conflation of sex/gender can encourage the reification of difference with women in the subordinate position. The conflation of the categories of race/sex/gender can make political work more difficult because citizens can use it to reassert the liberal abstraction that we are all just alike and so race/ethnicity and sex do not matter. This abstraction silently privileges the white male, middle-class person as the standard and ignores the conditions of difference that are a part of the fabric of the lives of women, persons of color, and the poor. There is merit in this concern. Furthermore, equating all cultures can lead to cultural relativism that makes citizens unable to judge wrongdoings. While most American citizens reject the values of Nazi Germany, harmful cultural practices can be justified on the basis of such observations as "that is just how their culture does it." While assuming that dehumanizing persons through racism violates a universal cultural value, bell hooks still makes use of postmodernism. She suggests that feminists use it to interrogate "whiteness" in order to deconstruct race as an ideology.[53] Taking up this challenge, Nancie Caraway uses postmodernism in *Segregated Sisterhood* to interrogate white racism in the women's movement. Caraway argues that "Talk. Endless talk" will transform us.[54] What Caraway, hooks, and postmodern feminists have in common is a concern with the way in which citizens' bodies become signs that locate citizens in a polis. Violating such locations can elicit punishment. Cross-dressing, passing, and other so-called "impersonations" carry dues unless the performance is done just for entertainment. It seems that U.S. citizens need to travel with their gender-ethnic identities on their sleeves for all to see. In this effort, they are assisted by J. C. Penney and Sears, who offer clothing designed for women of color, but also by cultural practices that delight us as we costume ourselves to express our individuality and our ethnic heritages. But can these body signs be performed in ways that undo racism and sexism while respecting cultural and sex-gender differences? Can category confusion assist in reforming political life?

Dealing with crossing gender/sex boundaries, Butler suggests that citizens can self-consciously perform genders and thereby articulate a contingent understanding of the sex-gendered persons that "we" can be:

> The choice to assume a certain kind of body, to live or wear one's body a certain way, implies a world of already established corporeal styles. To choose a gender is to interpret received gender norms in a way that reproduces and organizes them anew. Less a radical act of creation, gender is a tacit project to renew a cultural history in one's own corporeal terms.[55]

Seeing body performances as choices suggests that those choices can be made differently.

But such choices involve both asserting and surrendering power. Current social movements, including the women's movement, recruit members on the basis of ethnic, class, and gender categories—categories that are signaled through body markings. Jobs for African-Americans and Chicanos are created by using these identities as access to special groups. Just at the moment when Chicana, black, Native American, and Asian cultural perspectives have gained political force through the celebration of race-cultural identities, it seems that postmodern feminists have shifted attention away from such cultural heritages. But have they? Or are they asking us to hold such categories more lightly and to use them less to determine behaviors than to expand social relationships? Postmodern feminists do privilege the hybrids—those who inhabit in-between categories—and they advocate a contingent understanding of cultural practices. Does this move assist those who would demolish affirmative action and return to white privilege, or does this open up a new way of constructing a multicultural, multigendered polis?

While this hybrid rhetoric holds promise, living under the "hybrid" sign is not so easy. Certainly, the hermaphrodite figure serves as a warning. Western societies often cherish neat categories and heap honor on pure (clear) representations, while they dishonor mixes. Political dues may be extracted from persons who present themselves with a multiplicity of ethnic backgrounds. American society creates male and female codes of behavior with taboos, boundaries, that are not to be crossed. Catalogs, sizing, department store space arrangements—all carefully separate male things from female things so that we will not become "confused." Although a few items are unisex, they serve as infrequent reminders that citizens need primarily to stay in THE correct gender category. While some citizens enjoy testing such boundaries, sex-gender identities are deeply held and fragilely constructed. American citizens appear to fear that even small-rule infractions could break up our sex-gender system. Much of the anti-ERA rhetoric emerged in the form of defending the two-gender system against the feminists who would have us "all" be the same and even use the same bathroom. Because this argument is on the face of it so strange, I think it reveals that modern Americans fear a break-up of the sex-gender system itself.

By defining the position between two polarities as hybrids rather than as compromises or composites, postmodern feminists unsettle identity politics. For example, a Hispanic who is also Euro-American or a Euro-American who is also Hispanic can be well situated to facilitate dialogue between so-called Euro-Americans and Hispanics. The hybrid identity works to disturb American social order, which has taken racial-ethnic identities so seriously as a social, cultural, and political division among its citizens. The South defined a citizen with one black ancestor as black, and northern black/white sorting systems similarly reify persons by calling upon so-called racially pure categories. But now this categorization has been shown to be unfounded in that race is a social construct and not a legitimate biological distinction among persons. This does not mean that race does not matter, but it does mean that those who use this category need to recognize its social roots rather than use biology to justify its use. Cultural categories, in contrast, are more complex. What postmodern feminists do is trace the social-political formulations of the category race and the social evolutions of ethnic distinctions. By undoing cultural "purities," postmoderns focus on those whose background shows the intersections of cultures. Those whose heritage offers them two or even more ethnic identities can work to bridge cultures; their both/and (their in-between status) symbolizes the possibility of both coalition and community. But more importantly, many citizens have a multiplicity of heritages that they have acquired from birth families, from their socialization, from education, and from friendships. For example, Toni King, an "African-American scholar," identifies herself as both African-American and as Euro-American because she knows and lives by both cultural traditions.[56] I consider myself socialized by the culture of Hawaii, which helped shape my adult life. In the area where I lived and worked, native Hawaiian practices were foregrounded.

A multifaceted identity can encourage citizens to think of themselves in a complex way that includes the variety of experiences that shape habits and values—family relationships, cultural contexts, class situations, gender/sex, regions, and professional training. This means that black women do not have to choose to represent themselves in terms of gender *or* ethnicity. Lesbian Chicanas can represent themselves as both lesbian and Chicana and more.

Politically, such rhetorical moves can advantage those who inhabit in-between categories. For example, bisexual women might be reconstructed as women whose sexual variety provides a vantage point for healing tensions between lesbian and straight women. This moves away from classifying such a person as disloyal to either lesbians or straight women. The emphasis on hybrid identities harbors hope for those who were previously caught in between politicized categories. More importantly it offers promise for healing rifts and constructing coalitions that take citizens beyond the old essentialized categories of race-ethnicity, sex-gender, and sexuality. Understanding the self in more complex ways enables citizens to participate in more diverse communities that can cherish a wider range of differences. This does not mean becoming less vigilant in protecting citizens from the harms that come from racism, sexism, classicism, heterosexism, and other denigrations that discredit persons on the basis of social categorizations while failing to take account of their actions.

But complex visions of the self do not solve the ethical problem of how to evaluate actions. Certainly, those who consider homosexual acts as sinful will rightfully claim that they are taking account of actions in evaluating gay-lesbian lifestyles as wrong. But those who follow Butler might argue that the performance of the female is in some respects a choice about how to perform. If female identity is judged on the basis of performance, same sex interactions (interaction between two females) is more difficult to discern. This problematizes not only who counts as a female but what counts as same-sex sex. Sometimes a person might perform as a female while at other times a male. A problem still remains. Some citizens will evaluate the female performance (whoever performs it) as inferior to the male performance. This denigration of the feminine encourages persons to repress their feminine side. The question then is not simply about a multiplicity of selves, but it is also about what sorts of diversities to value in the multiplicity of selves that compose a community: "What philosophies, habits, symbols can we put on that will enable citizens to reconstruct our male/female identities? Are there some good feminist parts that have not yet come on stage? What genders will play them? Can we invent more genders in our sex-gender scheme? What political possibilities do we open up by recognizing the play of difference in gender and class, gender and race, gender and sexuality, class and gender, race and gender, sexuality and gender, and in any of the other categories we inhabit?"

In response to this I want to develop an ethic that begins with four basic assumptions: (1) that being human means being both male and female, and that both are valuable sources for understanding human talents; (2) that cultural differences can contribute to social order and a robust public life; (3) that wealth does not measure worth and that poverty does not mark worthlessness; and (4) that homosexual love makes important contributions toward building families and communities that are based on affection as well as on reproduction. With these assumptions in place, I will now discuss how an approach to a political ethic can be developed from the postmodern feminist conversation.

NOTES

1. Luce Irigaray, *This Sex Which Is Not One*, trans. Catherine Porter with Carolyn Burke (Ithaca, N.Y.: Cornell University Press, 1985), 205-18.

2. A cyborg is a being who is both human and machine.

3. Donna Haraway, "A Manifesto for Cyborgs: Science, Technology, and Socialist Feminism in the 1980s," in *Feminism/Postmodernism*, ed. Linda J. Nicholson (New York: Routledge, 1990), 196.

4. Haraway, "A Manifesto for Cyborgs," 223.

5. Donna J. Haraway, with paintings by Lynn M. Randoph, *Modest_Witness@Second_Millennium.FemaleMan©_Meets_OncoMouse*™ *Feminism and Technoscience* (New York: Routledge, 1997).

6. Robert M. Pirsig, *Zen and the Art of Motorcycle Maintenance: An Inquiry into Values* (New York: Bantam, 1974).

7. Haraway, *Modest_Witness*, 267-73.

8. Even in this oft-told story, there is a subtext that values the multicultural roots of American public life.

9. Haraway, *Modest_Witness*, 8.

10. Donna Haraway, *Primate Visions: Gender, Race, and Nature in the World of Modern Science* (New York: Routledge, 1989), 377.

11. Maxine Hong Kingston, *The Woman Warrior: Memories of a Girlhood among Ghosts* (New York: Vintage Press, 1976).

12. Haraway, *Modest_Witness*, 213-65.

13. Judith Butler, *Gender Trouble: Feminism and the Subversion of Identity* (New York: Routledge, 1990), 137.

14. Haraway, *Modest_Witness*, 3.

15. Simone de Beauvoir, *The Second Sex*, trans. H. M. Parshley (New York: Random House, 1952), 301.

16. Judith Butler, "Variations on Sex and Gender: Beauvoir, Wittig, and Foucault," *Praxis International* 5 (January 1986): 505-16.

17. Jean-Jacques Rousseau, *The Social Contract or Principles of Political Right*, trans. Charles M. Sherover (New York: Meridian, 1974), especially 47.

18. Thomas Hobbes, *Leviathan, Or, The Matter, Forme, and Power of a Commonwealth Ecclesiasticall and Civill* (New York: Collier Books, 1962).

19. I echo the title of Judith Butler's *Bodies That Matter: On the Discursive Limits of "Sex"* (New York: Routledge, 1993).

20. Haraway, *Modest_Witness*, 7.

21. Susan Rubin Suleiman, "(Re)Writing the Body: The Politics and Poetics of Female Eroticism," in *The Female Body in Western Culture: Contemporary Perspectives*, ed. Susan Rubin Suleiman (Cambridge: Harvard University Press, 1986), 7-29.

22. See Laura Mulvey, *Visual and Other Pleasures* (Bloomington: Indiana University Press, 1989); and Mary Ann Doane, *The Desire to Desire: The Woman's Film of the 1940s* (Bloomington: Indiana University Press, 1987).

23. Luce Irigaray, *This Sex Which Is Not One*.

24. Susan Bordo, *Unbearable Weight: Feminism, Western Culture, and the Body* (Berkeley: University of California Press, 1993).

25. Susan Bordo, *Unbearable Weight*, and for commentary on how fashion articulates social codes, Roland Barthes, *The Fashion System*, trans. Matthew Ward and Richard Howard (New York: Hill and Wang, 1983) and on relationships to the self and politics, see Henry S. Kariel, *The Desperate Politics of Postmodernism* (Amherst: University of Massachusetts Press, 1989).

26. Butler, *Bodies That Matter*, xii.

27. Butler, *Bodies That Matter*, 9.

28. Butler, *Bodies That Matter*, 138.

29. Butler, *Bodies That Matter*, 88.

30. The meaning here depends on the double meaning of the word "field," which refers to fieldwork in a foreign culture or distant locale, as well as academic fields. See Haraway, *Primate Visions* and Laurel Richardson, *Fields of Play: Constructing an Academic Life* (New Brunswick, N.J.: Rutgers University Press, 1997).

31. For a discussion of this field metaphor, see Donna Haraway, "Primatology is Politics by Other Means," in *Feminist Approaches to Science*, ed. Ruth Bleier (New York: Pergamon Press, 1986), 77-118, especially 81-89, and Haraway, *Primate Visions*, 13-15, 279-303, 382.

32. Trinh T. Minh-ha, *Woman, Native, Other: Writing Postcoloniality and Feminism* (Bloomington: Indiana University Press, 1989).

33. Trinh T. Minh-ha, *Surname Viet Given Name Nam*, produced, written, edited, and directed by Trinh T. Minh-ha, 1989.

34. For this question, I thank Robert Cahill, whose research on Hawaii illuminates the problematic intersection of ethnicity, territory, and human genesis.

35. Analysis by Michael J. Shapiro, talk at Denison University, spring 1997.

36. Thomas L. Dumm discusses the constitutive nature of this tension in *united states* (Ithaca, N.Y.: Cornell University Press, 1994).

37. Attempts to enforce a single English-language system within the United States are attempts to create this single culture out of the multiplicity of cultures that we are. Comments that "white" Americans make about themselves as well as the comments made about them often indicate a lack of awareness of the fact that white America represents a Euro-American cultural mix. Americans often fail to notice that hamburgers, pot roast, pasta, and french fries *are* ethnic foods.

38. Mary Hawkesworth, *Beyond Oppression: Feminist Theory and Political Strategy* (New York: Continuum, 1990).

39. Sara Ruddick in *Maternal Thinking: Toward a Politics of Peace* (Boston: Beacon Press, 1995) makes an argument about using the image of motherhood to develop an understanding of citizenship as caregiving and as peacemaking.

40. Metaphors work by strained comparisons. To say "man is a wolf" is to describe humanity poorly in that humans do not walk on four legs, while, nonetheless, suggesting something about the animal cunning that describes humans quite well.

41. Stanley Fish, *Is There a Text in This Class?: The Authority of Interpretive Communities* (Cambridge, Mass.: Harvard University Press, 1980).

42. Conversation with Peri Schwartz-Shea, University of Utah, fall 1991.

43. Semiotic language theory argues communication depends on a circuit of communication created by an interaction between a speaker and a listener. The listener decodes the speaker's message through the language system. This theory was developed from Ferdinand de Saussure's analysis of communication. For an analysis of the politics of this

communication process, see Eloise A. Buker, *Politics through a Looking-Glass: Understanding Political Culture through a Structuralist Interpretation of Narratives* (New York: Greenwood Press, 1987), 1-51.

44. Employing semiotics, feminists might want to imagine ways in which earrings might be seen as symbols that emphasize the listening skills that give women pleasure and insight. Native Hawaiian women will often tug gently on their earlobe to remind children of the importance of listening.

45. For an explanation of how community stabilizes meanings and interpretations, see Stanley Fish, "Normal Circumstances, Literal Language, Direct Speech Acts, the Ordinary, the Everyday, the Obvious, What Goes Without Saying, and Other Special Cases," in *Interpretive Social Science: A Reader*, eds. Paul Rabinow and William M. Sullivan (Berkeley: University of California Press, 1979), 243-66.

46. Hermeneutics argues that understanding depends upon life circumstances; see Eloise A. Buker, "Can Feminism Politicize Hermeneutics and Reconstruct Deconstruction?" *Social Epistemology* 5 (1991): 361-69, and "Feminist Social Theory and Hermeneutics: An Empowering Dialectic?" *Social Epistemology* 4 (1990): 23-39.

47. For an argument about the political struggle required for change, Gayatri Chakravorty Spivak with Ellen Rooney, "In a Word. *Interview*," *differences* 1 (1989): 125-28.

48. For this comment, I want to thank Rae Ellen Douglas, Denison Women's Studies major, Denison University, fall 1995.

49. It might also be useful to liberate religious imagery from an idolatrous relationship to the masculine. New typologies of mythic images for God might help do this.

50. Please note that although some feminist analyses have made a distinction between "sex," which refers to biological phenomena, and "gender," which refers to sociological phenomena, postmodern feminists challenge this distinction inasmuch as scientific constructs of sex depend upon and come out of cultural understandings of gender.

51. This image of dressing ourselves each day as male or female comes from Phyllis Turnbull, lecture and discussion, Honolulu, 1979.

52. bell hooks, "Critical Interrogation: Talking Race, Resisting Racism," in *Inscriptions* 5 (1989): 159-64.

53. hooks, "Critical Interrogation," 162-63.

54. Nancie Caraway, *Segregated Sisterhood: Racism and the Politics of American Feminism* (Knoxville: University of Tennessee Press, 1991), 203.

55. Butler, "Variations on Sex and Gender," 508.

56. Presentation by Toni King at Denison University, Granville, Ohio, spring 1997.

Chapter 10

Talking Our Way Along: Ethics and Politics

Is it possible to develop an ethics that avoids setting out universal principles? Does the postmodern feminist's rejection of universal principles make ethics impossible because it leaves us with no way to make decisions except personal preference? Calling on the insights of postmodern feminists, I develop a five-point model of ethics that responds to the question, "How can women and men compose ethical lives that value both differences and similarities?" First, I begin with a critique of universal principles as a basis for just decisions, and then I advocate replacing universal principles with a contextual moral code. Second, I argue that the liberal understanding of equality that advocates treating all persons "the same" before the law should be subordinated to a definition of equality based on a morality of care. This morality redefines equality by shifting from an emphasis on the distribution of resources through procedural rules to an emphasis on attending to individual differences through the responsiveness of citizen actions. Rather than depending on rules and their enforcement to create just situations, this moral code depends on the wise judgment of citizens who respond to one another without necessarily dispensing with rules and procedures. Third, I examine the way in which power can be understood as a desirable and just pursuit by understanding politics as an honorable and delightful activity. Assuming that being fully human requires involvement in public life, I abandon a utilitarian view of politics as a necessary "evil" and, instead, argue that the human spirit needs to participate in public life. Fourth, I examine the ways in which speech practices constitute an ethical code that integrates tradition with present immediate concerns. Fifth, I develop an antifoundational ethics that makes ethics dependent on a robust public life.

CAN POLITICS RECONCILE
UNIVERSAL PRINCIPLES AND ETHICAL CODES?

Postmodern feminists ask what constitutes "politics" as they anticipate that all ethical concepts are shaped by cultural and linguistic limits and so fall short of universal laws. They consider both liberal and socialist understandings of ethics insufficient. Avoiding both procedural and distributive understandings of justice, a postmodern feminist ethic emerges in the contexts of conversations about cultural practices that are expected to shape and continually reshape cultural practices.[1] Making these cultural practices explicit offers ways of examining them—deconstructing them—to illuminate how they distribute power and authority within a community. Postmodern feminism is not a source of values but a way of discovering the values already articulated in the myriad of cultural practices (habits) that compose daily life. Clarifying these values enables citizens to "come to terms with them."[2] Ethical practices are not secured by a universal set of principles, virtues, or patterns of resource distribution but evolve as citizens call on cultural habits to enable them to choose fair and just remedies to particular problems. The accumulated decisions of a people, their history and habits, compose an ethic that serves as a cultural constitution. This constitution guides citizens in ways not totally different from the U.S. Constitution. Ethics is achieved not just through the application of rules, but it requires the wisdom of citizens who administer to one another as they apply the constitutional habits to the activities in their daily lives.

But this ethic has two drawbacks. First, postmodern feminists offer their political workers a somewhat less inspiring reward by promising that things will be better-for-right-now, while modern American liberalism promises citizens that change will make things better-for-ever-and-ever as progress moves citizens toward an ever brighter future. Things get better and better. Furthermore, modern liberalism suggests that good politics will produce an eternally good set of practices that apply around the world. In contrast, postmodern liberal feminism offers some improvement and some good for the moment right around here. Its promises are limited to these times and this sort of place. Rather than immortal fame for political excellence, postmodern feminists offer momentary recognition that will fade. Many fear that such a modest reward will be insufficient to induce people to act as citizens.

The second drawback is that postmodern feminists place more responsibility on each citizen because they argue that citizens cannot merely apply rules but must make judgments. Justice is not a "thing" to be found but a quality of the interactions among citizens. Wisdom grows in a culture through the accumulation of interactions that produce habits that nudge citizens toward fair practices. Ethics involves not only judging others and judging oneself, but it also requires developing a critical viewpoint that asks how justice and injustice occur in daily life. From the perspective of contemporary liberals who understand justice as a set of codes, legal rights, and procedures, postmodern feminist justice is at worst ad hoc and at best ambiguous. One place where this postmodern ambiguity becomes especially difficult is in the area of equality.

American postmodern feminism emerges in a context that emphasizes that equality means treating all persons alike. The golden rule, "treat all persons as you wish to be treated," articulates the similarity of citizen needs. Because all citizens know what they require for fairness, each citizen has access to what others want simply by thinking about themselves. In situations in which citizens are alike, this works well. It works poorly where they are not alike. For example, the fact that U.S. citizens take the question "what do women want" seriously illuminates the difficulty. The question assumes that women are so different that their wants cannot be known. So, men cannot treat women as they (men) would want to be treated. There is truth in this because society has situated women differently from men. For example, the history of women's education, socialization, voting privileges, occupational opportunities, and rights differs from that of men. This can make it harder for men to learn what women want. If women's history and social circumstances are studied less than men's, as has been the case in the United States, it is harder for both women and men to know about women's situation, and so it is harder even for women to know what women want and need. While the question is often posed, "What do women want?" to discredit women, this question reveals how little society has attempted to find out what women want, to understand women's situations. Similar problems emerge in responding to the handicapped, so-called minorities, the poor, homosexuals, and others who are constituted as different from the "regular" folks—the white male, middle-class, Anglo-Saxon, ablebodied, straight persons. Normative values and equality based on similar treatment creates inequality for those who are in any way considered "different." As it turns out, the white, male, middle-class, Anglo-Saxon, ablebodied, straight person simply does not exist, for all persons deviate from this imagined norm. White males differ from the imagined norms as well.

Postmodern feminism does not solve the dilemma of difference by asserting that women are "different," but instead, they examine similarities and differences. Accepting assumptions that humans have similarities, postmodern feminists add a second level of questions that investigate how citizens also differ. Their point avoids the question whether women are similar to or different from men by showing how equality depends on reflecting on the twin questions of similarities and differences.

HOW CAN DIFFERENCE AND SIMILARITY CONSTRUCT A PLAYFUL PLURALISM?

While liberal pluralism promises ways of incorporating all persons into a republican, democratic society, certainly American women (who had been denied the vote, denied their day in court, and denied representation in legislatures) did not begin in 1776 on an equal footing with other citizens. In fact, if women are considered citizens, from 1776 to 1920 the majority of citizens in the United States were not eligible to vote because they were female. The democratic republic does not begin until 1920. Even today, liberalism has not yet produced a plural politics that fully includes women. Evidence of this exists in many forms but perhaps the most basic statistic that demonstrates the problem is revealed by the fact that in the late 1990s women compose only 10 percent of Congress and this figure has been considered so "large" that 1992 was declared the "year of the woman." The cry for equality with men that fueled the sixties' women's movement continues. Elaborate justification systems for treating women as inferior to men have just begun to lose credibility. Placing women into positions of public responsibility has only begun.

To gain a public voice, second-wave feminists emphasized the similarities between women and men. Equal pay, equal opportunity, and equal access to education exemplify the gains based on the argument that "we" are all alike and so need and deserve similar resources and rewards. But these gains also brought losses. To gain benefits, women have felt they had to become like men. African-American feminists pointed out how this focus on similarity encourages citizens to treat them like "white women." Even the metaphor "sisterhood" universalized and homogenized women's lives. Uncomfortable with the call to sisterhood, María C. Lugones and Pat Alake Rosezelle argue that it be replaced with a call to friendship.[3] In so doing, they show how postmodern feminists might displace the kin-blood image of female bonding (that is, sisterhood, which develops out of so-called "natural" family bonds) with the image of voluntary commitments (that is, "friendship"). This shift from an emphasis on similarity (including genetic similarity) to one on selective affinities is one example of how persons can be connected by both similarities and differences.

Bonding on the basis of similarity and difference encourages citizens to reject two assumptions that have made American politics difficult. The first is the assumption that there is one superior model of political life and that all others are subordinate to it. The focus on *one* (which appears in such phrases as "one nation under God") has created a hierarchy in which only *one* person or value can be at the top. Media discourse that presents "two" sides to a story continually implies that only one is correct. Some media even go so far as to invite audiences to call in to indicate the "correct" position. In a competitive system, the *one* that is best is supposed to *win*. This sort of cultural practice reduces persons and the categories that they represent to hierarchal rankings in which one side, group, person, or idea is better. One way is best. In contrast, postmodern feminists offer a different understanding of plurality and diversity. They emphasize that different contexts require different solutions. One way may be right in one situation but wrong in another. Thus, citizens need to be adaptable and flexible. They cannot acquire a moral code that will be sufficient for their entire life. Moral character requires constant attention. Citizens need to continue to grow and change. Said differently, persons do not *become* good Americans once and for all, but *Americans* continue to evolve as citizens. People are not either good or bad, but they make good and bad decisions. Persons are not converted once and for all to a good way of thinking; they must continually work on themselves. Beginning with an evolutionary understanding of citizens as changing persons, American citizens need twin, triplet, and so forth, models of the excellent person, organization, leader, or group. Excellence is to be found not in the one right way of doing things, but in creative responses in a context. Formula cannot be designed for all contexts and so good judgment and accurate interpretations are even more important than good rules and regulations.

The second assumption that has made American politics difficult is the way in which citizens emphasize conformity to create unity, solidarity, peace, and consensus. This drive for unity and conformity contradicts the basic liberal theory, which argues that conflicts and differences create better decisions. The separation of powers articulated in the Constitution demonstrates America's affection for conflict as a check and balance system. Even the concept of a federal system is itself a belief in the importance of diversity. Present popular versions of liberalism, however, seem to fear critique and differences, while employing a one-happy-family image of public life. But more often, difference is reduced to a debate between two sides that are to be quickly resolved. So persons who raise important critical questions are often labeled troublemakers, nonteam players, or complainers; sometimes the label is bitch, feminist, communist, liberal, or some other term. Citizens, especially female citizens, are taught to "go along, to get along" even when following this advice means economic losses for companies, dysfunctional government activities, and violations of personal integrity. Whistle-blowers need special protection because their failure to conform is often punished. Critical reflection puts a citizen outside "the" majority, "the" norm. The story is that being normal requires conformity to the style, values, beliefs, and practices of the majority. But, of course, women are the majority and so it is not the numerical majority to which they are expected to conform. Women are expected to conform to those who are considered the "normal, real main persons"—the minority who are male. So this "great" American story insists that deviations from the mainstream need to be minimized.[4] In contrast, postmodern feminists argue that public institutions, government, and commercial interests need to find ways to nurture the diversities that make them strong. Conformity and public agreement may signal fear, not loyalty, because loyalty depends on honesty.[5] Postmodern feminism offers a new story of critical reflection that values diversity and critical conversations.

It is not just left liberals, black politicos, Chicano activists, liberation theologians, socialists, environmentalists, or feminists who suffer from so-called "political correctness." Certainly, conformity makes politics impossible for conservatives as well because it attempts to reduce all answers to the one right answer.

Democracies and the U.S. founders have long feared this tyranny of the majority, but women's inability to gain power even though they are in the majority suggests that there is also a gendered tyranny of the minority. The term "political correctness" itself mocks politics as an activity and encourages citizens to withdraw from public life, leaving governance to those already in power, to the economic elites. "Political correctness" is a term used by those who want to assert the moral self-righteousness of their position by radically reducing public debate. The term suggests that moral decisions require no debate or deliberation. The "PC" label is one strategy for silencing public considerations of difficult questions like abortion, welfare, and sexuality. Moral self-righteousness is not a strength, but a political liability, because it encourages citizens to dismiss opposing viewpoints. Good political communities depend on the willingness of citizens to hear each other and to negotiate relationships that are open to reformulating judgments and opinions. This happens best when citizens anticipate a lifetime of living a public life with others in attempting to achieve fairness and justice.

What postmodern feminists most fear is that the drive toward comm*unity* will enforce unity and suppress differences, including differences within feminist communities.[6] Politics works best by recognizing differences while building on similarities. Thus, the postmodern feminist analyses of the intersections of race/ethnicity, gender, and class serve as examples of how to engage in reflective political work.[7] Such pluralities undercut the "purity" of any one position and so make both understanding and negotiation more likely.

Postmodern feminism offers to replace assumptions about unity and conformity with an understanding of human differences that embraces twin and multiple models of excellence that are shaped by constructive critical conversations. For example, in a confrontation between two persons or groups who understand themselves as different, the process would *not* be constructed so much as a *debate*, a term that implies that one group must win and the other lose, or as a *deliberation* that promises to produce the "one right way of living," but, instead, as an opportunity for opening oneself up to a *playful* process that promises transformation of the very self that constitutes the "I/we." But this is not so very new, for it is commonplace to begin conversations with others in a debate mode that stresses the categories I/you, we/they. It is, however, important to end such conversations with reformulations that incorporate all parties. This transformative approach differs from the model of compromise privileged in present interpretations of liberalism. Compromise suggests that the right way is to be found in a middle ground between two so-called extreme positions. The strength of a postmodern feminist interpretation of diversity is not in "appreciating" difference or in being "sensitive" to others. It lies in the ability to call on a variety of possible selves in order to respond to situations in a critical and fair way. It involves not only transforming others but transforming the self. From such an approach, citizens can negotiate encounters with each other to produce changes in each other, in themselves, and in the systems that make up their cultural practices.

This account of difference argues that encounters with others are opportunities for education that can transform the self. In such situations, citizens can play out new parts of them/ourselves as they continue to learn from a variety of critical conversations. This is not to argue that all selves should come forward. Some aspects of ourselves should be controlled, limited, subverted, and even eradicated; certainly the racist, sexist, homophobic aspects of ourselves as well as of our culture need to be undone. There are ethical judgments to be made about which selves should be privileged. What I am suggesting is not a loose and free play of difference without restraints, but instead a play that makes one's self part of the process of social change. Political activity encourages new parts of one's self to come forward.[8] The old adage "you are what you eat" can be rewritten as "you are what you perform," so one must be careful what one performs in order to be wary of making an ugly, unjust self. I am willing to say something about which selves should at this time be given special attention. As I suggested at the conclusion of the previous chapter, at this time in American history American citizens need to begin self-consciously to work with four ethical commitments in mind: (1) that both women and men have important contributions to make; (2) that cultural diversity contributes to American vitality; (3) that worth cannot be measured by wealth; and (4) that homosexual love makes valuable contribution to American understandings of family and politics.

HOW CAN POWER POLITICS
BECOME AN HONORABLE PURSUIT?

American liberalism contains a paralyzing contradiction: citizens are taught that power corrupts at the same time they are taught that as citizens they need to regularly exercise power. One argument against granting women the vote was that involving women in politics would corrupt them. Even voting power is seen as a potentially corrupting use of power. This contradiction is often resolved by rotating persons in and out of political office. Term limits is one such strategy. But this also imagines politicians as corrupt persons who will inevitably go into moral decline. Even though in the late twentieth century it may appear illogical to think that political power corrupts while economic power does not, this belief continues to degrade politics. Postmodern feminists are willing to deal with the question of their own use of power in order to respond to this contradiction, and many are ready to claim that their scholarly work is also political work.

For example, Donna Haraway, whose academic training is in biology, embraces both a postmodern epistemology and politics. She wants her work to be "simultaneously political theory, science fiction, and sound scholarship."[9] She affirms partiality and exclusivity as constitutive elements of the new evolving postmodern science, an ever-evolving story, while acknowledging, even celebrating, the political nature of the motivating energy:

My contention is that the intersection—coupled with other aspects of the "decolo-
nization of nature" that have restructured the discourses of biology and anthropology,
as well as other practices of international politics—destabilizes the narrative fields
that gave rise to both primatology and feminism, thereby generating the possibility
of new stories not strangled by the same logics of appropriation and domination, but
also not innocent of the workings of power and desire, including new exclusions.[10]

Her focus on politics makes three important points that move feminist politics
forward. First, her statement that her work is political makes it harder for power
to hide because she makes power relationships explicit at every level of public
life—personal, institutional, social, as well as governmental. Haraway shows
that the exercise of power need not embarrass feminists. Second, she invites feminists to see themselves as political persons who can and do exercise power on
behalf of a set of values and ethical commitments. Hence, rather than playing
"out-of-power" games, gaining energy from status as the poor outsider other,
feminists can also take up roles as policy makers and political actors. This is not
only important in avoiding victim feminism, but it is also important in developing and critiquing collective political strategies. Assuming the role of political
actors makes it easier for feminists to exercise power consciously and so to
engage in it more strategically. Becoming more conscious about themselves as
political persons encourages others to see feminists as power brokers, and so puts
feminists in a position to initiate actions rather than merely respond to them.
Third, it opens the way for feminists to replace the old image of politics as
"nasty" business with an image of politics as a vital part of life. Politics is not an
instrument for achieving happiness but is itself one of life's pleasures. It is this
third point that I want to develop. By rejecting the image of politics as "dirty"
business and of power as a necessary "evil," citizens can make politics a positive
part of everyday life. Encoding politics as "dirty" has made it difficult for both
liberals and conservatives to acknowledge their own exercise of power, and so
they cover it over with the pretense of neutrality and procedural purity. Both cry
out, "The rules made me do it; the law says so." Politics serves citizens in more
ways than merely providing public order and security. Even early liberalism
understood politics as a vital part of a citizen's life. But in the late twentieth century economics has crowded politics out of the lives of U.S. citizens. They are
too busy with their role in businesses to develop a personal life or a public life.
Reducing citizens to workers has manufactured mechanical beings whose lives
are unsatisfying. Healthy citizens need a public life as much as they need a personal life, food, and exercise. If a feminist politics can be developed that makes
politics an end in itself, a pleasure that is part of being female—part of being
human—then citizens will more easily become involved in politics. Often citizens are hungry for politics and public life without realizing it. If citizens can be
brought into policy formation, participation will be broadened, respect for government increased, and public life improved.

Part of the problem with everyday understandings of politics has been a focus on politics as an activity designed for getting things for one's self and one's "own" kind. One step in moving away from this understanding of politics can be found in the way that postmodern feminists decenter the self. They explain that the self is not an autonomous being separate from politics but that the self is the result of social-political-economic activity. Therefore, a part of remaking the self includes working on remaking the social order. This reformulates self-interest as a motivation for involving oneself in politics because it turns politics into an activity for making values rather than a mechanism for getting things. This postmodern version of the self encourages citizens to see their "selves" as tightly connected to public life. So, if someone or some part of the public harms an individual that affects all the citizens. But this notion is already a part of liberalism. For example, criminal acts are framed as crimes against the people; court cases identify the "people" as one side of the case. A model of politics that connects citizens with one another is vital for politics. If citizens can see that their own transformations depend on a good political system and that the way to change things about themselves that they don't like is to simultaneously work on themselves and public life, they will find politics more satisfying. This refocuses politics by transforming it from an activity that is designed to get things for the self to an activity that offers new possibilities for moral growth in everyday life. This leads toward the development of an understanding of a collective self that exists through communities and coalitions with others. But it might also help to remind citizens that communities also fall short of good practices. Like individuals, communities err and perform evil. Collectivity is no guarantee that good practices and justice will be achieved. Only focused diligence, accurate critique, honest dialogue, and kind courage can help citizens move toward ethics and away from evils in individual decisions and collective actions.

The understanding of politics as an arena for the expression and development of each citizen fits well with feminist understandings of public life. For example, it fits with relational feminism, which argues that women understand themselves in relationship to others rather than in regard to their separation from others. As Carol Gilligan's work demonstrates, it is not only the postmodern feminists who advocate contextual ethics.[11] However, relational feminism conceives of a self that is clearly bounded and fixed, while postmodern feminists imagine a self with permeable boundaries that separate the self from others. But they both emphasize the important role that public life plays in each person's life. Furthermore, the postmodern and relational self fit well with ecofeminism, which affirms human connections and dependency on other earthly beings and/or things. To respect the earth is to respect a political self that makes decisions not on the basis of self-centered ends, but on the basis of ethical commitments to a variety of beings and phenomena, including the self. A wide range of feminist theories advocates a strong politics that goes beyond a narrow liberal view of the political as individual selves making contracts with one another. Feminist politics imagines the body politic as an interwoven interdependent set of relationships. That interdependency is more than a mere convenience for the exchange of goods and services, and it is more than a mechanism for creating social order. Persons need public life in order to be full human beings. Politics is not a necessary "evil," but a vital part of human existence. Thus, participation in public life is not only a privilege but a necessary component of a full life.

This understanding of politics makes politics a vocation for all citizens. Part of that vocation is that each person needs to take responsibility for building a just, ethical public life. Although Americans have sold each other a mythic vision that happiness is found in a private family life, this vision does not work. First of all it depends on a view of happiness that is driven by material comforts and physical conveniences as well as family love. But more importantly, it depends on a vision of family love that makes "mom" into the self-sacrificing servant and "dad" into the hard-working boss who together produce homey comforts for themselves and "their" children; it depends on inequality and self-centeredness. While the founders may have had this in mind when they claimed that all persons had the right to pursue life, liberty, and happiness, it may be that these things go together and that without liberty—public political liberty—happiness cannot be obtained, even in a private family setting, without justice. If one citizen purchases happiness by enslaving or even using another, both will be unhappy, whether that takes place in a family, a work setting, or a community. Humans need fair and equal interactions with each other and anything less diminishes all parties. Those interactions depend on a shared public political life. So politics and justice are a part of each person's daily routine even if they do not give politics explicit attention. In this understanding of politics, power does not simply tempt and corrupt citizens but enables them to seek the good and just. Women and other adults cannot be denied political activity without damaging their spirit—the spirit that supports growth, moral development, and emotional expression. Public life is a part of being; politics is necessary to sustain a robust living self.[12]

HOW DO SPEECH PRACTICES PROVIDE MORAL GUIDELINES?

To understand the moral guidelines that postmodern feminists offer citizens, it is helpful to situate postmodern feminists' ethics in relationship to the philosophies of liberalism, marxism, and critical theory. Each of these philosophies calls on a particular discourse and set of beliefs to develop ethical guides for public and private life, and each of these philosophies offers strategies for change. Modern liberals call on rationality and legal procedures, and so they turn to the law and constitutional amendments for social change, and they depend on citizens to *figure out* that a good life for their families depends on an orderly society. Liberals believe that natural law and rationality can offer a foundational guide for the good life and so modern secular moralists try to recover enduring principles to guide civilization. This has been one of the most prominent views of ethics in modern America. While many feminists rely on the law, it has not been sufficient for formulating feminist social values. In contrast, marxists examine the material conditions of human existence and consider a moral good life one that allocates material resources and work fairly. Thus, marxists seek social change through the transformation of economic conditions. While many feminists use a marxist framework, changes in material conditions and work have been, like the law, unable to address gender inequities.

Critical theorists like Jürgen Habermas depend on free speech and public critiques to interrogate cultural practices and to allocate more authority to the people. Habermas links marxism, psychoanalytical thought, and liberal principles of free speech. The term critical theory has grown in use, because many universities teach critical thinking, and by that, they do not mean the theories put forth by the Frankfurt School and now advocated by Jürgen Habermas. This term has come to mean a willingness to challenge patterns of authority by calling on a skeptical approach to received knowledge and so-called common sense. One way to engage in such a challenge is to assume a marginalized social position for social analysis. While feminists embrace critical theory, critical theory discourse has been less able to include feminism and women in the conversation. Postmodern feminists call on language itself as the medium for moral decision making and so politics involves creating new symbols and rhetoric. Postmodern feminists focus their skepticism on gender issues and concentrate their negative evaluations on the ways in which patriarchy has generated inequalities in gender, race/ethnicity, and sexuality. They pay close attention to the way that occurs through symbolic representations in social life. They seek the foundation for ethics in language traditions and reflections on them. Such reflection is facilitated by examining speech practices, because through speech a community of people articulate and preserve their moral codes. Words and speech express emotions, political values, and moral judgments. This means that speech practices and reflections on them are intimately connected to the development of public policy.

For example, Dvora Yanow examines the narratives of a community in Israel to show how the community formulated public policies by shaping public space.[13] She goes beyond simple participant observation or in-depth interviews to show how a community creates meanings that in turn support public practices and policies; and in doing this, she shows that the retelling of a people's experiences occurs through retelling stories, constructing public space, and forming public policies.[14] Because people construct symbols to create meanings, decoding speech reveals the speaker's moral position, values, and beliefs. Not only does this make it possible for citizens to understand the moral codes of others, but by listening to themselves citizens can see their own codes clearly and then can embrace, modify, or reject those codes.

For postmodern feminists the question, then, is how to determine what part of a code or moral template is to be embraced, modified, and rejected. Because language is ambiguous, it does not determine decisions. Language offers a medium through which some choices can be understood, in other words—stood under. In listening to postmodern feminism, I come to understand ethics as a matter of responsible choices rather than the result of finding and applying a sacred or secular code. This echoes early Greek traditions that argued that citizens, not codes, produce good ethical practices. Good public actions and moral habits (codes) are formed by citizens who negotiate with each other by being willing and able to change themselves in the process of that negotiation.

Understanding politics as negotiation emphasizes the responsibility that each citizen has to participate in the process. This definition of public life may be similar to Aristotle's notion of politics as the art of the possible. Ethical actions and just practices flow from the possibilities that citizens create by negotiating life with each other. For such negotiations to work, public conversations need to occur in ways that include articulations of diverse viewpoints. Public conversations and negotiations do not necessarily avoid difficulties by silencing some people so that others can speak. However, the end goal cannot be consensus. That would give one person or one small group a veto over all actions and might prevent communities from acting at all. Such value conflicts will continue to occur. Nevertheless, postmodern feminism suggests the way to deal with such conflicts is through public conversations, which can produce ethical solutions to difficulties.

In my model of political ethics, it is not useful to encourage citizens to "find" or "create" universal principles that apply to all persons in all places, for this universal dream about the end of politics is also a dream about heaven-on-earth, the perfection of human existence. Attempts to create heaven-on-earth are not only an unmanageable burden, their success would be the end of human existence. If citizens set aside this heaven-on-earth dream, they can content themselves with being responsible for finding temporary, contingent solutions to problems. While such solutions may in some measure go beyond immediate concerns, they will not solve all the world's problems for all time. While some will call such a model "situational ethics," in a post-Kuhnian, post-Gadamerian time, a more laudatory label is "contextual ethics." My understanding of political ethics is that ethical decisions can best take place in the context of citizens engaging in public conversations with each other about what to do in particular situations. By proposing that politics involves negotiation, I am suggesting that ethics emerges in the interactions among citizens as much as it does in the application of rules, which serve as the backdrop for such interactions.

This is a democratic model of politics because it means that citizens who act in everyday life situations are as important as congressional representatives and senators. Both citizens and congressional representatives work to slowly recompose the U.S. "constitution." Focusing on the politics of everyday life holds all citizens accountable for the political actions they commit with their speech acts. Even jokes articulate social values, and humor is an important part of political change. A central political virtue in this ethic is the willingness to speak about an issue and the willingness to listen carefully to others as they speak. Listening also involves listening to oneself to clarify moral positions either to take them with greater confidence or to discard them when they no longer "sound right." Citizens may do more to reduce injustice by listening carefully than they do by enforcing rules and punishing those who violate them. But clearly a combination of rule enforcement and listening provides more points at which to administer justice. Furthermore, the back-and-forth conversations that both articulate and question current values can facilitate public conversations, helping to clarify those values and improving their ability to make justice happen.

HOW CAN AN ANTIFOUNDATIONAL ETHICS PROVIDE A HOME BASE?

Contextualized ethics asks citizens to rethink the connection between ethics and politics by grounding ethics in the experiences of their cultural situations. Politics is foundational in that it involves the community of interacting citizens, but this foundation is contingent rather than eternal. It exists in the moment in a particular historical geographic location. Reevaluating ethics in this way asks citizens to go beyond principles, empathy, and social analysis to reflect on how ethics might be achieved in particular situations. Each case presents a different situation; some are very different when they involve different historical periods or locations distant from each other and others are very similar in cases that involve the same historical period and locale. But in this ethical understanding principles are not eschewed, for claims can be made for moral guidelines that hold for "local" moral imperatives. While these guidelines are not necessarily universally applicable, they can establish just practices for a particular community, and they may well apply to more than one community. Such principles are components of local cultures—be they universities, corporations, towns, or nations.

This emphasis on local communities reconstructs the image of the cosmopolitan citizen as someone who is well-traveled, internationally known, and environmentally aware, but it finds the hero and heroine in persons who are committed to the place they inhabit. For consumers, this focus emphasizes products that are characteristic of one's locale. It cautions against bad habits that see the neighbor's lawn as greener, or foreign cultures as more exotic, and so, richer. It discourages shopping around to find the "one best" object. Such shopping around can be a version of the hopeless quest for utopia and can make citizens too ready to abandon commitments to local communities in order to move on. But travel in the sense of cultural critique is a part of the process I am advocating. While I am not opposed to "travel," too often citizens travel to demonstrate their status and wealth and to affirm their own self-centered values. Such travel can avoid the transformative imagination that other forms of "travel" can produce.[15] According to my position, travel is not out; but travel to gain status or escape responsibilities is out. By traveling through the imagination in a variety of ways to gain insights into other viewpoints, citizens can gain a critical reflection on the culture of their "hometown" that they can use to make that hometown better.

WHAT DOES POSTMODERN
FEMINISM OFFER AMERICAN CITIZENS?

Postmodern feminism brings politics down to the everyday because it involves the politics of daily living. Avoiding the crisis model of politics, postmodern feminists do not wait for problems to emerge but problematize a variety of aspects of everyday life. Crisis politics in America brings citizens out of their private sanctuary to fix problems, only to return them to the private realm once the crisis passes. Unfortunately, this often provides a superficial quick fix, and so the crisis replays itself over and over. By attending to politics as a part of daily life, citizens can avoid thinking about politics in terms of responding to a crisis. Responding to public life only when crises arise is an unworkable model of citizenship. Part of the negativity that goes with the word politics comes from the fact that citizens label crisis in relationships "politics" instead of understanding that public life, politics, shapes relationships in positive ways. Making politics part of everyday work can enable citizens to understand that office politics, academic politics, and other political situations as parts of life rather than annoying distractions. Building good public relationships can sustain citizens in the variety of organizations that provide them with opportunities for working with others. Understanding politics in this way can make citizens happier and legitimate strategic moral considerations about their own conduct in organizations and in their everyday practices.

Postmodern feminism encourages rejecting the American ideology that argues that speech can do no harm. The speech-does-no-harm viewpoint is a version of the speech-has-no-power view of modernity. Some argue that the First Amendment protection of "free speech" means that almost all speech, including hate speech, is ineffective in exercising political force.[16] But advertisers spend a great deal of money on television ads, which use speech to persuade viewers to act. If speech is as powerless as some say, these advertisers act quite foolishly. It does not seem reasonable to conclude that speech is an effective instrument for selling goods but ineffective in motivating persons to act on behalf of social and political values. Debates about hate speech illuminate the crisis in American politics over the contradiction that speech matters very much (which is manifest in the rule of law, which is itself speech) and that speech must remain unregulated (which is manifest in the belief that speech does no harm to persons). The title of the edited work, *Words That Wound*, itself attempts to undo the second half of this contradiction.[17] Postmodern feminism does not encourage citizens to develop speech codes. Instead, it encourages citizens to examine the speech codes that are already in place to see whom they harm, how they restrict citizens, and whom they privilege. In this way, postmodern feminism encourages reflection about speech at a level that is deeper than legal regulation.

If speech is considered ineffective, citizens may find themselves biting their tongues and/or suffering unjust speech acts because such speech acts are considered trivial. This has been especially true for female citizens and persons of color. And citizens do not have to tolerate sexist, racist jokes to prove that they are good sports. Calling on postmodern feminist arguments, citizens can playfully call people on their jokes, recognize the problem of speech in their own critical response to sexist speech acts, and above all speak out rather than be silenced. Of course, even silences can be strategically powerful. In practice, American citizens recognize the power of speech, and so limit the speech of even the marginalized who can use speech to harm the powerful. Citizens can inflict political harm on each other, and the state attempts to limit that harm. But all citizens need to watch their own tongues so that they do not injure others through careless or malicious speech acts.

Postmodern feminist thought draws attention to the politics of language, speech, and symbol making. Of course, such attention includes problematizing how feminists constitute "woman" and critically examining theories of identity that threaten to turn "woman" into the "one true being." But postmodern feminism invites citizens to realize multiple identities by acting with others in a variety of coalitions. Public actions with others who are different enable citizens to understand that within themselves are a multiplicity of identities, including a multiplicity of genders. So, I find that postmodern feminism encourages me to take up different identities. For example, I do not need to be only female or only Irish-American or only a political scientist; I can mix and match various identities to compose myself. Politics is not simply about getting things but about deciding on a set of relationships to bring to the foreground and a set of ethical values to re-present in actions, in public performances.

In inviting citizens to reflect on their language and the ways in which they perform a variety of identities, postmodern feminism depends on a praxis model of the relationship between knowledge and action. Postmodern feminism shows how genuine knowledge emerges only after citizens act out our/their theories. This attention to language as a political phenomenon may be difficult for citizens because it politicizes everyday discourse. On the other hand, it reveals many opportunities for political action in the everyday activities that compose public life. There is no need to wait for new national laws or new economic structures before creating a better politics. Actions are not deferred, but take place in the here and now in the words that citizens speak or fail to speak. At the same time, postmodern feminists emphasize that our choices are limited by cultural situations and the identities that those situations invent. An advantage for feminists is that, unlike their nonfeminist counterparts, they have already realized how much their "subjecthood" is invisible, denigrated, and culturally constrained. In this sense, much of postmodernism has been anticipated by second-wave and even first-wave feminism. Postmodern feminism understands human agency as choices that take place in a cultural context. Persons are capable of exercising power. And persons are continually evolving and changing within that cultural context as it changes them and as they change it. But power lies in moral action, not in creating an eternal mark on the world.

WHAT DOES THIS MEAN FOR ETHICS AND POLITICS?

The interpretation of postmodern feminism that I have presented is a simple model that contains two types of ethical commitments. First, it affirms that women, people of color, the poor, and homosexuals are parts of society. This means that postmodern feminists deconstruct the symbols and language practices within Western patriarchy to reconstruct politics in a way that treats more persons, including women, as full citizens. While speech and language do not alone determine public values, they are powerful factors in politics. Second, my version of postmodern feminism affirms that genuine understanding does not take place until citizens have acted out theories and that it is through such actions that theories are reformed. Acknowledging that such action takes place in speech as well as in other forms, postmodern feminists invite citizens to put on various identities. Even our bodies can be used to say new things as we recompose "our"selves.

Most importantly, postmodern feminists invite citizens to see themselves playing parts that enact feminist stories. Coalition politics brings out new selves as individuals and as communities when citizens are willing to engage in the back-and-forth, interactive, even spontaneous qualities of play. Such play enables citizens to put off our quest for final universal answers and to take on civic responsibilities as continuous struggles to make ethical decisions. Thus, we can turn, instead, to putting forth questions. Asking questions is a way of engaging in politics that urges citizens to negotiate with each other to formulate agendas that respond to issues at hand.

While others search for the end of politics, postmoderns embrace a playful politics of the moment that emerges through negotiating relationships. Rejecting the radical dream of an earlier matriarchal society, rejecting the liberal feminist dream of continuous progress toward a gender-just society, rejecting the marxist hope for the classless social order, and setting aside Adrienne Rich's "dream of a common language," postmodern feminists focus on local strategies and limit their goals to disrupting social orders as they play with language to keep politics alive, to keep the human spirit growing in both its public and private selves—to enable the personal to be political and the political to be personal.[18] In creating a permeable boundary between personal life and public life, I hope that postmodern feminism can lead the way in respecting the differences between these two arenas while encouraging citizens to develop an ethic that moves between them; that ethics can contain some ways to play with gender that enable citizens to develop a new understanding of themselves as gendered persons who create gendered public lives that contain, affirm, reject, and critique the male/female distinction.

Postmodern feminism gives me the sense that what people say to me matters and that what I say matters; this awareness makes life richer. Politics is not elsewhere—in Congress, in the court, in the United Nations, or even on the battlefield. It is in the everyday interactions of my life. As I speak to reconstitute political life with women as full citizens, my political actions recompose my political citizenship.

NOTES

1. In *The Philosophy of the Limit* (New York: Routledge, 1992), Drucilla Cornell makes a similar argument about the importance of judgment in making moral decisions.

2. In conversations that took place from 1989–91, Henry S. Kariel used this phrase to show how postmodern feminists articulate their position, which is one step in producing a reflective hermeneutic that permits citizens to share self-understandings. See also Henry S. Kariel, *The Desperate Politics of Postmodernism* (Amherst: University of Massachusetts Press, 1989).

3. María C. Lugones and Pat Alake Rosezelle, "Sisterhood and Friendship as Feminist Models," in *The Knowledge Explosion: Generations of Feminist Scholarship*, eds. Cheris Kramarae and Dale Spender (New York: Teacher's College Press, 1992), 406–12.

4. Theoretical discourse that utilizes the language of normative behavior and deviancy contributes to these fears.

5. Jean Bethke Elshtain, "On Patriotism," *Power Trips and Other Journeys: Essays in Feminism As Civic Discourse* (Madison: University of Wisconsin Press, 1990), 163–77.

6. For a postmodern analysis about community and unity, see William Corlett, *Community without Unity: A Politics of Derridian Extravagance* (Durham, N.C.: Duke University Press, 1989).

7. For analyses of similarity and difference in the intersection of race and gender, see bell hooks, Cornel West, Henry Louis Gates, María C. Lugones, and Patricia Williams.

8. For an application of this play of difference in feminist political theory, see Iris Marion Young, "The Ideal of Community and the Politics of Difference," in *Feminism/Postmodernism*, ed. Linda J. Nicholson (New York: Routledge, 1990), 300–323; and Iris Marion Young, *Justice and the Politics of Difference* (Princeton, N.J.: Princeton University Press, 1990).

9. Donna Haraway, "Primatology Is Politics by Other Means," in *Feminist Approaches to Science*, ed. Ruth Bleier (New York: Pergamon Press, 1986), 81–82.

10. Donna Haraway, *Primate Visions: Gender, Race, and Nature in the World of Modern Science* (New York: Routledge, 1989), 288.

11. Carol Gilligan, *In a Different Voice: Psychological Theory and Women's Development* (Cambridge, Mass.: Harvard University Press, 1982).

12. For the development of a political ethical self, see Michael J. Sandel's understanding of the encumbered self, *Democracy's Discontent: America in Search of a Public Philosophy* (Cambridge, Mass.: Belknap Press of Harvard University Press, 1996).

13. Dvora Yanow, *How Does a Policy Mean?: Interpreting Policy and Organizational Actions* (Washington, D.C.: Georgetown University Press, 1996).

14. Yanow, *How Does a Policy Mean?*, 1–33.

15. In "Playfulness, 'World'-Travelling, and Loving Perception," *Hypatia* 2 (1987): 3–19, María C. Lugones develops the metaphor of travel to explain how feminists can connect in cross-cultural ways.

16. For a summary of this debate and a new reflection on it that transcends the First Amendment issues versus speech codes, see Judith Butler, *Excitable Speech: A Politics of the Performative* (New York: Routledge, 1997), which responds to Mari J. Matsuda, Charles R. Lawrence III, Richard Delgado, and Kimberlé Williams Crenshaw, *Words That Wound: Critical Race Theory, Assaultive Speech and the First Amendment* (Boulder, Colo.: Westview Press, 1993).

17. Matsuda, Lawrence, Delgado, and Crenshaw, *Words That Wound*.

18. Judith Butler, *Gender Trouble: Feminism and the Subversion of Identity* (New York: Routledge, 1990), 149, and Elspeth Probyn, "Travels in the Postmodern: Making Sense of the Local," in *Feminism/Postmodernism*, ed. Nicholson, 176–89.

Chapter 11

Feminist Stories and a New Politics: Justice, Truth, and Ethics

FEMINIST POLITICS: JUSTICE, TRUTH, AND ETHICS

The connection between law and justice is important because the law enables citizens to talk about justice in public forums. In my analysis of the law and justice, I have argued that court cases serve as public stories. These cases can serve as the basis for public discussions that go beyond the outcome of the case to social patterns that the case illuminate. For example, *Roe v. Wade* did more than illuminate Jane Roe's problem; it illuminated the problem of women's access to abortions, which is why the Supreme Court took the case. While this issue was vital for women's safety in the United States, the case did more than simply prevent states from denying abortions to women in the first trimester. The case helped the entire nation focus on women's issues; it helped move women's issues from the private sector to the public. Similarly, Catharine MacKinnon encourages citizens to discuss pornography by bringing the issue to light through legislation and litigation. While who wins and which side makes the smartest feminist move are important, the most vital concern for feminist politics is how each case can bring women's concerns into American public discourse. Litigation is one way of getting citizens to talk about public issues. While this is certainly not the only way to organize public policy conversation, it has served this purpose because it brings together issues of justice and politics by focusing on concrete situations. Because court cases have implications for general policies, a focus on a particular case can help sharpen discussions. Despite the bias courts have against female experience, even courtroom situations can be used to get women's stories out. Clearly, feminist activists have used litigation to this end, and while it has not always produced the best solution, it has been an effective avenue for raising important social concerns. If feminists become even more aware of the way the courts make issues public, this forum can be even more useful in achieving justice for women and men.

In discussing feminist jurisprudence, I have argued that legal discourse can serve to get women's stories told in public. The law begins with individual cases and individual situations, but presents them in public forums and so politicizes those situations—that is, it makes them political matters. In this sense, the law moves from the personal individual level to the political. Robin West, in exploring the benefits of narrative, juxtaposes rights talk with narration. She argues that in the context of the courtroom, narratives create situations in which a community endeavors to understand a situation:

> When we tell stories, we not only convey information, but we share a piece of history; we expand not only our knowledge of what happened, of what someone did, but also of why and how they did it, of how it felt, why it seemed necessary, how it fit into a worldview.[1]

In other words, the narratives take the issue beyond that of who should win what in court. It takes matters beyond the issue of rights, which are primarily constituted by placing limits on government action. Courtrooms can be public forums for talking about conflicting social values and the contradictions in political structures. Courts may not so much resolve disputes as they air troubles. Cases like *Roe v. Wade*, O. J. Simpson's murder trial, and *Cleveland Board of Education v. La Fleur*, illuminate social tensions. Trials bring issues to light and enable citizens to talk about them in terms of a concrete case. Unfortunately, that talk can be narrowed to questions concerning the guilt or innocence of a particular individual. This can be frustrating and counterproductive because the public often does not have sufficient access to the details to render such a judgment. But the public does have sufficient information to reflect on the moral issues surrounding such issues as sexual harassment and the conflicts that compose those moral concerns. Feminists' concerns can guide the public beyond discussions of the guilt or innocence of a particular person and cases can then be used to discuss larger issues. Such discussions can empower the public to make judgments about women's situations and to remedy practices that promote gender injustices.

For feminists, this forum is vital. Even though the law has been shaped by patriarchal discourse, feminists have found ways to use the law to reform public discourse. Getting women's stories told in public can change the way the public talks about justice; and public talk can, in turn, change legal practices. This can happen even if the court case is lost. Litigants can gain satisfaction from the political victories that evolve through this public exposure, even as they experience the pain of legal defeat. As I mentioned in the section on jurisprudence, the Anita Hill example shows how moral judgments about sexual harassment have been reformed by her story, and the O. J. Simpson trials have refocused America's moral judgment on wife abuse and domestic violence. MacKinnon and Dworkin's work on pornography puts issues on the table in feminist terms and even though feminists disagree about the right direction to take on pornography, the public debate is framed through feminist discourse. This is a different situation than confronted the 1970s feminists, who had a time getting a serious public hearing. While feminism still lacks legitimacy, the terms of the discourse have changed. Feminists can use the courts as public forums to develop female-friendly, gender-inclusive discussions about political practices.

It is not an accident that some of the most popular recent media cases involve feminist concerns because feminist discourse encourages contesting values and airing conflicts. Examples include sexual and racial harassment, constitutional rights to privacy, employee protections, and protection of free sexual expression. Such discussions can help citizens understand these conflicts in the context of creating a just public life together and in the context of their own individual lives.

Feminist jurisprudence shows how stories do political work. First, the courtroom situation offers two stories that are often opposing narratives. This legal format then makes it possible to construct a third narrative that incorporates parts of the old stories but weaves them into a new story. The new story offers a new world view, a new mythos, for citizens to live by. For example, the public has used the Anita Hill story to construct a new story that encourages corporations and public sector organizations to work toward eliminating sexual harassment. In the new story, the corporations and organizations in the public sector become key players in taking responsibility for seeing that their employees are aware of how sexual harassment harms workplace relationships and productivity. The story moves from the private sphere, where the locus of responsibility is with individuals, to the public sphere, where the locus of responsibility is with organizations and groups. I have argued that legal discourse can get stories into the public and make it possible for the public to tell new stories that promise to help citizens avoid old injustices and render more fair judgments. Each case calls forth a third narrative that can enable citizens to become primary actors in creating new sets of circumstances that avoid the old traps. Such narratives will create new traps and call forth yet more stories to move citizens into new relationships with one another.

In this way, the courts can serve as arenas in which feminist narratives can be told, and so feminists can assume leadership positions in helping the public articulate the conflicting values and moral codes that such narratives reveal; certainly abortion represents such a value conflict. While the issues these conversations address are difficult, a democratic public must be prepared to discuss such difficulties. Lady Justice may today be better at helping citizens tell stories than she is at balancing a scale.[2] Telling such stories and then discussing the conflicting moral claims involved in them can enable citizens to make better judgments in their private and public lives. I am encouraging citizens to use the law as a forum for public discussions. This requires citizens to listen empathetically to each other by employing both reason and emotion, to review the conflicting values in situations, and to consider the cultural circumstances that shape contexts.

I have emphasized that what is important about the law from a political viewpoint is not the case or even the establishment of precedents. The law cannot by itself deliver justice to women. But what the law can do for women is to encourage American citizens to talk in public about the justice of women's situations. This talk can offer reflections and rules that guide citizens toward finding and internalizing more just practices for daily life. By providing citizens with a language for talking about justice, the law offers citizens ways of thinking about and sharing understandings of sex/gender issues. Whatever impulses have kept alive the phrase "the personal is political," this phrase helps articulate the role stories have in this legal process, because stories can move from personal experiences to public political concerns. Thus, the law can serve as a forum for making personal stories public and for talking about them in terms of justice. The law can offer feminists a forum for talking about justice for women and men. This is no small matter. I have argued that it is important that feminists frame such discussions in moral terms to encourage citizens to consider the ethical construction of their personal and public lives—to frame such conversations directly about justice. While legal cases tell stories and so help focus on the connection between justice and politics, feminists use stories in other arenas.

The connections that I have made between science and truth are important because truth is essential for political action. Political actions that are not based on the truth fail. Yet, if truth is understood as a cosmological certainty, a metaphysical set of laws, truth is separated from politics. Modernity and the epistemological strategies developed by logical positivism have created such a separation. It is not so much that politicians lie, as it is that modern American citizens think that the distinction between lying and truth has little relevance for political discourse. Feminist science offers hope in reconnecting truth and politics. To do this, feminist scientists have turned to stories to explain how science connects truth and politics. I have argued that by thinking about science as narratives, readers can understand how science provides true and accurate reports without elevating science to a place of worship. Such elevation not only strips science of political commitments but it also turns science into an abstract force. While scientists do pursue objective truth claims, they do so in the context of social life. Connecting social contexts and public life makes it possible for citizens to turn to science for understandings of what is true in the context of particular social locations, cultural values, and historical situations. This places scientists in the same plane with other citizens who come to public policy with a set of issues that they hope to realize and expertise for realizing them. While science cannot serve as the sole arbitrator of truth, scientific expertise contributes to public life by offering not only details about physical/natural phenomena, but also models for the critical exploration of truth claims. It is only when scientific truth claims are given cosmological status as the *only* avenue to truth that science becomes a tool of ideologues. Understanding science as storytelling helps citizens avoid using science as ideology. Thus, feminist scientists urge citizens to treat science as narratives because they provide true understanding of social life.

I have argued that feminist scientists offer citizens a new way of thinking about how to talk about the truth by breaking down the distinction between facts and values, between myth and reality, and between true stories and fictional narratives. Facts emerge as true in the context of a value system within a historical-cultural context. Facts depend on theories. Scientists rely on that value system and the theories that inform it to form their research. Approaches in anthropology and cultural studies, which understand myths as basic, sacred narratives that articulate a people's world view, help forge these general connections between fact and theory and between myth and social practice. This does not mean that the material conditions of human bodies and the world do not limit the social construction of social understandings. Myths, facts, and social practices become meaningful in the context of such material limitations; they do not erase them. Scientific truth is not arbitrary; a society cannot become whatever it wants to become. Nor is science relativistic in that truth depends on the beliefs of individual persons. Truth emerges in the context of a community's quest for knowledge, which takes place in the midst of the lives of its citizens and so myths can explain social practices, and social practices can give rise to new myths. Such myths form the basic world views that compose knowledge production. By speaking about science as a narrative made by scientist citizens who are part of a particular mythic world view, scientists can understand the ways in which imagination shapes both writing and reading science. Feminist science uses the metaphor of story to make this point in order to open up conversations about truth claims that include scientific discourse.

Using the metaphor of narrative to explain scientific epistemology makes scientists part of public life rather than separate from it. The story metaphor encourages scientists to act as citizens and to offer their insights on public policy issues. But equally important, this story metaphor invites scientists to broaden their gaze so as to include themselves in their observations. This story metaphor can help give scientists the authority to make judgments about the types of relationships that projects foster as well as about the methods that projects employ. However, this metaphor does not bestow exclusive authority on scientists for determining "the truth." No one approach to understanding the world can be so privileged. No one approach can be made the final arbitrator of truth. Just as the medieval power of the church needed to be reduced to one position among many, so science needs to be reduced to one position among many to avoid epistemological hegemony and the ignorance that such hegemony produces. Intellectual work thrives on the conflict of interpretations.[3] The story metaphor may make it easier for citizens to take a number of conflicting interpretations seriously.

Feminist scientists demonstrate that the story metaphor needs to reflect self-consciously on how gender enters into the images, tropes, and metaphors of scientific discourse to open up scientific discourse so that scientists and citizens can speak with one another. This assumes that both scientists and citizens are willing to reflect on how science shapes and is shaped by contemporary values, belief systems, and ideologies, including those based on race/ethnicity, sexuality, class, age, etc. The story metaphor can be used to talk about the practices that compose daily life and the priorities that might be used to recompose it.

The connection between politics and ethics exists in the ways in which postmodern feminists enable citizens to reflect on the ethical dimensions in their daily lives. Narratives have been an explicit part of postmodern feminist analyses from its inception. Borrowing from narrative theory in philosophy and the concrete political experiences of telling stories in the women's movement, postmodern feminists were in a handy position to talk about storytelling.[4] Rejecting grand narratives and turning to local narratives, postmodern feminists have engaged in cultural studies to uncover the power dimensions that constitute women as women and so shape gender relationships. Postmodern feminists argue that the constitution of everyday life creates foundational patterns that shape politics.[5] Even though this is not separate from the U.S. Constitution, it can be even more important than the Constitution even with its voluminous legal interpretations because habits guide everyday practices. While constitutional moves can create dramatic changes, changes can also come about as the result of one situation and one small action that ripples through the polity. Rosa Parks, who refused to give up her seat on the bus, and Ida B. Wells, who refused to leave her seat on the train, offer two models of how one action can set in motion major political changes. These changes take place not only in the political system itself but also in the lives of the women who serve as leaders in this way. While it is true that others must become involved to create such an extensive ripple, the process begins with an act that often appears quite small.

STORIES, FEMINISM, AND POLITICAL EXPERIENCE

Stories served feminists in the early sixties days as a form of consciousness raising as each woman told her story to a small group. Women talked away their invisibility and created solidarity with each other. This worked because women could genuinely connect with each other, and it worked in nonfeminist circles because Americans had developed a healthy respect for experience. This respect was encouraged by America's homegrown philosophy, pragmatism, which established the authority of experience. John Dewey, William James, and other pragmatist architects taught the importance of testing theories by living them and then retheorizing out of those lived experiences.[6] Theory, real life actions, and experience were stages in the process of knowing, and knowledge required all three. Because experience itself had been given a privileged place in understanding the world, American citizens were ready to pay attention to women's experience. Pragmatism, feminism, and praxis became important to women's studies because of the way this explained how theories shaped actions and how social action shaped theory.

It was then not surprising that second-wave feminists thought it important to build theory and social interpretations on the basis of life experiences, and narratives proved a way to communicate such experiences. Challenging much of what had been accepted as truth, women's narratives produced new theories, and these theories gave birth to a new body of knowledge—feminist scholarship and feminist theory. So women's studies, an interdisciplinary discipline, has come to serve as an organizing center for systematic revisions of paradigms, new epistemologies, new theoretical dialogues, and the development of new strategies of interpretation. This new body of knowledge has touched nearly every discipline and has played transforming roles in many of them—especially in the social sciences and humanities. The stories got out. They changed things, including how academics think about what they know. Pragmatism's reliance on experience and women's dramatic tales of experience made such transformations possible.

At the same time, the rise of postmodernism began questioning how experience worked. The notion of an unmediated experience came under scrutiny. Reports of experience seemed as much framed by cultural norms as by the unique events of an individual's life. Maybe the experiences women reported arose because they expected them to arise. They did not constitute a separate discovery by many women located in different places but a shared ideology that created expectations that themselves shaped experience. Life copied art, and art was shaped by cultural practices. Experiences were not so much the reports of actual "real" events as they were learned patterns of expectations and interpretation. For example, teachers who were told that some students had potential to outperform others later reported that these same students had risen above the others. This story explained the self-fulfilling prophesy. But this is only one small part of the extent to which experience as a raw category was challenged. The Cinderella tale shaped little girls' expectations of themselves in love relationships to the extent that they had a Cinderella-like experience. Even tales of abuse came under review as events that could be created as well as actually remembered. Experience was subject to interrogation and no longer served as the anchor for the truth. This issue was not politically neutral because women had used the report of their experiences to correct scholarly errors. Now a new body of scholarship, some of it supported by feminists, was questioning the accuracy of those reports. If experience was now to be considered a sort of fiction that may or may not be accurate in its details, women's credibility was once again in danger.

Even postmodern feminists saw this problem.[7] Hence, the term "unmediated experience" became important because it attempts to blend pragmatism, which relies on experience, with postmodernism, which argues that experience is itself shaped by cultural practices and symbols. Postmoderns have been careful to point out that they are not simply talking about the experiences of marginalized groups but are instead problematizing the notion of objectivity, which is embedded in the concept of an unmediated, raw experience. Without giving up the primary role of culture in shaping experience, feminists began to explain how experience could still be used to understand social truth even in its mediated state. Sandra Harding provided part of the basis for this link, and her respect for both Nancy Hartsock and Donna Haraway provided the epistemological spirit that could serve to recredit experience. Harding's development of ethnoscience explained how objective truth can depend on cultural practices rather than universal laws for its epistemological anchor.[8] This move made it possible for feminists to continue to talk about experiences without making the claim that those experiences offered a final or fundamental truth that made all other interpretations false. Experience counts, but it no longer counts as a trump card. Some feminists are uncomfortable with this understanding of experience. Others find it politically useful because Nazis and others whose agenda conflicts with feminist values were beginning to use their experiences as trump cards. Experience had been especially useful to women and others who were in out-of-power situations because it encouraged listening to unfamiliar situations. But experience failed to provide a sufficiently critical edge to move citizens toward ethical political judgments. Trading experiences does not always produce true understandings and may not move citizens toward ethical reflection.

While experience was being reframed, its link with storytelling was also altered. Stories were being separated from "real" life reports; fictional narratives and poems continued to contribute importantly to feminist theory and politics. Alice Walker's *The Color Purple*, a novel, and Maxine Hong Kingston's *The Woman Warrior*, an autobiography that contains mythic and fictional narrations mixed with "real" life reports, became standard works in feminist theory. Audre Lorde explained that "poetry was not a luxury" and the role of imagination, fiction, poetry, dance, and other artistic articulations took center stage as ways of performing theory. Audre Lorde, Adrienne Rich, Susan Griffin, Ntozake Shange were read simultaneously as theorists and as poets. Women's stories conveyed theory. Philosophy could be accomplished through poetry as well as through arguments; feminist scholars looked to both philosophy and literature departments for colleagues who generated new theory. This was even more central in political philosophy because politics itself relies on poetry as well as on social science to articulate central issues.

This does not mean that feminists divorce politics from truth. Truth is not necessarily to be found in so-called "real" life reports but may be communicated through scenarios, examples, and fictional representations that illuminate abstract concepts and reveal philosophical truths. Storytelling, whether told through imaginative examples or through so-called "real" life reports, can move citizens closer to reflective understandings of their world because all stories—both real and imagined, both "true" accounts and fictionalized accounts—do more than simply report experiences. Thus, stories offer something that goes beyond personal experience. The shift from real life accounts to narratives that include fictions is politically important because it acknowledges the way in which stories convey ethical codes. Stories can be used to hear how the storytelling envisions the world without necessarily accepting that all the claims within the narrative represent accurate reports of world events. This does not mean that it does not matter which events are actual and which imagined. It does mean that there are other ways to listen to stories besides searching for the correlation between world events and the actions presented in the story. Because stories are already understood as interpretations of the world, stories need not be heard as recreations of real life events but instead can be seen as ways of highlighting the meaning of events. This gives stories a different epistemological base that suggests that all stories convey a truth about the conceptual understandings of the storytelling. In this sense, all stories are telling because they explain how citizens might live well together. Stories are more than oral histories; stories are more than reports. Feminists began to listen to stories to understand the ethical concerns that the stories reveal.

While second-wave feminists used stories to engage in feminist consciousness raising, before the 1960s women were telling stories to pass on their wisdom to their children, to other women, and to men. The image of the woman storyteller is a common one in American culture, although this image often pictures her doing this as private work. Moving women's storytelling from a private intimate setting to a political one has helped bring women's wisdom into public political conversations. Dale Spender helped second-wave feminists reflect on the history of women's knowledge, which has been preserved through a variety of narratives. Spender begins *Women of Ideas*, an 800-page work with Aphra Behn (whose first play, *The Forced Marriage* was performed in 1670), and she concludes it with her own comments on second-wave feminism, which she labels with the subheading, "The Old, Old Story" (a part of the section called, "Reinventing Rebellion"). [9] The old story is one in which a male literary critic finds an article by two feminists lacking because the women do not appear attractive in their picture. Telling such "old" and oft-repeated stories has encouraged women to make their pain public, seeking new grounds for political resistance and rebellion. Acknowledging that her work represents only a small sample of women's ideas, Spender shows her readers how women tell stories to articulate their thoughts and feelings. Some of these narratives are fictional, some are autobiographical, and some are historical; all are designed to articulate the truth about women's situations in order to change them. In times of intense misogyny, homophobia, and racism, these narratives preserve women's wisdom; they are telling. Recent publications like Patricia Bell-Scott's *Life Notes: Personal Writings by Contemporary Black Women*, Mary Catherine Bateson's *Composing a Life*, and Carolyn G. Heilbrun's *Writing a Woman's Life* demonstrate the ways current feminists as well as others seek to understand women by listening to them report their experiences.[10] Earlier works like the dairies of Ida B. Wells, the essays by Teresa of Avila, the *History of Woman Suffrage* by Elizabeth Cady Stanton, Susan B. Anthony, and Matilda Joslyn Gage and others, also preserve women's interpretations of their life experiences. Jill Ker Conway's *Written by Herself* is an anthology of autobiographies of women who challenged the practices of science, art, politics, and slavery in America.[11] This work illuminates how narratives reveal women's political work. The emphasis on personal experience and life narratives within second-wave feminism has demonstrated how stories can encourage public conversations about difficult and painful topics. The life stories of women in the sciences and in other disciplines have inspired those disciplines to become more gender inclusive. English and modern languages have revised their canons by incorporating female writers and poets; history has revised its content by examining women's contributions to societies; and science has reflected on its methods by examining the lives of such persons as Nobel Prize winner Barbara McClintock.[12] Ida B. Wells recorded her life stories in diaries that now serve to teach others about politics. Coming-out narratives have enabled the articulation of lesbian experiences in ways that convey the delight that comes with an affirming self-understanding, the pain that comes with prejudice, the insight that comes by connecting personal difficulties with political injustices, and the transformations that come with a new political movement.[13] A variety of narratives including those about heterosexism, sexism, domestic violence, sexual harassment, racism, and other public problems have helped the American public understand these issues. For example, lesbian narratives have helped heterosexuals see the political harm caused by punishing people because they love someone of the same sex, and coming-out stories offer ways of discussing these matters with friends and family. Because stories are mainstays of academic feminism and vital for feminist politics, it is important to reflect on how stories perform political work.

STORIES AND POLITICAL PERFORMANCES

Stories offer feminists two important political virtues: (1) the integration of emotional and rational analyses and (2) a means for productive dialogues among diverse citizens. Because stories encourage citizens to listen intently and empathetically to each other, they work well in creating conversations among persons whose experiences differ. In other words, stories can provide a forum that mediates the experiences of persons situated differently within sociopolitical systems. This gives stories their enduring quality, but more importantly, for feminist politics it makes it possible for women to access the experiences of women from a variety of historical periods, cultural contexts, marginalized situations, and social classes.

Stories and the Integration of Emotion and Reason

First, stories present information in ways that encourage storytellers and listeners to reflect on both the emotional and rational aspects of events. Unlike the empirical research design, which also has its own sort of credibility, the story has emotional dimensions; its data are not faceless and unindividuated as are the data presented by empirical analyses. Because stories highlight the lives of a few persons, they encourage readers to identify with them almost as they might identify with a neighbor. Such identification can inspire citizens to act on behalf of their neighbors' needs. At the same time, telling the story in public encourages listeners to reflect on a range of individual cases that form patterns in public life. This encourages citizens to address a problem at the level of its manifestation as a pattern rather than to help one person at a time. However, citizens can do this without being tempted to design solutions for all persons in the world. The private story made public can jolt citizens to act not only on behalf of an individual but on behalf of individuals who are similarly situated. By telling stories about their experience of discrimination, both black and white women awakened America in the 1960s and introduced a new political era. Similarly, the individual narratives of blacks, Hispanics, Hawaiians, Chicanos/Chicanas, and others have helped citizens experience the pain of racism and the joy of solidarity with those who work to eradicate racism. The narratives of abused children, battered wives, and harassed employees have transformed American public policies at both the national and local levels. Stories offer a strategy for social change, and feminists have encouraged women to seek public forums—the electronic media, magazines, newspapers, and large public assemblies—to tell "their/our" stories—stories of rape, incest, sexual harassment, job discrimination, and addiction.

Unlike the news story or the research report, personal narratives incorporate a person-to-person reporting format, and the narration process itself creates a connection between the storyteller and the listener, which is augmented by avoiding the depersonalized third-person voice sometimes assumed by the media and scientific style reports. In ways that philosophy seldom can, stories can make us cry and laugh; they move us. Thus, they can move citizens to action. This motivation may be especially important at times when citizens need to feel empowered.

However, simply moving citizens to act does not solve political problems. What matters is moving citizens to act in ways that support a better public life. In this regard, stories can both help and hurt. Plato was quite suspicious of the emotional qualities of narratives, and so he did not want poets in his republic because of their ability to sway public opinion. Stories can also be used to move citizens to enact greater injustices. Certainly, Hitler used stories for this purpose. Those critical of current feminism, like Daphne Patai, Christina Hoff Sommers, and Camille Paglia, argue that feminism—both academic feminism and feminist politics—is dominated by emotion, sentiment, victim ideology, and antifemale beliefs.[14] Patai explains how many feminists have experienced attempts to silence them by other feminists who don't want feminism represented in a particular way. These critics suggest that narrow feminist ideologies hold women captive and present unfounded conclusions about women. Narratives that blend emotion and reason can fuel such ideologies. Such errors, like weeds, seem to grow alike in liberal, conservative, left, and radical academic environments. Feminists, like others, err. On the other hand, American ideologies often demand perfection in women while imperfections in men and antifeminists are more easily forgiven.

While Plato argued that poetic narrative power could encourage citizens to select immoral actions over moral ones, I have suggested throughout this text that becoming more aware of the emotional dimensions of our situations makes citizens more able to make just and fair decisions. Privileging reason and suppressing emotions does not work. Taking account of both reason and emotion can enable citizens to make better decisions. Encouraging reflection about personal and public passions, experiences, feelings, thoughts, and reasons, create a better basis for judgments. It is often more dangerous to ignore, suppress, and/or control emotions than it is to deal with the emotional elements that compose even explosive situations.

Narratives invite the listener to understand the position of those in the story and to identify with them. That empathy can encourage citizens to care about one another. If listeners "take stories to heart," narratives can help citizens to look up close and put themselves into the situations of those in the story, thus, creating a bond between the listener and those whose lives inform the narrative. This can lead citizens to consider reformations—reformations of themselves, of public policies, and of the everyday cultural practices that guide the sociopolitical system. Focusing on the self as part of political reform can discourage the sort of domination that distance nurtures.

Dialogue and Diverse Citizens

Second, stories encourage citizens to expand their horizons beyond their own experience. The language of story creates openness by asking citizens to listen to another very intently without focusing on a counterargument. In this way, stories support the development of empathy and community among persons who may have very different backgrounds, experiences, values, and images. For example, stories bridge discipline differences within the academy by enabling analysts to blend fact and fancy, experience and fantasy, and description and imagination. This sort of bridge can help literature departments that work with fiction and social science departments that focus on facts to speak with each other about the articulation of the truth. Perhaps the recent interest in autobiography demonstrates the ways in which the personal narrative serves as a dramatic case of what is true of stories in general. Making this bridge, stories can bring together systems of information that are normally kept apart, such as science and literature— the former focused on facts and the latter focused on fantasy. And they can be useful in bridging cultural differences.

This process works because storytelling encourages listeners to suspend skepticism. While skepticism has been valuable in critical feminist thought, it has liabilities in that listeners may become skeptical before they understand a situation. Suspending suspicion and skepticism can help a citizen understand unfamiliar viewpoints before they move onto a critical analysis of them. For example, for a long period of time, citizens were skeptical about sexual harassment because they did not want to believe it happened and because it was so unfamiliar to them that they could not make sense of reported incidents. In other words, skepticism made it harder to hear the victims' reports. Because telling a story involves suspending judgment until the story is completed, it can offer the listener a more solid base from which to under-stand, that is, stand under the experiences of those in the story. Furthermore, stories can satisfy citizens' desires to gain experiences that stretch beyond the boundaries of their own lives, because stories communicate both emotional and factual dimensions. For example, Minnie Pratt's essay about overcoming racism illustrates how she was able to get beyond her own historical cultural roots. She "traveled" in the way María Lugones suggests, so that she did not simply meet "others," but met them as unrealized parts of herself.[15] Lugones and Pratt offer a view of feminism that is dynamic and playful rather than static and unitary. As I have suggested, the term used in Hawaii—"talk story"—encourages cross-cultural communication by adding a personal narration to interactions that help citizens understand the cultural context each brings to the interaction.

Narratives can bridge other types of differences as well. For example, narratives can facilitate dialogues between experts in a field and other citizens. Stories enable citizens to claim their own expertise as narrators of their experiences. The ability to tell a story does not depend on educational certifications, class privilege, or other specialized skills, even though there are differences among individual storytelling talents. But this sort of education is easier to obtain, especially for those without economic resources, than is the education required to communicate through genres often used by social science and philosophy. Because stories value local discourses, it may be the case that a story listener will find a story told in a dialect different from his or her own more engaging rather than less so. The poor are often quite able to explain their experiences through narratives even though they may be less able to use social science methodologies to analyze their situation. In this sense, telling a story is often a more accessible genre. More important, telling a story grants for a moment a certain amount of authority to the storyteller. Thus, for those out of power, storytelling may be particularly valuable.

A third way in which the narrative form enables conversations between different groups occurs in the academy. The narrative form offers a mode of discourse and analysis that is multidisciplinary. While literary scholars have for some time studied what can be called stories, and historians have for some time understood themselves as telling stories about the past, more recently philosophers from a variety of perspectives have begun to suggest that their work is performed by telling stories.[16] Feminist scholars have for some time self-consciously used narratives to do their work. For example, Bettina Aptheker in *Tapestries of Life*, demonstrates not only the ways in which stories bring feminists into contact with the dailiness of women's lives, but also the range of feminist theorists who call upon the image of story to explain their work.[17] Aptheker's analysis shows how story serves as a feminist method of analysis throughout various feminist discourses.

For empirical social scientists, the use of story for analysis begins with the use of scenarios as a mode of communicating possible situations to respondents or as a mechanism for communicating possible outcomes of the interaction of a multiplicity of variables. From the scenario, which is a brief, highly stylized narrative, social scientists have begun to use stories in survey research and to collect narratives as ways of understanding cultures. Certainly, anthropologists were leaders in this methodological strategy, but others have followed, and now one can find, especially in oral history, ethnography, and other phenomenologically influenced methods, a reliance upon story as an important form in which information is communicated.[18] For example, Emily Martin uses stories and metaphors very effectively to show how working-class women talk to their children about menstruation.[19]

Story has also played an important role in religious studies, and feminist spirituality has relied on narrative as an important way in which religious understandings can be shared. Certainly, Carol Christ's *Diving Deep and Surfacing* demonstrates the important role of story in religious studies. Liberation theology itself works to render authority especially to those who lack material resources. Hence, inviting these people to tell stories is especially important and the accessibility of story is vital.

For feminist scholars, these interdisciplinary features of the narrative form are important because stories can serve as a common point of departure for interdisciplinary conversations. This is especially important for feminist scholars who work in interdisciplinary contexts. Hence, narratives can offer a common process for revealing information even though disciplines might vary in how they extract information from such narratives.

Thus, an emphasis on stories can support democratic conversations because the process of storytelling encourages listening to one another with a generous spirit. Although this generous spirit need not avoid critical reflection, it does avoid the sort of skepticism that begins with the assumption that a report is a lie. It rejects the assumption that the other lacks authority and legitimacy until they prove themselves worthy. The assumption in active listening is that the storyteller has a message to deliver and that the message has truth and import, although the listener may discover that a narrative was a lie. The first assumption is generous. While at first glance this might look like Pollyanna feminism, it is not. This sort of assumption is common practice in the United States. In fact, citizens cannot maintain skepticism about the myriad of information that comes their way. What happens instead is that citizens often use skepticism to scrutinize those who are out of power while simply accepting the dominant view. I am arguing for extending this acceptance to those in the margins. Furthermore, the mechanism of so-called objective descriptions and skeptical approaches often endangers critiques because combative questions silence intellectual exchanges. Neither academic feminists nor feminists in other settings will stay in a conversation for long if its form or telos is verbal combat. Feminists alert to the problems of the permanent other are often intolerant of playing subordinate roles.

THE POLITICS IN READING, TELLING, AND ENACTING STORIES

Postmodern feminism explains how ethics is composed by citizens in the activities of their daily lives. Daily actions work together to shape and reform how citizens think about ethics. So daily speech plays a part in forming the codes that guide citizens in their lives together. In this way, speech shapes politics. Speaking is a political act. Speech and its multiplicity of forms including painting, sculpture, architecture, dance, and gestures, express the values of a people. The accumulation of the speeches of a people form their grammar, which encodes the ethics of their everyday lives together. Stories are enacted at the level of daily life as local narratives which spin an ethical code that is preserved and shaped by the myths of a people. These myths are to be respected as they offer ways of connecting the events of daily life with historical traditions, cosmologies, and political philosophies. But the story metaphor can enable citizens to hold such myths more contingently, more playfully. Stories acquire this power especially in the latter half of the twentieth century because stories are seen as outside the rigid bounds of reason and the "business" of public life; they are feminine. They may be considered feminine because they are not rigid, but it may also be that women have called on stories because other avenues of power were blocked. This feminine quality has made it easier for citizens to tell stories playfully and to listen to them playfully.

To read a story playfully means using the story as a way of understanding some aspect of life. Playful readings avoid turning stories into fanciful commandments. Stories are calls to action but not blueprints for it. A good political response to a story does not require the reader to do what the story tells the reader to do. Readers need not take up the cause of the heroes or heroines of the tale. Stories are not colorful commandments that offer citizens political rules. But stories can enable citizens to gain broader understandings of situations and to reflect on possible outcomes of actions that they might choose. Stories are political to the extent that they enable citizens to understand each other and to appreciate the contributions that each makes to the common good as well as the temptations that each faces to reject a common good.

Playful, contingent understandings of rules help make change possible. Narratives can help shake a rigid law into a guiding principle that itself evolves and changes as circumstances alter. Recontexualizing rules and traditions enables them to continue to flourish and change. Just as political scientists speak about the living Constitution, which the American legal system continues to adapt, so the rules, traditions, and habits of a people are "alive" and thus continue to evolve and change. Living in an environment free of such rules and guidelines would be unhealthy and it is quite likely impossible. It would be equally unhealthy to avoid adaptations of such rules and principles in the course of daily life. Stories help citizens talk about the polity that is composed between no rules (anarchy) and rigid obedience to rules (authoritarianism). Ethics involves negotiating that in-between ground so as to be fair to as many citizens and other beings as possible.

Such negotiation begins with the self. Postmodernism encourages citizens to understand themselves in terms both of similarity and difference and to continue to recompose themselves in the process of acting politically. Thus, politics, while not a tool for accomplishing tasks, is necessary for individual and collective self-development and growth. In expressing their political selves, citizens articulate the good and the ill within themselves and in others. By listening carefully to the ways in which citizens constitute their lives through the various forms of communication, citizens can make their ethical codes explicit and discuss them. Such discussions will always be limited by the cultural context and the inequalities of power within that context. Recognizing the limitation is a recognition of the fact that all stories cannot be told at once nor can all stories be heard at once. Some stories will rule while others wait. Feminists understand what it means to wait and how painful that can be. Waiting for some two thousand years, Western feminists have only recently found a public voice for women. But this long wait has made feminists aware of the importance of listening. Feminists continue to find ways to make the personal political in order to forge a place in public life for women.

Postmodern feminists give narratives a different sort of status. They take personal narratives one step further by suggesting that parts of these narratives come from the collective mythos of a people. Understanding narratives as articulations of the myths present in a culture suggest that new narratives can produce a set of new cultural practices. New narratives can reform understandings of the past, present, and future in ways that open up new political practices.

The multiplicity of viewpoints offered by thinking about life in terms of stories fits well with contemporary feminist concerns. Because stories integrate emotions and reason, they bridge differences among feminists and can move feminists toward collective, collaborative action. Listening to each other's stories supports relationships and offers avenues for building connections that honor both commonalities and differences. While it is important to understand the reasons why so many feminists call on stories, I have focused on the image of conversation rather than that of narration. In considering feminist conversations about the law, science, and the postmodern, I have wanted to connect the political implications of feminist conversations, which themselves shape public stories.

GOING BEYOND STORIES

Stories and ethical reflections, however, are not enough. Getting public stories told is not enough. Narratives are not a way to avoid political differences. They are not a method for finding the truth to resolve conflicts and make good decisions. The dream that some method can provide humans with salvation from all error disappears with the eclipse of positivism. But citizens do need to find ways to talk about the truth, that encourage moral reflection, political action, and forgiveness.

I have suggested throughout these chapters that politics requires reflection on personal and public values, a willingness to correct both private and public behaviors, and the ability to forgive those who offend us. In this regard, a playful politics involves an element of forgiveness. But forgiveness without change merely excuses bad behavior and thereby encourages it. Correction without forgiveness creates hostilities, giving birth to new wrongs that replace the old ones. But forgiveness does not mean forgetfulness, and forgiveness cannot occur until injuries and offenses have been discussed. Injustices need to be identified and remembered in order for the practices that perpetuate them to be addressed and changed. It is the commitment to social change that makes forgiveness possible and facilitates healing. Forgiveness is not a response to an apology but takes place in response to a new way of being that rights old wrongs. Changes in individuals and social life are the preconditions for forgiveness. Social changes signal that a story has been heard. Once the tale is told, once the truth is explored, once the new narratives are articulated, feminists call citizens to enact a new story that institutionalizes the wisdom in that social change.

While feminists have sometimes been uncomfortable with the language of morality, we have been clear about the connection between politics and justice. Even feminist scholars cannot avoid the realization that their work has immediate relevance and that it has political significance. But any understanding of injustice is incomplete and even damaging unless citizens act to change those injustices. Naming is important but insufficient for change to occur, and while telling new stories is important, it too is not enough. To build a public life together, citizens need to act collectively on behalf of those new stories, to enact them. This collective action might take the form of speech, but to be strategic, this speech needs to be directed toward social change. The affirmation of feminist values is not enough, nor is the negation of patriarchy. Without collective action, feminist communities become apolitical places for sharing stories. While affirmations and patriarchal critiques nurture individuals, they do not offer the vital opportunities for growth that can be realized through political work.

First- and second-wave feminists demonstrated a fierce political courage. Only by taking the risk to enact values can feminists find ways of continuing to grow both personally and politically. Those risks need to be formulated by reflections on justice, truth, and ethics, and those reflections need to take place in the context of a generous spirit toward all, including ourselves, who inevitably fall short of our expectations. Public life requires citizens to make basic commitments to one another in the context of the variety of interactions that compose the life of a people. Those citizens need to offer affection, affirmation, constructive critique, and love, because without those qualities, political associations that are aimed at social change are too painful. Such basic commitments cannot be fully encoded in the law or constituted by language or preserved by narratives. The commitments are forged in the context of living a public life with others. This brings me back to my introduction where I avoided the pronoun "we" because I was concerned that this term was unpersuasive and perhaps even manipulative. I now want to return to this term and argue that we move toward the formulation of a "we" that affirms the ways in which "we" as a variety of political communities exist with each other and so need to find ways to exist in solidarity with each other.[20] While it has been important to problematize "we" and to articulate the divisions that make that word stick in the throats of many, it is also important to find ways in which we can connect with one another in communities and in coalitions. Without a "we" there can be no "us" or even an "I" because each of us becomes a full person, a full citizen, in the context of living with, and for, others.

To create a public life, citizens need to develop the discipline of negotiating with each other in a generous and playful spirit. Politics is not a zero-sum game because the end of politics is the end of human existence. But justice, truth, and ethics are not enough; citizens need to seek them in the context of a community in which each citizen offers the others affection and respect. Feminism has taught me that politics works best when stories are formulated with love, boldly told, and compassionately enacted.

NOTES

1. Robin West, *Narrative, Authority, and Law* (Ann Arbor: The University of Michigan Press, 1993), 425.

2. Eloise A. Buker, "'Lady' Justice: Power and Image in Feminist Jurisprudence," *Vermont Law Review* 15 (1990): 69–87.

3. Paul Ricoeur, *The Conflict of Interpretations: Essays in Hermeneutics*, ed. Don Ihde (Evanston, Ill.: Northwestern University Press, 1974).

4. For a review of the literature on narrative that excludes feminist theories of the narrative, see Martin Kreiswirth, "Tell Me a Story: The Narrative Turn in the Human Sciences," in *Constructive Criticism: The Human Sciences in the Age of Theory*, eds. Martin Kreiswirth and Thomas Carmichael (Toronto: University of Toronto Press, 1995), 61–87.

5. While I am aware that postmoderns hesitate in eliciting the image of a "foundation," I want to suggest here that there are certain foundational concerns within the postmodern perspective.

6. Timothy V. Kaufman-Osborn, *Creatures of Prometheus: Gender and the Politics of Technology* (Rowman & Littlefield, 1997), and *Politics/Sense/Experience: A Pragmatic Inquiry into the Promise of Democracy* (Ithaca, N.Y.: Cornell University Press, 1991); for connections between praxis and political theory, see Richard J. Bernstein, *Praxis and Action: Contemporary Philosophies of Human Activity* (Philadelphia: University of Pennsylvania Press, 1971).

7. Furthermore, the work of Richard Rorty linked postmodern theory and pragmatism in ways that credited story even as it questioned experience; see especially *Contingency, Irony, and Solidarity* (New York: Cambridge University Press, 1989).

8. Sandra G. Harding, *Is Science Multicultural?: Postcolonialisms, Feminisms, and Epistemologies* (Bloomington: Indiana University Press, 1998).

9. Dale Spender, *Women of Ideas: And What Men Have Done to Them: From Aphra Behn to Adrienne Rich* (Boston: ARK, Routledge, 1982), 35, 728.

10. Patricia Bell-Scott, *Life Notes: Personal Writings by Contemporary Black Women* (New York: Norton, 1994); Mary Catherine Bateson, *Composing a Life* (New York: Atlantic Monthly, 1989); and Carolyn G. Heilbrun, *Writing a Woman's Life* (New York: Norton, 1988).

11. Jill Ker Conway, ed., *Written by Herself: Autobiographies of American Women: An Anthology* (New York: Vintage Books, 1992).

12. Evelyn Fox Keller, *A Feeling for the Organism: The Life and Work of Barbara McClintock* (San Francisco, Calif.: W. H. Freeman, 1983).

13. Trudy Darty and Sandee Potter, eds., *Women-Identified Women* (Palo Alto, Calif.: Mayfield Publishing Co., 1984).

14. Daphne Patai and Noretta Koertge, *Professing Feminism: Cautionary Tales from the Strange World of Women's Studies* (New York: Basic Books, 1994); Christina Hoff Sommers, *Who Stole Feminism: How Women Have Betrayed Women* (New York: Simon & Schuster, 1994); and Camille Paglia, *Sexual Personae: Art and Decadence from Nefertiti to Emily Dickinson* (New Haven, Conn.: Yale University Press, 1990).

15. María Lugones, "Playfulness, 'World'-Travelling, and Loving Perception," *Hypatia* 2 (summer 1987): 3–19; and Minnie Bruce Pratt, "Identity: Skin Blood Heart," in Elly Bulkin, Minnie Bruce Pratt, Barbara Smith, *Yours in Struggle: Three Feminist Perspectives on Anti-Semitism and Racism* (New York: Long Haul Press, 1984), 9–63.

16. See Rorty, *Contingency, Irony, and Solidarity*; Alasdair MacIntyre, *After Virtue: A Study in Moral Theory* (Notre Dame, Ind.: University of Notre Dame Press, 1981); and Jostein Gaarder, *Sophie's World: A Novel about the History of Philosophy*, trans. Paulete Moller (New York: Harper Collins, 1994).

17. Bettina Aptheker, *Tapestries of Life: Women's Work, Women's Consciousness, and the Meaning of Daily Experience* (Amherst: University of Massachusetts Press, 1989), 37–74.

18. Eloise A. Buker, *Politics through a Looking-Glass: Understanding Political Culture through a Structuralist Interpretation of Narratives* (New York: Greenwood Press, 1987).

19. Emily Martin, *The Woman in the Body: A Cultural Analysis of Reproduction* (Boston: Beacon Press, 1987).

20. For discussion of the importance of "we," see Jean Bethke Elshtain, *Democracy on Trial* (New York: Basic Books, 1995), 128–31.

Index

abortion, 2, 20, 34, 50–51, 63, 89–90, 106, 151, 174, 194, 207, 209
academic, 3, 9, 57, 77–78, 89–91, 96, 152–53, 158, 177, 180, 195, 202, 213, 216–18, 221
affirmative action, 160, 182
African-American, 91, 93, 158–59, 166, 182, 183, 192
Altmann, Jeanne, 85–86
ambiguity, 112, 191
Anglo-Saxons, 159, 168, 191
antifeminist, 2, 149, 160, 218
antifoundational, 189, 201–2
Anthony, Susan B., 215
Aptheker, Bettina, 220
Arendt, Hannah, 24, 131
Aristotle, 24, 200
authoritarianism, 222
authority, 12, 17–18, 20–30, 36, 38, 41–43, 52, 64, 67, 78–79, 90, 95, 101–6, 123, 126–27, 140, 153, 190, 199, 211–13, 219–21

Bartlett, Katharine, 55–56
Bateson, Mary Catherine, 215
Bauman, Zygmunt, 147
Beauvoir, Simone de, 170
Bell-Scott, Patricia, 215
Bender, Leslie, 56–57
blacks, 34, 48, 49, 59–60, 91–93, 139, 158–59, 176, 182–83, 193, 215, 217; black movement, 2, 158; black feminist thought, 53, 158
Bleier, Ruth, 102–4
Bordo, Susan, 171
Bumiller, Kristin, 52, 55
Butler, Judith, 158, 147, 169–73, 182, 184

canon, 216
capitalism, 80, 105, 140
Caraway, Nancie, 181–82
Chicano, 182, 193, 217
children, 10, 30, 35, 40–41, 79–80
Christianity, 64, 105, 151, 165
class, 10–11, 91, 191, 49–50, 183–84, 194, 216, 219
Cleveland Board of Education v. La Fleur, 208
Coeur d'Alene, 49
Collins, Patricia Hill, 93, 158
consciousness-raising, 54, 56–57, 59, 90, 212
Conway, Jill Ker, 216
Cook, Judith, 90–91
Cornell, Drucilla, 35, 150
cosmology, 102, 114, 144
Cott, Nancy, 94
Crenshaw, Kimberlé Williams, 53
cross-cultural, 218–19
cyberspace, 167, 173–174

day care, 2
decenter, 144, 156–60
deconstruction, 35, 146–48, 150, 157–58, 160, 165
Defries, Emma, 139–40
deliberative democracy, 131
democracy, 6–8, 10, 12, 20, 105, 117, 131
Derrida, Jacques, 35, 147–49, 153
dialectic, 21, 66, 111
discursive practices, 14
domestic violence, 21, 208–9, 212
double burden, 2

ecofeminism, 151, 197
EEOC v. Sears, Roebuck & Co, 71

Eisenstein, Hester, 150
Eisenstein, Zillah, 30–31, 35, 149
Elazar, Daniel J., 38–39, 41
Elshtain, Jean Bethke, 131, 149, 224
empowerment, 23–25, 28, 43, 54, 69–70,
    82, 93, 153, 208, 217
Enlightenment, 66–67, 78, 104–5, 120, 122,
    133, 145, 154, 167
epistemology, 75, 77–78, 80–81, 85–86,
    88–91, 93–97, 101–4, 110–14, 120–23,
    126, 132, 140, 148, 155–56, 158, 211,
    213–15
essentialism, 92–93, 138–40, 151–52,
    158–60
ethics of care, 25–27, 32–35, 39–41, 57,
    168–69, 175–76, 189–90, 218–19
ethnicity, 8, 10–11, 35, 69, 79, 112, 130–31,
    137–40, 160, 175, 181–83, 194, 199, 212
Euro-American, 34, 93, 139, 166, 169, 183

family, 15, 29–30, 33, 35–41, 81, 139–40,
    160, 171–72, 176, 183, 192–93, 195, 198
Fedigan, Linda, 88, 95
femininity, 13, 30, 34–35, 51, 58–59, 78–81,
    111, 129, 132, 147, 151, 165–66, 169,
    178–81, 184, 221
feminist imagination, 2, 112
feminization of poverty, 1
feminization of the self, 1
first-wave feminism, 1–2, 27, 8, 204, 223
Fish, Stanley, 147, 176– 77
Flax, Jane, 155
folktale, 101–4
Ferguson, Kathy, 147
Fonow, Mary Margaret, 90–91
Foucault, Michel, 25, 76, 146–47, 148–49,
    153, 171
Fraser, Nancy, 147
freedom, 2, 5, 36–37, 51, 126, 141, 173
Freeman, Jo, 27
Frontiero v. Richardson, 50
fundamentalism, 5, 112, 151–52, 158, 177

Gadamer, Hans-Georg, 147
Gage, Matilda Joslyn, 215
Geertz, Clifford, 97
genealogy, 35, 146–48, 171
Gilligan, Carol, 33–35, 102, 149, 197
Ginzberg, Ruth, 103
Griffin, Susan, 214

Habermas, Jürgen, 76, 199
Haraway, Donna, 85, 88, 91, 95–97, 102,
    106–8, 111–13, 120, 147, 154, 165–70,
    195–96, 214

Harding, Sandra, 90, 92–95, 97, 102, 106–7,
    109–11, 120, 214
Hartsock, Nancy C. M., 24–25, 92, 158, 214
Hawaii, 10–11, 76, 137–41, 152, 159, 174,
    183, 217, 219
Hawkesworth, Mary, 175
Heilbrun, Carolyn G., 215
Hekman, Susan, 147, 158
hermeneutics, 9, 13, 66–68, 72, 114,
    146–48, 177; feminist hermeneutic,
    34–35, 50
Herschberger, Ruth, 102
heterosexual, 8, 11, 29, 33, 35, 37, 50, 92,
    159, 171–72, 179–81, 216
Hill, Anita, 53–54, 208–9
Hitler, Adolf, 217
Hobbes, 170
homosexual, 2, 33, 35, 184, 191, 195, 204
hooks, bell, 90, 131, 158, 181
Hrdy, Sarah Blaffer, 86
Hubbard, Ruth, 102

identity, 10–11, 50, 79, 93, 130, 138–40,
    158–60, 166–72, 183–84, 203–4
immanence, 165–67
indigenous people, 152, 174
individualism, 7–8, 63, 159
Irigaray, Luce, 165, 171
Irish-American, 10, 138–39, 159, 174, 203

Jewish, 49

kahuna, 139–40
Kanter, Rosebeth Moss, 102
Keller, Evelyn Fox, 85
King, Toni, 183
Kingston, Maxine Hong, 168–69, 214
Kuhn, Thomas, 76

lesbian, 2, 34, 37, 40, 53, 91–92, 158–59,
    170, 172, 179–81, 184, 216
Lévi-Strauss, Claude, 146–147
liberal feminism, 9, 120, 149, 190, 204
Littleton, Christine A., 31, 32, 53
Longino, Helen, 111, 120
Lorde, Audre, 214
Lugones, María C. 192, 219

MacKinnon, Catharine, 30–31, 32–35, 48,
    51–53, 71, 149, 207, 208
marriage, 36–41
Martin, Emily, 94–95, 220
marxism, 9, 21, 94, 140, 146, 149, 151,
    153–54, 159, 161, 198–99, 204
marxist feminism, 8–9, 21

Matsuda, Mari, 57
McClintock, Barbara, 216
masculine, 9, 13, 20, 29–32, 34–35, 47,
    51–53, 59, 63, 76, 78–81, 102, 111, 121,
    129–30, 132, 147, 153, 159, 165, 169,
    178–81
multiculturalism, 2, 137, 145, 175, 182

Native American, 32, 34, 91, 174, 182
Native Hawaiian, 11, 76, 137–40, 174, 183,
    217
neo-Nazi, 49
neoconservative, 2, 29–30, 38–39, 54, 80,
    109, 145, 160, 167
Northwest Coalition against Malicious
    Harassment, 49–50
Nussbaum, Martha, 8

Paglia, Camille, 149, 217
parental leave, 2, 40
Parks, Rosa, 212
Patai, Daphne, 217
Pateman, Carole, 36–37
Phelan, Shane, 147
Pirsig, Robert M., 167
Plato, 217–18
positivism, 13, 64, 76–77, 81–82, 87, 95,
    101–2, 107, 117, 140, 145, 148, 210, 223
postfeminist, 160
poverty, 1, 10, 33, 40, 106, 184
pragmatism, 114, 212–13
Pratt, Minnie, 219
praxis, 6, 14, 66–67, 94, 203–4, 212–13
pregnancy, 2, 20, 31, 34, 127–28, 168, 173–74
pro-choice, 89–90, 173–74
pro-life, 89, 173
Promise Keepers, 39

radical feminism, 11, 120, 149–51, 172
rape, 9, 20, 52–55, 69, 85–86, 94, 217
relativism, 78, 81–82, 90
representation, 1, 9, 12, 29–32, 43, 76, 79,
    81, 87, 101, 129–30, 132, 138, 147, 158,
    167, 170–73, 175, 176, 178, 182,
    191–92, 199, 214
reproduction, 79–80, 85, 151, 165–66,
    171–74, 179–81, 184
revolution, 111, 149–52, 160, 177
Rich, Adrienne, 54, 158
Richardson, Laurel, 96
Ricoeur, Paul, 96–97, 147
Roe v. Wade, 20, 50–51, 207–8

Rorty, Amelie, 55
Rorty, Richard, 87–88
Rosaldo, Michelle, 54
Rose, Hilary, 94–95, 112
Rosser, Sue, 120
Rousseau, 170
Ruddick, Sara, 93

Saussure, Ferdinand de, 177
Schneider, Elizabeth, 32
second-wave feminism, 1–2, 8, 10, 20,
    26–27, 94, 102, 106, 148, 149, 153, 167,
    178–80, 192, 213–15, 223
semiotics, 97, 146, 152, 171, 176–78
Shange, Ntozake, 214
Shultz, Vicki, 57
Simpson, O. J., 59–60, 68, 208
social contract, 35–41
Socrates, 54
Sommers, Christina Hoff, 149, 217
Spender, Dale, 215
Spivak, Gayatri Chakravorty, 147, 151,
    157–58, 160
standpoint theory, 13, 54, 86–87, 91–93, 96,
    110
Stanton, Elizabeth Cady, 215
State v. Wanrow, 31–32
straight, 91–92, 170, 184, 191
Suleiman, Susan Rubin, 171

totalitarianism, 7, 152, 158, 177
transcendence, 91, 165–67
Trinh T. Minh-ha, 174–75

vice, 13, 58, 112
virtue, 9, 13, 24, 25, 28, 50, 58, 64–65, 66,
    139, 190, 201, 216
Voegelin, Eric, 76

Walker, Alice, 94, 214
Warmke, Georgia, 147
Weedon, Chris, 157–58
Wells, Ida B., 53, 94, 176, 212, 215–16
West, Cornell, 90, 131
West, Robin, 57, 208
white, 10–11, 49, 53–54, 80, 91–93, 139,
    152, 158–59, 166, 180–84, 191–92, 217
Williams, Patricia J., 57–58
Wishik, Heather Ruth, 54–55

Yanow, Dvora, 199
Young, Iris, 1310

About the Author

Eloise A. Buker is professor of Women's Studies and Political Science at Denison University where she serves as director of the Women's Studies Program. Her teaching and published research are in the areas of political theory and feminist theory with a focus on the intersection of language and politics, cultural studies and ethnicity, women and political leadership, and also empirical methods and postmodern feminist analyses. Her book *Politics through a Looking-Glass*, which examines the politics of storytelling in two different American cultural contexts, won the National Jesuit Book Award for the best book in the social sciences for 1987. Her next book-length projects will focus on how women move from private life to public leadership and how feminist hermeneutics can be used for transformative political work.